AIR PLANTS

AIR PLANTS

EPIPHYTES AND AERIAL GARDENS

David H. Benzing

Comstock Publishing Associates | *a division of*
Cornell University Press
ITHACA AND LONDON

First published 2012 by Cornell University Press

Printed in the United States of America

Library of Congress Cataloging-in-Publication Data

Benzing, David H.
  Air plants : epiphytes and aerial gardens / David H. Benzing.
     p. cm.
  Includes bibliographical references and index.
  ISBN 978-0-8014-5043-3 (cloth : alk. paper)
  1. Epiphytes. I. Title.
  QK922.B45   2012
  581.6'3—dc23   2011046584

Cornell University Press strives to use environmentally responsible suppliers and materials to the fullest extent possible in the publishing of its books. Such materials include vegetable-based, low-VOC inks and acid-free papers that are recycled, totally chlorine-free, or partly composed of nonwood fibers. For further information, visit our website at www.cornellpress.cornell.edu.

Cloth printing   10 9 8 7 6 5 4 3 2 1

Pursuing a career that combines daily immersion in a much-beloved subject with curious and talented undergraduates and engaging colleagues around the world is nothing short of rare good fortune. I dedicate this book to the possibility that what I have been able to enjoy will endure and, most important, that the natural world will survive for individuals lucky enough to be similarly captivated by its beauty and mystery.

Contents

Color plates follow page 48

Preface

My first encounter with an epiphyte occurred during a birthday celebration in the home of a childhood friend. About a dozen of us eight-to-ten-year-old kids had been herded onto a side porch to enjoy cake and ice cream. Despite all the commotion, I noticed a small, fuzzy gray object tethered by string to a piece of polished wood, which in turn was suspended from the ceiling far from rain or sunshine. "It's an air plant," my friend's mother responded when I inquired; "it's called that because it gets everything it needs from thin air. We ordered it from a catalog," she added. Skeptical, but unwilling to challenge an adult, and certainly not a friend's mother, I returned my attention to the party.

Now I realize that the piece of wood that supported the object that so fascinated me was a sawed-off, debarked cypress knee, one of those tacky souvenirs that heat-seeking tourists used to buy in southern Georgia and Florida before freeways put out of business the roadside vendors who sold them. And almost certainly its bound captive was a single shoot of the once quite common Florida bromeliad *Tillandsia paucifolia*. The vision of that scaly, cigar-shaped plant, lacking a respectable root system, and its alleged, even stranger manner of growth, remains with me today. Much later it would become one of my most heavily chosen subjects for investigations of epiphyte biology.

Encounter number 2 occurred a few years after the birthday party, while my family, including two maternal grandparents, was vacationing in south Florida. It was April, and flowers and recently expanded foliage were everywhere. One especially bright day, my grandmother instructed me to accompany my grandfather as he was about to leave our motel on yet another of his mysterious errands. What I didn't know was that my presence was intended to deter his visit to one of the local saloons. She believed, erroneously it turned out, that her husband wouldn't leave his only grandson alone and too young to drive in a parked car in a strange city.

That bright sunny day, my grandfather chose a watering hole across the street from a small cypress swamp that hosted abundant *Tillandsia fasciculata* in full bloom. His mission required several hours, more than enough time to fix in my mind's eye the brilliant orange-red spikes of the most spectacular of Florida's bromeliads: the cardinal air plant. I can just as clearly recall wondering how the plants that produced these magnificent inflorescences managed their gravity-defying lifestyle. What striking beauty combined with such an odd way to grow! Were they parasites? Wild pines, the locals called them; just look at those upright, spiky leaves, they said. Did I think back to that birthday party? I don't remember.

Interest in plants didn't count for much among my adolescent, typical middle-American friends. It was only as an undergraduate that I considered botany as a possible career. That decided, my PhD dissertation concerned the origin of the flowering plants, but it was the adaptive biology of epiphytes that became the subject of my research and writing through 41 years as a professor at Oberlin College in northern Ohio. Four technical books and many dozens of research reports produced over this period means it's high time to communicate what I have learned about the epiphytes to individuals other than undergraduates and colleagues.

Epiphytes, or air plants, or whatever you wish to call them, not only warrant attention for their aesthetics and suitability for culture, they also demonstrate with uncommon clarity many of the basic principles of botany. Accordingly, epiphytes were prominent contributors to my lectures and laboratories for Oberlin College students. These aspects of plant biology illustrated in Oberlin classrooms, the plants themselves, and their habitats constitute the subjects of this book. Read it and witness the epiphytes in all their impressive variety and novelty. Do this, and you will also end up with a greener proverbial thumb.

Acknowledgments

This book could not have been written without inspiration and information gained from countless colleagues as well as support from Oberlin College and various public and private granting agencies over the past 45 years. Special thanks go to The Marie Selby Botanical Gardens in Sarasota, Florida, to Toni Renfro and her husband, Bill, Elton Leme, and Harry Luther plus the many Oberlin alumni who assisted me during their undergraduate years and occasionally beyond. The Marie Selby Botanical Gardens along with Wesley Higgins, Bruce K. Holst, Stephen Maciejewski, Phil Nelson, Kevin Swagel, and Yuribia Vivas graciously provided images. Images without attribution and all of the drawings are from the author.

With Special Appreciation of The Marie Selby Botanical Gardens

AIR PLANTS

1   What Is an Epiphyte?

Different kinds of habitats host decidedly different kinds of plants. Species that live in deserts compared with those native to wetlands are adaptively distinct, and they in turn differ from those native to the understories of dense tropical forests. Hundreds of such ecologically defined categories exist, no small portion of which have already inspired book-length treatments. Other groups remain more obscure, and not necessarily because of small size or lack of importance. A particularly glaring omission is the absence for the nonspecialist of a comprehensive introduction to what are known as the "epiphytes."

Defined literally, an *epiphyte* is something that perches on a plant (*epi* = upon, *phyte* = plant). To a botanist, this unspecified something is another plant, and the *phyta* is its host or *phorophyte* (i.e., its support plant). Vines depend on phorophytes as well, but their roots maintain lifelong connections to the ground. Also excluded from the definition are the normally self-supporting terrestrial species whose occasional members only "accidentally" end up suspended in the crowns of larger plants (Figure 1.1). The approximately 28,000 kinds of officially anointed epiphytes grow this way on a more regular basis.

The botanically certified epiphytes include some of the humblest members of the plant kingdom, familiar examples being the single-celled algae whose dense colonies often color otherwise somber bark greenish to yellowish gray. Some of their aquatic relatives colonize submerged vegetation such as the surfaces of seagrass foliage. Thousands of kinds of more advanced, but still nonvascular species known as liverworts and mosses (bryophytes), especially in the humid tropics, further enlarge and diversify this category (Figures 2.4, 3.2). The most spectacular of the epiphytes, and those to which this book is dedicated, possess vascular systems and the other attributes that distinguish the "higher" from the "lower" plants (Figure 1.2B).

Few city dwellers realize how much the vascular epiphytes brighten their everyday surroundings. Some of the most frequently seen of the indoor plants normally anchor in the canopies of trees and shrubs in the wild or, if *cultivars,* come from wild stocks that grow this way. Not the slightest hint of their more natural mode of living is evident when the subject is confined to a soil-filled container or viewed in most garden settings. Several exceptions stand better chances of being recognized for what they truly are, most notably Spanish moss (*Tillandsia usneoides*) and the mistletoes displayed during the Christmas holiday season (Figures 1.3, 5.6).

Seeing epiphytes thriving on trees and shrubs, and even on foreign objects like telephone wires, has prompted professionals and laypersons alike to ask the same questions (Figures 1.3, 1.4): Is it possible that these plants live on air, and do they ever harm their hosts? How do so many of the orchids manage to survive with roots that cling to nothing more sustaining than naked bark (Figure 2.2)? What about the dense festoons of Spanish moss illustrated in Figure 1.3? Isn't the shrub involved being smothered? And what happens in the pools of water located in the centers of bromeliad shoots (Plate 7C; Figure 7.5E)? Science has provided at least partial answers to all these questions and many more.

The vascular epiphytes have already received considerable scrutiny, mainly because of their unusual lifestyle, but much else about them is botanically more mundane. As with plants of every other description, they need carbon-based food, more than a dozen mineral nutrients such as nitrogen and phosphorus, and substantial amounts of moisture. They must also reproduce, disperse, and endure all sorts of environmental assaults. It's just that many of the epiphytes go about accomplishing one or more of these universally required tasks in unconventional and, to the curious, fascinating ways.

Unless specified otherwise, the term *epiphyte* from here forward is reserved for the vascular types that regularly anchor on woody hosts—that as *arboreal* plants they engage in a genuinely elevated lifestyle. Indeed, the members of this group are the botanical world's supreme aerialists. No less impressive is the fact that nearly one in every ten species in one way or another manages to spend a substantial part of, if not its entire life, separated from the ground, totally dependent on other sources for the vital commodities just enumerated.

Getting to Know the Epiphytes

Getting to know the epiphytes requires some familiarity with the basic organization of higher plants and their development and operation. How, for instance, do leaves and roots acquire resources and otherwise interact with the environment? How do plants respond to sporadic threats like attacks by predators, and what measures prepare them for more routine challenges such as seasonal drought? In other words, how have 400 million years of evolution shaped botanical form and function to match conditions in the diverse habitats that make up the green landscapes of our planet?

Figure 1.1. *Pilea pumila,* a terrestrial herb, growing as an accidental epiphyte on the trunk of a fallen riverside cottonwood tree (*Populus deltoides*) in northern Ohio.

The vascular plant body consists of two roughly equally sized organ systems (Figure 1.2A). The upper half, known as the shoot, extends upward into the atmosphere, while the lower portion remains buried below ground. Shoot systems consist of stems that bear food-making leaves; flowers and fruits develop when it is time to reproduce. The subterranean half amounts to a less-ordered array of roots. The two parts communicate by way of a vascular system that shuttles substances from where they are absorbed or manufactured to where they are used. Being unable to flee, plants use chemicals and physical barriers to discourage herbivores and pathogens.

Being fixed in place poses another challenge for plants. Species, being populations comprising individuals with finite life spans, must produce and disperse enough offspring to compensate for mortality. Spores permit the ferns and their similarly primitive *pteridophytic* relatives to colonize new sites and maintain occupancies elsewhere (Figure 9.1). Seeds do the same for the pteridophytes' more recently evolved *spermatophytic* relatives. The ways vary in which the higher plants engineer the unions of sperms and eggs that precede spores and seeds, with the flowering plants being most precise when it comes to selecting mates and dispersing their young to suitable locations (see Chapter 9).

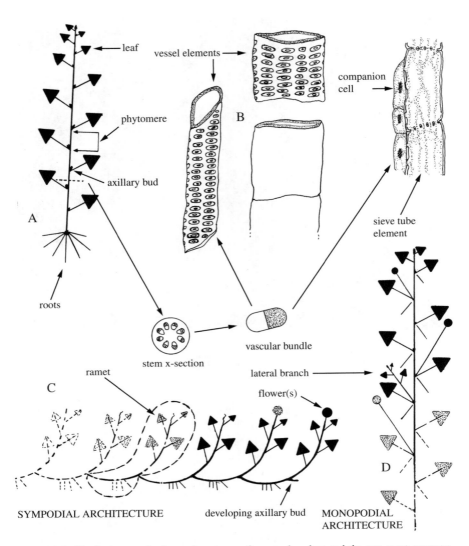

Figure 1.2. The basic organization and anatomy of a vascular plant and the two most common body plans among the epiphytes. **A.** Architecture of a unitary-bodied vascular plant such as a tree. **B.**Types of conducting cells that make up the phloem (right side) and xylem (left side) systems of vascular plants **C.** Sympodial body plan **D.** Monopodial body plan.

Figure 1.2 further illustrates how the upper half of the typical vascular plant is decidedly modular, that is, comprising repeating structural units. Note that each branch of what for the adult is usually a many-divided shoot consists of a stack of *phytomeres*. One phytomere consists of a node, the point at which one or more leaves are attached, the associated axillary or lateral bud(s), and the

Figure 1.3. Spanish moss (*Tillandsia usneoides,* Bromeliaceae) on *Citrus* in central Florida. Photo by Linda Grashoff

associated stem segment. Atop each branch is an *apical meristem* that consists of a cluster of embryonic stem cells. The apical meristem produces phytomeres until cued to switch to making sex organs or to simply abort. Regardless, a plant must branch if its leafy half is to expand beyond the single-stemmed, juvenile condition shown in Figure 1.2A.

A root is also tipped with an apical meristem that fosters growth in length, but the organ itself lacks the pronounced modularization exhibited by a leafy shoot, and it bears no lateral appendages comparable to leaves or axillary buds. Branching occurs when the smaller secondary meristems that develop well behind the apex of a parent root grow out to become the same number of secondary roots (Figure 4.3 lower left). Rarely do they emerge with the regularity exhibited by leaves and axillary buds on shoots.

A large majority of the epiphytes lack the clear-cut root-shoot differentiation embodied in the architecture of the conventional vascular plant illustrated in Figure 1.2A; instead, they root *adventitiously,* meaning more or less randomly

Figure 1.4. Ball moss (*Tillandsia recurvata*, Bromeliaceae) growing on a telephone wire in central Florida.

along much of or the entire lengths of their shoots. This arrangement allows many epiphytes to more extensively utilize their substrates. The species with rhizomatous shoots are especially well equipped to spread laterally. *Rhizomes,* as these streamlined, often scale-covered shoots are called, are especially prominent among the arboreal ferns and the monocot-type epiphytes and particularly the orchids (Figures 7.2D, 8.3B, 9.4B,E).

Figure 1.2B also illustrates the *phloem* and *xylem,* conducting cells that make a higher plant a vascular plant. The phloem *sieve tube elements* and their adjacent, narrower companion cells remain thin walled and alive at maturity, whereas the water-conducting vessel elements lay down thick rigid walls before dying, as required to sustain high-volume fluid transport. Unlike phloem, xylem vascular cells must sustain tensions (negative pressures) powerful enough to pull mineral-charged solutions upward. Flow proceeds from one superposed vessel element to the next across paired *perforation plates* in the end walls. Vertically aligned, thin circular to oval areas known as *pits* that facilitate horizontal transport mark the lateral walls. A relatively modest positive pressure pushes the sugar-laden phloem sap through similarly

Figure 1.5. Colony of lithophytic *Vriesea* sp. growing on a low granitic dome in southeastern Brazil.

aligned series of sieve tube elements, each of which bears a perforated *sieve plate* at each end.

Numerous non-epiphytes also deviate from the arrangement exhibited by the land-dwelling stereotype depicted in Figure 1.2. Many root into or on media other than earth soil, and sometimes conventionally structured root or shoot systems are missing, although rarely both in the same species. The lithophytes anchor on bare rock, whereas the aquatic types such as the duckweeds spend their entire lives afloat on the surfaces of ponds and slow-moving streams (Figure 1.5). The familiar aquarium plant *Elodea,* except for its tiny flowers, grows totally submerged. It no longer produces more than an occasional root, which probably is not needed anyway, because water and nutrients readily enter through its finely built shoots.

The individual organs of the epiphytes also often depart from those of the more typical soil-rooted plants. Roots in some instances have acquired characteristics usually associated with foliage, and, for others, leaves have diverged in the opposite direction. Like *Elodea,* many an epiphyte experiences the same medium, which is air rather than water, around most of its body (Figure 2.2). Consequently, the need for shoots and roots that diverge in structure and

function is relaxed compared with that needed by our standard land plant occupying two different kinds of space: the atmosphere, which is the source of
life-giving solar energy but is also dangerously dry; and the soil, which is wetter
but lacks the sunlight needed to sustain photosynthesis.

The epiphytes are adapted to a wide variety of growing conditions, similar to
plants that root in the ground. Many aerial habitats are too hostile to sustain any
but the most stress-tolerant types, and they represent only a couple of families.
Where life is easier, meaning more reliably warm and humid, aerial gardens are
botanically more diverse, in addition to being wonderfully lush and colorful. Who
occupies these most accommodating of sites is also broadly egalitarian. Epiphytes
of high evolutionary status commonly occur with others much farther down the
taxonomic hierarchy, for example, lowly liverworts and mosses cheek to jowl with
the far more specialized and stress-tolerant bromeliads and orchids (Figure 3.2).

Body Plans

A large majority of the epiphytes conform to one or the other of only
two of the dozens of "body plans" that have evolved among the higher plants
(Figure 1.2C,D). Shoots possessed by individuals that exhibit *sympodial*-type
architecture branch in a way that yields series of subunits called *ramets,* each of
which consists of multiple phytomeres. The resulting body is developmentally
limited or *determinate* on one level of organization and open-ended or *indeterminate* on another. On the finer of these two scales, the individual ramet produces a species-specific (genetically specified) number of phytomeres, and once
that quota is met, growth ceases. Whole shoots, because they consist of ramets
that beget ramets, operate free of this constraint. So equipped, an individual
might live forever were it not for inevitable events such as being eaten or being
dispatched by a pathogen.

Ramets progress through a three-phase life cycle, the first phase consisting
entirely of vegetative development. Phase 2 involves only reproduction, both
flowering and seed production. Decline and death constitute phase 3. Phase 1
usually requires a year for what begins as a lateral bud to become a fully leafed
and rooted ramet. Flowering occurs by way of a single terminal or one or more
lateral *inflorescences* (branch segments specialized to bear flowers). Hormonal
changes triggered when an apical meristem aborts or starts to produce sex organs initiate the next round of branching. Postreproductive ramets survive for
one or two additional years.

An environmental cue, usually a photoperiod that heralds a change of seasons, triggers branching and flowering for most of the sympodial epiphytes.
Annual fluctuations in temperature and light intensity probably stimulate many

of the exceptions. Regardless of the nature of the cue, the sympodial plant develops in a fashion that is both seasonally (temporally) and architecturally discrete (modular). To be sympodial, herbaceous, and arboreal to boot means that the subject is most likely a monocot-type flowering plant. Most of the monocots are constructed according to this pattern, which explains why the epiphytes, being overwhelmingly members of this taxonomic group, most often are sympodial (see Chapter 7).

The epiphytic orchids demonstrate how conservative in addition to common the sympodial body plan can be. The bulbophyllums, for example, produce ramets that bear only one or a pair of leaves at the summit of a single swollen phytomere that makes up the bulk of what is called a *pseudobulb* (Figure 7.2D). A consistently lateral rather than terminal inflorescence further contributes to the group's architectural uniformity. Evolutionary divergence within this more than 1500-member genus of primarily epiphytes has involved mostly the reproductive rather than the vegetative apparatus (Plate 2A,B). Consequently, differentiating closely related species of *Bulbophyllum* is nearly impossible without flowers.

Epiphytes that conform to *monopodial*-type architecture branch less frequently than the sympodial-bodied species. Here, the shoot consists of more numerous phytomeres produced by longer-lived apical meristems (Figure 1.2D). In other words, the development of the individual leafy branch, unlike its sympodial counterpart, is *indeterminate.* Moreover, inflorescences always arise laterally from axillary buds rather than from the tips of main or "long" shoots. Rooting is adventitious, as with the sympodial types, and being herbaceous as well, the monopodial epiphytes also die progressively at the rear as they grow forward. Vines, like the *Vanilla* orchids, illustrate monopodial growth in its extreme (Figure 7.2E).

Architectural reduction all but obscures the body plans of the most structurally specialized of the epiphytes. The monopodial organization of the so-called shootless orchids is difficult to discern owing to greatly telescoped internodes that bear what now are tiny, scalelike leaves (Figure 2.2). Flowers and fruits, however, have changed less from their conditions in leafy ancestors. The root system, however, having taken on the additional task of making the food formerly provided by normally expanded foliage, has become more prominent. Spanish moss, a sympodial-bodied member of family Bromeliaceae, is comparably abbreviated but in the opposite direction. Each of its miniaturized ramets consists of just three leaves topped by a single blossom (Plate 3C; Figure 7.6F). Why these plants have become so streamlined is considered in Chapter 7.

A modest minority of the epiphytes possess a *vascular cambium* whose presence allows stems and roots to thicken by adding woody tissue. When this laterally (as opposed to apically) positioned meristem is active, an epiphyte can become a shrub, small tree, or even more. The massive roots and expansive crowns produced by the strangling hemi-epiphytic figs wouldn't be possible were this layer of embryonic stem cells missing, as it is among the monocots and pteridophytes, or if it were less prolific (Figures 2.8, 3.1). Chapter 7 describes how the capacity to thicken helps differentiate the eudicot-types from the remaining arboreal angiosperms. Chapter 4 explains why more than modest woodiness is unsustainable for an epiphyte in all but the most humid of aerial habitats.

The body plans illustrated by the spore-bearing or pteridophytic epiphytes parallel and deviate from those possessed by their seed-producing cousins. None is woody, and except for the members of the primitive genera *Psilotum* and *Tmesipteris,* all incorporate leaves, stems, and roots (Figure 9.10). Shoots branch less regularly among the pteridophytes, owing in part to the absence of typical axillary buds. The fern frond occurs in a vast array of shapes and sizes and, depending on the species, can perform functions in addition to photosynthesis (Figures 9.3, 9.4). Variety on both counts still falls well below what the flowering plants have achieved. Less is known about roots except that none employed by the spore producers performs as many operations or exhibits the kind of specialized anatomy that so effectively serves the arboreal aroids and orchids (Figure 4.3).

The epiphytic lycophytes, which also reproduce with naked spores instead of seeds, are otherwise not fernlike (Figures 2.4, 9.10). New shoots arise exclusively from the bases of older, usually pendent axes. Those of the canopy-dwelling huperzias divide symmetrically prior to producing terminal cones (Figure 9.10). Divisions of this distinctly dichotomous type occur within the apical meristem and yield two equally proportioned daughter axes. Each determinate shoot of *Psilotum,* although a distant fern relative rather than a lycophyte, exemplifies the kind of whole plant architecture that results from repeated dichotomous divisions (Figures 9.9, 9.10). Unlike the broader, more elaborately vascularized leaves (*megaphylls*) that serve the more advanced pteridophytes and the seed plants, the *microphylls* featured by the lycophytes amount to simple *enations,* each of which is equipped with a single undivided vein (Figure 9.10).

Most of the epiphytes probably possess one or the other of just two of the many existing body plans in part because of where they grow. Aerial habitats would be friendlier for plants with single, upright shoots atop similarly discrete root systems if their substrates tended to be more horizontal than precipitous. Instead, most of the arboreal species exhibit branched constructions that better match their needs to creep over and hang from narrow, elevated perches (Figure 1.2C). The more unitary, vertical alternative is essential for the forest dominant, but not nearly so for the plants that anchor in its crown. Why else would all but the primary hemi-epiphytes and a few others possess adventitiously rooted, sympodial or elongated monopodial shoots or pteridophytic versions of this arrangement?

The Epidermis

Plants rely on a surface layer or *epidermis* to acquire resources from the atmosphere and to block or mitigate many of its threats. Although usually quite thin, it is an exceptionally complex tissue that consists of diverse kinds of cells whose occurrences and functions vary depending on location. For example, the *stomata* (sing. *stoma),* each of which features a prominent pair of guard cells, occur at highest densities on the lower surfaces of leaves (Figure 4.1A,B,C,D,F). The distributions of minute scales and hairs (*trichomes*) are less consistent, and depending on abundance and nature, they provide a variety of services. Mostly they discourage herbivores and slow water loss or reflect excess light.

The epidermis says more about where a plant lives and how it operates under prevailing conditions than does its body plan or even the characteristics of its foliage (see Chapter 4; Figure 4.2). This is especially true of the epiphytes, thousands of which, for example, possess leaves densely covered with absorptive trichomes or bear foliage shaped and arranged to collect litter and moisture (Figures 4.4, 5.5; Plate 3C). An even larger number of aroids and orchids achieve air-worthiness largely by deploying roots surrounded by an equally specialized epidermis known as the *velamen* (see Chapter 4; Figure 4.3; Plate 8B).

Other Notable Features of the Epiphytes

The epiphytes constitute a valid ecological category for one reason: where they grow. If they rooted in the ground instead, their "habit" would switch from arboreal to terrestrial. Almost everything else about their kind, such as how they conduct certain vital processes, is varied, more so in fact than for trees and many of the other common forms of vegetation. Variety is especially pronounced relative to the ways in which they acquire and use water and nutrients and interact with animals. To differ so much in such fundamental ways seems odd, considering that most of the 28,000 species of epiphytes conform to just two body plans.

The epiphytes offer exceptional opportunities for investigators interested in the mechanisms by which plants survive climate-imposed stress. Much the same can be said for the intricate symbiotic relationships that occur between certain species and animals, especially ants, some of which have few rivals for importance in woodland communities. More alluring for the horticulturist and hobbyist is what the epiphytes offer for pleasure and profit. Individuals simply curious about the natural world can enjoy these plants by learning how elegantly they accomplish under tough circumstances what all land-based flora must do to survive.

While it is true that plants generally satisfy life's demands more passively than animals, the exceptions can be exquisitely dynamic. The ways in which reproduction occurs illustrate this fact particularly well and especially among the species that most deftly manipulate their pollinators and seed dispersers. Photosynthesis and the management of moisture and nutrients pale in comparison, but even here the epiphytes exceed most other types of vegetation for botany in action. Some of the most bizarre of these performances are exemplified by species featured in this volume. Readers interested in elegant expressions of typically rather humdrum botanical processes should find the following chapters particularly compelling.

Starting at the Beginning

Epiphytism was not an option for the earliest land plants because, being so recently emerged from a watery world, they lacked the capacity to cope more effectively with a challenge that remains in place today. They couldn't afford to absorb CO_2 in any but the most humid of terrestrial environments (Figure 4.1). Performing photosynthesis under more arid conditions without drying out would require two additional innovations: a shoot surface provisioned with stomata and otherwise sealed with a waxy cuticle, and a vascular system to transport water and dissolved minerals upward from the ground and the products of photosynthesis in the opposite direction (Figure 1.2B).

Being so poorly prepared to stave off desiccation also severely limited the size of the first botanical pioneers of land. Modest stature—no more than a few centimeters of height—was essential to stay close to the ground and adequately insulated from the full force of the atmosphere's powerful capacity to evaporate water. Initial habitats were swamps and the edges of lakes and streams in a world substantially warmer and more humid than the one we know today. In no way were these most primitive of the land dwellers even remotely suited to endure the conditions that most of the modern epiphytes experience on a routine basis.

Figure 1.6 illustrates one of the most ancient of the land plants. Approximately 410 million-year-old *Aglaophyton* possessed the bare essentials to survive on land: rudimentary conductive tissue, stomata and cuticle, a body minimally differentiated into aerial and subterranean portions, and a simple reproductive apparatus based on the production of tiny spores within saclike organs called *sporangia* (sing. *sporangium*). In effect, the body of *Aglaophyton* consisted of little more than a series of dichotomously branched stems crudely adapted at one end to operate in soil and at the other to function in the atmosphere. No evidence of the modern shoot's modular construction or specialized appendages was evident (Figure 1.2).

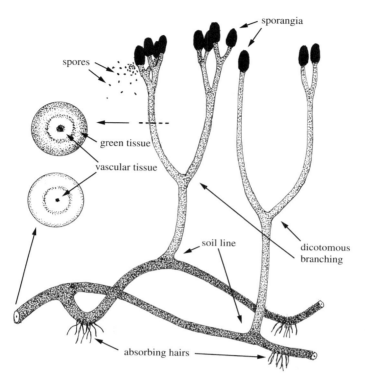

Figure 1.6. *Aglaophyton,* an early, protovascular plant. Note its structural simplicity, particularly the absence of differentiated root and shoot systems, leaves, roots, and modular construction. Also shown is its pteridophytic "free sporing" manner of reproduction.

Today's land plants grow just about everywhere except in regions covered by permanent layers of ice and snow. Success across such a broad range of often punishing habitats would be impossible without structural and physiological refinements that far exceed those possessed by *Aglaophyton* and its similarly ancient relatives. Organs specialized for specific functions, like leaves for photosynthesis and roots for absorbing nutrients and water, had to evolve before descendants could invade regions too hostile to accommodate their more vulnerable antecedents. Epiphytism set the bar even higher, often requiring substantial refinements of these second-generation appendages.

The vascular plants have had the better part of one-half billion years to exploit multiple kinds of habitats and perfect corresponding devices and mechanisms to reproduce and obtain water and the other essential resources. Modern botanical diversity also reflects the ways in which organisms have adjusted to each other—plants to plants and plants to animals. These even higher-order adaptations could not evolve until the most fundamental challenges facing photosynthetic organisms on land, especially drought, had been solved by early arrivers like *Aglaophyton*. Epiphytism also remained beyond reach until some of the flora that had colonized land had become robust enough to provide the necessary aerial perches.

Geological History

The fact that proportionally more of the lycophytes and ferns than seed producers grow above ground suggests that epiphytism has a long history. None of the surviving spore-bearing species, however, is even remotely constructed like the earliest land plants. Members of predominantly epiphytic *Psilotum* and *Tmesipteris* are simple bodied enough to almost qualify, but their

Figure 1.7. *Botryopteris forensis*, a long extinct, epiphytic seed fern (redrawn from Rothwell 1991).

leafless, rootless condition more likely reflects adjustment to the rigors of aerial life rather than echoing times long past (Figures 9.9, 9.10A,B, 9.11). Status as evolutionary relics used to be cited to explain what botanists now know is only superficially *Aglaophyton*-like architecture.

Forests that existed during the geologic period known as the Carboniferous, some 290–355 million years ago, already harbored epiphytes, but how extensively, paleobotanists cannot say. Fossilized remains do not reveal much about how a plant lived or the identity of its rooting medium. It is known that trees as large as many of those that support the modern epiphytes had evolved by the Upper Devonian period about 360 million years ago. Fernlike but seed bearing and long extinct, *Botryopteris forensis* rooted to the trunks of *Psaronious*, another extinct genus of plants that resembled the modern tree ferns (Figure 1.7). The *Tmesipteris* specimen shown in Figure 9.11 was probably growing much as *Botryopteris forensis* did more than a quarter of a billion years ago.

Geographic Distribution

More than half (about 55%) of the epiphytes live in the Americas (the New World), in part because neither Bromeliaceae nor Cactaceae ranges beyond this region except as terrestrials, barring a single *Ripsalis* cactus (see Chapter 8). More of the responsibility for this asymmetry, however, lies with the heavily epiphytic, pantropical families (e.g., Araceae, Gesneriaceae, Orchidaceae), a majority of which experienced their most robust arboreal radiations in Neotropical woodlands. Only a handful of these more widespread families include superior numbers of Old rather than New World epiphytes, and in two of these cases, only two genera each account for most of the inequality (*Dischidia* and *Hoya* in Apocynaceae and *Hydnophytum* and *Myrmecodia* in Rubiaceae).

Episodes of global cooling accompanied by severe aridity that repeatedly diminished the extent of tropical wet forest during the last 2.5 million years further explain the uneven distribution of epiphytes. Africa experienced the greatest impact and accordingly has the most epiphyte-impoverished of the three continental floras (Australasia and the American tropics being the other two). The Andean uplift more than compensated in the New World by massively expanding forested lands in western South America. Rain-soaked uplands dissected by deep valleys fostered explosive proliferations of species whose products account for the record diversities of epiphytic aroids, bromeliads, gesneriads, and orchids and more reported from montane sites ranging from Peru northward into Central America.

The epiphytes of the Southern Hemisphere occur from its mild and moist midlatitude regions to the Equator, and diversity trends in the same direction.

Most extreme among the pole-ward outliers are members of the orchid genera *Earina* and *Winika* extending as far south as the Steward Islands, located at 47°S off the coast of New Zealand's South Island. *Sarcochilus australis* and *Drokrillia striolata* of the same family inhabit climatically similar woodlands in Tasmania. The bromeliad *Tillandsia usneoides* penetrates to 38°S in Argentina. Rain forests in New Zealand and central Chile support the highest concentrations of temperate-zone species, enough at one Chilean site to account for about a tenth of the local vascular flora.

Distributions relative to latitude follow a similar pattern on the other side of the Equator, although fewer epiphytes are involved. Species that venture farthest north include several ferns and lycophytes native to the Pacific Northwest of North America and *Tillandsia usneoides* into maritime Virginia. Other records for poleward ranges occur in Japan and North Korea. High-diversity hotspots for arboreal flora at midlatitudes north of the Equator include certain south-facing slopes of the Himalayas, particularly at the eastern end, southern Japan, and rain forests in western Washington State in the United States and adjacent Canada. Ferns tend to dominate at higher latitudes in both hemispheres.

Some families contribute more of their epiphytes than others to temperate-subtropical instead of tropical forests (e.g., Bromeliaceae, Orchidaceae, and the higher ferns more than Araceae, Cactaceae, and Piperaceae). Families that field midlatitude epiphytes in the Southern Hemisphere tend to have tropical affinities. Proportionally more genera, if not families, with pronounced northern ranges and largely terrestrial memberships overcontribute north of the Equator (e.g., *Thallictrum* of Ranunculaceae, *Ribes* of Saxifragaceae, and *Smilacina* and *Maianthemum* of Convallariaceae). Epiphytes that scale the flanks of tropical mountains to heights visited by frost present a more mixed picture.

Cold hardiness is best developed among the parasites (Figure 5.6). Dwarf mistletoes of genus *Arceuthobium* attack conifers in the boreal forests of North America and Eurasia. Similarly, diminutive species infest cacti in some of the driest deserts of South America, where the term *forest canopy* barely applies. The free-living types probably lack equivalent frost tolerance owing to their greater exposure to lethal freeze-desiccation. Except for flowers and fruits, the most specialized of the mistletoes reside inside the host body; nevertheless, like the nonparasites, the mistletoes reach peak diversities in what ecologists designate *ever-wet* tropical forests. Even here, however, they never account for more than a few percent of the local vascular species.

Unlike their host-tapping counterparts, the free-living epiphytes sometimes equal more than a third of the total inventory of vascular species, and they usually occur in greater densities (Table 3.1; Figure 3.4). Individual trees growing under particularly favorable conditions may support more than 100 different kinds of epiphytes. One tree examined in Costa Rica had been colonized by at least 125 species representing 52 genera and 21 families, or about 1% of the vascular flora native to that floristically rich country! More impressive yet, fully 25% of Ecuador's indigenous species are either epiphytes or hemi-epiphytes.

Finally, stray individuals representing species that lack the means to be more consistently epiphytic find their way into forest canopies from the deep tropics well into both temperate zones. Why they behave this way usually accords with some unrelated aspect of their biology. *Solanum dulcamara,* a semiwoody vine in the nightshade family, is one of the most common of the accidental epiphytes in northern Ohio. As a wetland species, it does quite well on moist media irrespective of its location. Being fleshy fruited, knotholes and additional pockets of moist suspended humus fall within its long list of acceptable sites. The mechanically dispersed seed responsible for the *Pilea pumila* specimen illustrated in Figure 1.1 was almost certainly washed onto the fallen cottonwood tree trunk serving as its riverside host.

Use by Humans

Epiphytes figure prominently in ornamental horticulture, but except for the hemi-epiphytic orchid *Vanilla planifolia* and a couple of large-fruited cacti ("dragon fruits," genus *Hylocereus*) that grow the same way, none provide food, fiber, or chemicals in commercial quantities. Additional species yield minor fruits for local markets and likely will not gain greater attention without further domestication (e.g., several members of the mulberry-like genus *Coussapoa*). Perhaps some currently obscure drupe or berry produced by an epiphyte will emerge as yet another miracle source of health-promoting agents from the tropical rain forest! The practice of harvesting Spanish moss to stuff upholstery gave way long ago to use of synthetic alternatives. More modest applications continue, such as its use for lining flowerpots and Easter baskets.

Easily met requirements for growth, appropriate dimensions for container and landscape culture, and often-colorful foliage, floral bracts, and flowers account for the immense popularity of many of the epiphytes in developed countries (Plates 1–7). Likewise, many a rural house and garden across the tropics features transplants from nearby woodlands. Christmas celebrations and other religious ceremonies consume countless epiphytes, mostly bromeliads, in many parts of Latin America. Similar choices commonly decorate household shrines and roadside sites of fatal accidents. Individuals in places like southern Mexico are being encouraged to reduce pressures on wild populations of bromeliads by propagating endangered species in private woodlots.

Many of the most valuable of the cultivated cacti, philodendrons, gesneriads, and orchids have epiphytic origins like those of the ornamental bromeliads, and markets for their kind continue to expand in the developed world. Guatemala and Mexico exported some 72 million bromeliad plants as far back as 1989, mostly to Western Europe, Japan, and North America. High dollar value is second only to habitat destruction as a threat to the wild populations of numerous species of bromeliads, cacti, and orchids (see Chapter 11).

The epiphytes warrant closer scrutiny as potential sources of therapeutics in addition to use as ornamental cultigens. About 15% of the 670 medicinal plants employed by the Shuar Indians of Ecuador, for example, grow above ground, according to one authority. Herbaceous vines and lianas outnumber the epiphytes, largely because so many belong to the pharmacologically well-endowed families Apocynaceae, Bignoniaceae, Convolvulaceae, and Fabaceae. Araceae, Bromeliaceae, Gesneriaceae, and Orchidaceae account for the largest numbers of epiphytes listed, many for other than medical utility. Exceptions include numerous Gesneriaceae, especially several of the epiphytes characterized by red-pigmented leaves that suggest efficacy for gynecological problems (Plate 7A).

Conservation

Epiphytes differ in their vulnerabilities to extirpation for a variety of reasons, abundance and geographic range being most decisive. Species that occur widely throughout low-lying, relatively moist landscapes such as South America's Amazonian watershed are relatively secure. Special features such as the capacity of Spanish moss to colonize hosts with shoot fragments and its broad range across two continents essentially eliminate vulnerability (Figure 1.3). Quite the opposite applies to the many other species, especially in Orchidaceae, that occupy narrow geographic ranges with few individuals in places such as the northern Andes. Epiphytes are overrepresented in CITES (Convention on International Trade in Endangered Species) appendixes I and II.

Undoubtedly, the number of extirpated epiphytes is already substantial and certain to rise, if only because habitat conversion for human use is going to continue. Should predictions about climate change prove accurate, losses will mount even faster. Rising concentrations of CO_2 and nutritive nitrogen in the atmosphere are more likely to compound than to moderate the effects of climate change. Should the worst of these possibilities materialize, the consequences of what will be much-diminished epiphyte diversity and abundance will ripple through ecosystems to the extent that these plants influence systemwide processes like nutrient cycling, as described in Chapter 3.

What follows in the remaining ten chapters is an examination of the vascular epiphytes, both the parasites and the free-living types, although more comprehensively of the latter. All the subjects introduced in this brief overview and more are presented in fuller detail. Some of this information can help growers refine protocols for cultivating the more difficult to manage of the epiphytes. Most of the discussion, however, is guided by the premise that fundamental aspects of epiphyte biology, namely nutrition, water balance, reproduction, and influences on other organisms and ecosystems are entertaining and worth knowing for their own sake.

2 The Types of Epiphytes and Their Evolutionary Origins

Chapter 1 describes the epiphytes as operationally varied and taxonomically diverse. It also reports that some of the most specialized of their kind perform vital tasks in ways that differ from those practiced by plants that root in the ground. Especially noteworthy are the ways in which, under often difficult circumstances, many of the arboreal species obtain mineral nutrients, perform photosynthesis, and succeed in reducing the threat of drought to manageable proportions. Several of the quirkiest of these attributes position the epiphytes to play key roles in the lives of the other organisms that share their ecosystems.

The ecological category represented by the epiphytes has no scientific name, nor does it enjoy recognition in the more familiar Linnaean classification system that groups individuals into species, species into genera, genera into families, and families into classes, and so on. Figure 2.1 illustrates how the Linnaean scheme is designed to depict evolutionary history (*phylogeny*) and to a lesser degree, genetic relatedness. This purely hypothetical *clade* (a term that describes a group of species, all of which have descended from a common ancestor) includes 12 *lineages,* only 11 of which include living members, the twelfth having become extinct.

Note in Figure 2.1 that species numbers 1 and 2 share a common ancestor, and that they and species 3 and 4 are derived from a more ancient common antecedent, and so on down the tree. The ultimate common ancestor, the one shared by all 12 lineages, forms the trunk of the entire phylogenetic tree. Note also that species 1–4 are assigned to genus A, whereas species 5 and 6 make up genus B. These six in turn share a still more distant (older) ancestor and so represent a still more inclusive clade, which according to this genealogy constitutes a family. The other six species make up two more genera and a second family that together with the first family form a taxonomic order, the next higher (more inclusive) Linnaean rank.

Also note in Figure 2.1 that leafy tanks emerged twice within this hypothetical clade as its 12 component lineages descended from the succession of common ancestors or *stem* lineages enumerated above. It essentially experienced a redundant

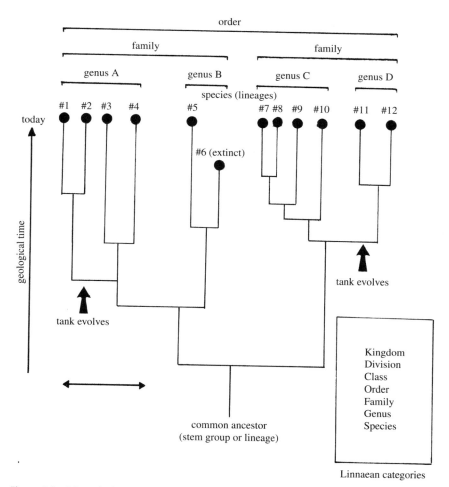

Figure 2.1. A hypothetical phylogeny consisting of 11 surviving and one extinct lineage illustrating how the Linnaean hierarchy of taxonomic ranks relates to genetic relationship and evolutionary history (phylogeny). Also indicated is an example of convergence or homoplasy involving the repeated evolution of tank-forming shoot architecture as it occurs in family Bromeliaceae.

evolutionary event (a *homoplasy*) as its membership expanded and diverged through geologic time (underwent an *adaptive radiation*). As a result, only 4 of the surviving 11 species possess this feature, and they belong to two genera (A and D) whose members are less closely related to one another than to members of B and C, respectively. Likewise, species numbers 1 and 2 and 11 and 12 represent one adaptive type, whereas the other eight, lacking the same tank-forming shoot, belong to another.

All seven of the higher taxa (four genera, two families, and one order) depicted in Figure 2.1 are valid because their members (species) share common ancestors at appropriate levels, that is, each is *monophyletic;* however, should a taxonomist mistakenly assume that tank-type architecture within this clade indicates phylogenetic relationship, species 1 and 2 and 11 and 12 would end up assigned to a single invalid or artificial genus. Being composed of parts of two separate clades rather than one, it would technically be *polyphyletic.* A taxon is no more acceptable when it fails to represent an entire clade. Reassigning species number 8 to either genus B or genus D would make what's left of genus C *paraphyletic* and also invalidate B or D!

Plants can also be grouped using attributes other than levels of shared ancestry and genetic relationship, as indicated in the opening paragraph of this book. While a rose belongs to family Rosaceae, it is also a member of additional categories, for example, semiwoody shrubs, plants with winter deciduous foliage, and plants possessing fragrant, ornamental flowers. The epiphytes can be broken down according to the ways in which they overcome adverse conditions in aerial habitats (Tables 2.1–2.6). Rather than being relegated to genera, families, and so on, this less formal system differentiates the 28,000 arboreal species into *adaptive types.* The fact that evolution tends to be redundant or homoplasious explains why plants that share the same labels in this performance-based classification, contrary to Linnaean-style practice, vary widely by genetic and phylogenetic relationship.

Two realities complicate attempts to classify the epiphytes according to the ways they operate without roots that penetrate the ground. One is the absence of discrete boundaries between certain compensating adaptations. Many species unquestionably fit a particular adaptive category, for example, the tank-bearing bromeliads that rely on moist, nutrient-rich materials impounded in leafy tanks as substitutes for earth soil (Figure 5.4). A second category includes the non-tank-forming "atmospheric" members of the same family that tap precipitation directly with foliage covered by dense layers of absorbing scales (Figures 4.4, 4.5; Plate 3C). The problem arises when choosing a label for relatives that combine both features. Nature's boundaries are often blurred, and such is the case here.

The epiphytes further defy classification into adaptive types because their assignments shift with the criterion applied. For example, two species that obtain

Table 2.1. Epiphytes differentiated by nutritional mode

Nutritional mode	Qualifying groups
Free livers (self-feeding or autotrophic)	All of the other epiphytes
Parasites (the mistletoes)	A. Hemi-parasitic (partially parasitic)
	B. Holo-parasitic (fully parasitic)

moisture in the same way can deviate when it comes to the ways in which they obtain mineral nutrients (compare Tables 2.3 and 2.4). They may also part company according to the way they manufacture food, some employing CAM-type photosynthesis and others the C_3 syndrome, as described in Chapter 5. Similarly, epiphytes with near-identical requirements for rooting media in some cases shed their foliage during the driest part of the year as required to operate as *drought avoiders,* whereas others with more robust, longer-lived or evergreen leaves function according to a mechanism known as *drought endurance* (see Chapter 4).

The epiphytes differ most fundamentally in the ways they obtain mineral nutrients, water, and manufactured food—whether as shoot parasites (mistletoes) or as "free livers." If the latter, they conduct photosynthesis and obtain moisture and the additional raw materials required for life, such as nitrogen and phosphorus, from sources other than the vascular system of another plant. No other criterion so profoundly determines how an epiphyte lives and how it affects its neighbors (Table 2.1). The free-living types exhibit the greatest adaptive and taxonomic variety and account for more than 90% of the species, so this is where we will begin.

The Free-Living Epiphytes

As a group, the free-living epiphytes endure just about every extreme of climate short of deep frost; as individual species, they tolerate far less, and as we shall see, even less than many of the nearby soil-rooted plants. Requirements for rooting media are similarly precise, for instance, restrictions to the surfaces of trunks or substantial branches as opposed to twigs, or to nests constructed by arboreal ants (Figure 3.1). Consequently, the number of arboreal species and adaptive types that can occur together in one habitat, be it the crown of a single free-standing tree or a hectare of forest, depends in large measure on the heterogeneity of its growing conditions, including its aerial substrates.

Table 2.2. Nonparasitic epiphytes differentiated according to type of substrate

Required substrate	Subtypes
Humus	A. Knothole or rotten wood B. Suspended humic soil
Ant-nest	—
Bark	A. Twig B. Trunk, large branches (naked)
Relatively independent of their substrates (the "atmospherics" or air plants)	—

Figure 2.2. *Harisella filiformis* (Orchidaceae), a "shootless" twig epiphyte. Photo by Bruce K. Holst

Members of one subset of epiphytes comprising primarily bromeliads, orchids, and a few similarly prepared ferns never occur on any but slender stems, their seeds and spores apparently failing if dispersed to more robust supports (Figure 2.2). A larger, more taxonomically mixed collection of species does the opposite, being intolerant of all but the rougher or more weathered surfaces characteristic of thicker axes (Figure 2.3). Some of these associations occur

Figure 2.3. *Encyclia tampensis* (Orchidaceae), a bark epiphyte. Photo by Linda Grashoff

regularly enough to justify labels such as "twig," "trunk," and "bark" epiphytes (Table 2.2; Figures 2.3, 3.1). Other species, the bromeliad *Tillandsia recurvata* being a prime example, defy such designations, rooting on all manner of media, including trunks, twigs, and even telephone wires (Figure 1.4).

Thousands of epiphytes reside exclusively in ever-wet forests owing to their need for bark made more hospitable by overgrowths of moisture-retaining mosses and lichens (Figure 2.4). It is appropriate to label this kind of rooting medium a suspended humic soil because its composition parallels the sodden deposits of decomposing plant remains that support bog and fen flora. Likewise, it is reasonable to apply the adjective *humus* to the epiphytes that require such substrates. Not surprisingly, some of the humus specialists have bog-dwelling relatives, certain members of Ericaceae (the blueberry and *Rhododendron* family) being familiar examples (see Chapter 8).

Figure 2.4. A branch bearing humic soil and abundant nonvascular plants in which epiphytes are rooted, most conspicuously a tank bromeliad and a lycophyte, in a Costa Rican wet forest.

Aerial substrates in turn dictate some of the qualities of the plants that use them. Not only must a twig epiphyte be small enough to avoid overburdening its delicate support, it must also produce offspring quickly before its typically short-lived axis fails, irrespective of how much weight it happens to bear. Accordingly, the species that make up this adaptive category possess body plans that are markedly abbreviated to promote rapid maturation (Figure 2.2). Trunk and branch epiphytes, being on average more substantial, require more time to reproduce, and they often live longer, which is not as great a liability on more durable anchorages (Figure 2.3).

Requirements for the conditions that knotholes and rotten branches provide further differentiate the humus-type epiphytes (Table 2.2). Some species root interchangeably in suspended organic soils and comparable terrestrial media. The *Psilotum* specimens anchored in small cavities in a *Taxodium distichum* (bald cypress) trunk damaged by fire in Figure 9.9 were accompanied by others growing just as vigorously in humus-filled crannies in nearby eroded limestone. *Dendrobium speciosum,* along with a couple of additional Australian orchids, falls at the other end of the spectrum, requiring deposits of organic material that only certain species of *Eucalyptus* provide.

Several thousand free-living epiphytes create moist, leafy chambers for the debris-feeding animals (*detritivores*) and microbes that help them harvest nutrients from impounded litter (e.g., the tank bromeliads, Figures 2.7, 5.4, 7.5E), or they intercept the same materials in tangles of roots as "trash basket" species (Figure 2.6). Still other epiphytes obtain what they need by encouraging plant-feeding ants to colonize dry leaf and stem cavities provided for this purpose (Figures 5.3, 7.5A, 8.3F,H, 8.4, 9.4B,E), or they root in the soil-like nests and runways built by members of the same insect group (*ant nest-garden* types, Figure 6.2). A sizable collection of additional species, owing to their heavy dependence on nutrients derived directly from canopy washes, free-falling precipitation, and aerosols, make up the *atmospheric* category (Figures 1.3, 1.4, 2.2).

Devices and mechanisms employed to maintain adequate hydration provide the criteria for another series of adaptive categories (Table 2.4). Humidity determines where the epiphytes differentiated on this basis can live. An impoundment capable of serving as a reservoir will not suffice unless precipitation is

Table 2.3. Nonparasitic epiphytes differentiated according to the source and method of obtaining mineral nutrients

Source and mode	Subtypes
Prey users (carnivores)	A. Passive traps (e.g., *Nepenthes*)
	B. Active traps (*Utricularia*)
Ant-fed	A. Ant-house
	B. Ant-nest
Litter dependent	A. Leafy tanks
	B. Trash baskets (root or leaf-root based)
Directly from atmosphere	A. Foliar trichomes
	B. Velamentous roots
Substrate dependent	A. Humus via roots
	B. Naked bark via roots

Figure 2.5. Litter collected by a trash basket–type *Anthurium* sp. (Araceae) in Venezuela.

both abundant and reasonably well distributed through the year. Where droughts tend to be more severe, backup supplies must be sequestered within succulent foliage, stems, or roots (Figure 4.1D,G). Still other species avoid problems during dry weather by jettisoning their foliage before it becomes too serious a liability (Figures 2.6, 9.6). CAM-type photosynthesis, which conserves tissue moisture by allowing plants to fix CO_2 at night, is nearly the rule among the evergreen epiphytes that inhabit even moderately arid sites (see Chapter 5).

Fidelity to aerial instead of terrestrial substrates further differentiates the epiphytes into operationally distinct categories. Like the *Psilotum* just described, not all the species that grow on other plants do so consistently, and how regularly this happens distinguishes three degrees of faithfulness (Table 2.5). If only bark or some other suspended medium is acceptable, then the appropriate label is *obligate* epiphyte. The *accidental* types fall at the opposite end of the continuum, soil or rock being the rule except for the occasional individual that accidentally ends up rooting on a phorophyte instead of in the ground or on the side of a cliff.

To be a *facultative* epiphyte, which is the third category, is to utilize bark less frequently than always, but more often than accidentally. How regularly a

Figure 2.6. Trash basket–forming *Cyrtopodium punctatum* (Orchidaceae) in south Florida. Many of its deciduous leaves have already been shed as preparation for the dry season. Photo by Wesley Higgins

host is involved tends to shift across the geographic ranges of the facultative types, moisture being the primary arbiter of which option works best at a particular location. Climates cool and wet enough to promote dense growths of nonvascular plants and lichens cause living conditions to converge in the canopy and below. Likewise, extreme aridity inhibits soil formation to the extent that a fair number of the *xerophytic* (dry-growing) epiphytes encounter suitable conditions whether their seeds land on bark or on the ground. Facultative epiphytism is least common where aerial and terrestrial substrates diverge most.

Several thousand species that represent about two dozen flowering plant families, most notably Araceae and Moraceae (the figs and relatives), root sequentially as individuals on bark and in terrestrial soil. These are the *hemi-epiphytes,* so-called because they routinely switch substrates around midlife. Although differing from the facultative types by being regular bark users, they are not confined to this medium. Whether a hemi-epiphyte operates above the forest floor

Figure 2.7. A tank bromeliad in southern Venezuela supporting a carnivorous *Utricularia* sp. with its inflorescence and some foliage and associated traps exposed.

early or later during its life determines whether it belongs to the *primary* or *secondary* hemi-epiphyte category, respectively (Figures 2.8, 3.1, 7.8D; Table 2.6).

Assigning a lifestyle is not always possible; populations of certain aroids in particular often include epiphytic and hemi-epiphytic individuals, both primary and secondary types, and still others that maintain continuous contact with the ground. Lacking woody stems pretty much denies the pteridophytes access to primary hemi-epiphytism, but the other option is widely practiced,

Table 2.4. Nonparasitic epiphytes differentiated according to ways in which water is acquired, stored, and used

Source and related characteristics	Subtypes
From humus via roots, foliage evergreen, little storage capacity, C_3-type photosynthesis (severely to moderately drought vulnerable)	A. Hygrophytic (e.g., many filmy ferns) B. Mesophytic
Directly from the atmosphere via impoundments (external storage), C_3 or CAM-type photosynthesis (moderately drought vulnerable)	A. Leafy tanks B. Root or root-foliage collectors
From multiple sources, abundant moisture stored in succulent organs (internal storage), CAM-type photosynthesis (highly drought tolerant)	A. Succulent foliage B. Succulent stems
Directly from the atmosphere via specialized foliar trichomes or velamentous roots, CAM-type photosynthesis (highly drought tolerant)	A. Root dependent B. Leaf dependent
From humus or trash basket via roots, seasonally deciduous, C_3-type photosynthesis (drought avoiding)	—
From the atmosphere or humus via roots or foliage, desiccation-tolerant (poikilohydrous), C_3-type photosynthesis	—

Table 2.5. Nonparasitic epiphytes differentiated according to how faithfully they root on hosts as opposed to some other medium

Designation	Frequency of association with a host
Accidental	Only the rare individual
Facultative	More than rarely but not always
Obligate	Always

but again not consistently. Many a climbing fern, given its short roots, is about as likely to become a full-blown epiphyte as a secondary hemi-epiphyte. The hemi-epiphytes overall warrant more attention, considering how frequently they substantially augment the structural complexity of canopy habitats. Also needed is a more through assessment of the changes that occur in these plants as they shift dependence between aerial and terrestrial supplies of moisture and nutrients.

Figure 2.8. Strangling fig (*Ficus* sp., Moraceae) in the Western Ghats of Tamil Nadu state, south India.

Table 2.6. Nonparasitic epiphytes differentiated according to whether they normally spend all or only part of the life cycle rooted on another plant

Duration of association with host	Subtypes
Holo-epiphytes (entire life cycle)	—
Hemi-epiphytes (part of life cycle)	A. Primary (including stranglers) B. Secondary

The Biological Underpinnings of Epiphytism

A complete answer to the most vexing of the many questions that remain about epiphytism continues to elude researchers: Why is this lifestyle obligatory for thousands of species that represent so many families? Attributes that clearly help plants operate free of contact with the ground, such as the absorbing foliar trichomes of Bromeliaceae and the velamen-equipped roots of Orchidaceae, also serve terrestrials that utilize similarly unyielding substrates like solid rock (Figure 1.5). Even more puzzling are the numerous species in families such as Ericaceae and Melastomataceae that provide no clues whatsoever as to why they seldom or never root in terrestrial soil.

None of the characteristics associated with epiphytism, if not required for life in aerial habitats, characterize all the plants that live this way, the nearest to an exception being gravity-defying anchorage by tough durable roots. Only a couple of bromeliads no longer develop such organs, and they remain aloft either by draping over a phorophyte or by grasping nearby twigs with stiffly curled foliage (Figure 1.3). The mistletoes also lack root systems, this part of the body having been replaced by the tough, specialized invasive organ described in Chapter 5.

Other requirements for success in the forest canopy, particularly those concerned with reproduction, are achieved in multiple ways, although not with equal frequency. Most of the seed bearers require third-party interventions—almost always to pollinate and frequently to launch offspring encapsulated in fleshy fruits. The ways in which the arboreal types that bear flowers discriminate among potential mates also parallel what their terrestrial relatives do: the same animals provide services at both locations and in much the same ways. Only the trends differ, such as the disproportionate reliance by the epiphytes on nectar-seeking birds, as described in Chapter 6.

Many of the epiphytes, like their counterparts on the ground, depend on animals that consume soft fruits to disperse their seeds. Others equip their embryonic offspring with air flotation devices, or make them small enough to require no embellishments (e.g., the orchids; Figures 7.2, 7.3, 8.3E,G). Size may be the attribute most closely tied to lifestyle, the epiphytes on average producing smaller dispersal units than those released by their terrestrial relatives. Large, predominantly canopy-based genera such as *Codonanthe* of Gesneriaceae (the African violet family) further demonstrate the loose prescription for reproductive success in aerial habitats: some of its members utilize birds while others use ants or both types of animals (see Chapter 6).

Options narrow when it comes to the ways in which a plant can acquire key nutrients and maintain proper water balance while perched on a host, but even here much of what existed earlier remains unchanged. Roots for all but the arboreal contingents of a few families continue their roles as absorbing devices as they did for terrestrial ancestors. The same probably applies to the ways in which foliage conducts photosynthesis. Nevertheless, it is important to point out that the vegetative bodies of many of the epiphytes have evolved special features in response to the special conditions that prevail in many aerial habitats, as detailed in Chapters 4, 5, and 6. Most powerfully affected on this score are the dry-growing species.

How Epiphytism Evolved

Epiphytism is a derived condition that has evolved repeatedly from a taxonomically mixed ancestry that itself required different kinds of rooting media (Table 2.7; Figure 2.9). Having such a complicated history explains why the modern epiphytes operate in so many different ways and range from lowly lycophytes to the most highly specialized of the flowering plants. Lithophytism likely preceded epiphytism on numerous occasions, and the species that currently exploit rocks and bark interchangeably almost certainly demonstrate what these transitions looked like midstream (Figure 1.5). Some of the other routes are not so obvious.

Progressions that began with accidental through facultative to obligate epiphytism were probably most common. Whether well traveled or otherwise, neither this pathway nor the transition from rocks to bark explains the manner in which the secondary hemi-epiphytes arose, or how after achieving this status some lineages went on to generate full-blown epiphytes (holo-epiphytes). The primary hemi-epiphytes almost certainly followed still another avenue as their terrestrial ancestors became competent to colonize aerial habitats.

Secondary hemi-epiphytes germinate on the forest floor, after which they creep up nearby trees. Lacking vascular cambia, hence unable to replace aging vascular tissue, they die from rear to front, losing contact with terrestrial soil and ultimately forfeiting their initial status as vines (Figures 3.1, 7.8). From this point forward, they operate as total aerialists except when still younger roots

Table 2.7. Taxonomic groups that include substantial numbers of nonparasitic epiphytes

Plant type	Genus or higher group	Number of species of nonparasitic epiphytes
Lycophytes	—	225
Ferns	—	2400
Gymnosperms (naked-seeded plants)	Ginkgo	0
	Cycads	1
	Conifers	0
	Gnetaleans	4
Angiosperms (flowering plants)	Apocynaceae	140
	Araceae	1350
	Araliaceae	80
	Bromeliaceae	1500
	Cactaceae	150
	Clusiaceae	92
	Cyclanthaceae	86
	Ericaceae	675
	Gesneriaceae	560
	Marcgraviaceae	90
	Melastomataceae	650
	Moraceae	525
	Orchidaceae	15,000
	Piperaceae	710
	Rubiaceae	223
	Solanaceae	56

grow long enough to continue contact with the ground. This is an arrangement that in most respects parallels the adventitiously rooted vine-type habit that occurs widely among numerous predominantly woody tropical families.

Every time a secondary hemi-epiphyte progresses beyond its terrestrial to its aerial phase, it illustrates in quick time how its adaptive type originated. Not replayed during a single life cycle is a subsequent change that amounted to crossing another adaptive threshold, this time from secondary hemi-epiphytism to holo-epiphytism. Complete departure from the ground emerged this third way when what had been a vine-type shoot became telescoped and its now congested foliage reoriented to achieve a more or less vertical posture. The resulting funnel-shaped architecture is well illustrated by the bird nest–type anthuriums and philodendrons that approach the tank bromeliads as litter collectors (Figure 2.5).

Speculation about which evolutionary pathways led to epiphytism of one type or another raises a more fundamental question: Why did this lifestyle emerge in the first place? Contrary to the notion implicit in the language chosen by certain authors, the epiphytes did not "move up" into the forest canopy to "escape"

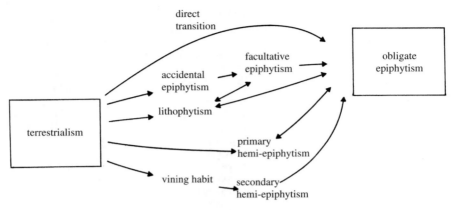

Figure 2.9. Evolutionary pathways leading from terrestrialism to epiphytism and hemi-epiphytism.

shade. More appropriate is the axiom: nature abhors a vacuum and, provided opportunity, eventually fills it. Vascular plants were going to colonize arboreal habitats simply because trees came on the scene and the adaptations that allow smaller plants to invade their crowns were widely accessible in the Darwinian sense. What likely cannot be determined is which of the adaptations that made the transition from ground to phorophyte possible evolved explicitly to serve this purpose.

Small-bodied plants reap different benefits and face distinct challenges depending on whether they anchor within or below a forest canopy that casts dense shade. Only the hemi-epiphytes, because they spend time in both locations, stand to make the best of and minimize the worst of the botanical consequences of these two options. Most successful in this respect are the stranglers. These are the species that earn their reputation by robbing canopy giants of their hard-won places in the sun (see Chapter 10). The most vigorous of their kind can kill a host following transition from modest-sized epiphyte to massive self-supporting tree (Figure 2.8).

The most aggressive of the primary hemi-epiphytes probably evolved from small to medium-sized woody epiphytes with long roots. Genus *Ficus* of family Moraceae holds the record for lethality, but it also includes some shrubby epiphytes and vines. *Clusia* of the tea family more or less parallels the figs for woodiness and growth habit, but its hemi-epiphytes less often kill. Most of the remaining primary hemi-epiphytes produce substantially less or no woody tissue and represent families like Araliaceae and the ferns. While they succeed in intercepting light that otherwise would nourish their hosts, they stand little chance of displacing them.

The Taxonomic Affiliations of the Epiphytes

The epiphytes occur unevenly across the plant kingdom. Close to one-third of the spore bearers, but a far more modest fraction of the seed producers, grow this way. Nor is epiphytism uniformly developed among the Linnaean families and orders (Table 2.7; Figures 7.1, 9.8). The conifers do not participate in this lifestyle beyond fielding a few accidental epiphytes, mostly in cool wet temperate forests. Panamanian *Zamia pseudoparasitica* alone within its roughly 250-member order, to which all the cycads belong, normally anchors above ground (see Chapter 10).

The flowering plants present the most mixed picture of all (Table 2.7; Figure 7.1). More than 80 of the approximately 400 families that make up this most recently diversified of the major clades of vascular plants contain at least one epiphytic member. Of these 80, only 32 contain 5 or more species, and fewer than half of the remainder account for the vast majority. At least half of all the arboreal species are orchids, this number constituting close to three-quarters of that family. Araceae and Bromeliaceae contribute about 3000 more, further ensuring that few communities of epiphytes are dominated by other than monocots or ferns. Why these two groups are so successful in aerial habitats is explored in Chapters 7 and 9, respectively.

Many fewer of the *eudicotyledonous* angiosperms anchor on other plants, and here again just a handful of families, especially Apocynaceae, Cactaceae, Ericaceae, Gesneriaceae, Melastomataceae, Moraceae, and Rubiaceae contribute most of the species. Piperaceae, which is a relatively primitive family that forms part of the "basal" angiosperm complex within the phylogenetic tree that depicts flowering plant history, is another major source of canopy-based stock (Figure 7.1). Conversely, quite a few of the largest of the eudicot families, such as Asteraceae (the composites) and Fabaceae (the herbaceous legumes) include no more than a dozen or so epiphytic members.

Genetic Heritage and Evolutionary Options

Plants native to challenging habitats typically exhibit traits that reveal the most demanding of the conditions under which they grow. The astute observer does not need a degree in botany to recognize that a thick spiny stem helps a barrel cactus tolerate drought and foil thirsty herbivores. A pondweed that spends its life submerged in turbid water requires an entirely different arrangement. Being relegated to spaces where dim light rather than drought limits growth calls for delicate foliage to conduct adequate photosynthesis. Similarly, it is hard to imagine architecture superior to that of a tank bromeliad for exploiting a perch in the crown of a tall tree (Figures 5.5, 7.4, 7.5B,C,E).

Few epiphytes possess more than a minority of the most common of the attributes that allow their kind to live unconnected to the ground. While succulence coupled with CAM-type photosynthesis and adventitious roots occur widely, such is not the case for absorbing hairs, cavities in stems or foliage for housing plant-feeding ants, leafy impoundments, or velamen-equipped roots. Two families that include thousands of arboreal members each underscore this point. A majority of the epiphytic bromeliads, but not a single orchid, employ leafy tanks to secure moisture and nutrients. Conversely, none of the former possess roots equal to those of the latter for performing multiple functions while suspended in air. Epiphytes representing additional families rely on still other suites of adaptations, further evidence that genetic legacy influences which solutions are adopted during the course of evolution to solve a given problem.

The adage "what precedes constrains what follows" applies to all forms of life; capacity for change is universal, but only within limits imposed by genetic history—by *phylogenetic constraints*. How powerfully this inherent filter narrows options for structural change within a lineage of plants depends on how deeply the trait in question is embedded within its *genetic architecture*. Leaf shape and size more readily respond to natural selection than overall body plan, which is far more fundamental in determining how and where a plant can grow. Phylogenetic constraints affect physiology as well. Studies have shown, for example, that at least some of the chlorophyll-free parasites (holo-parasites) retain the genes that mediated photosynthesis for their green ancestors, but in much degenerated condition.

Genetic legacy also accounts for the redundant nature of the evolutionary process illustrated in the phylogeny pictured in Figure 2.1. The architecture needed to collect useful materials is shown as having evolved twice. The capacity to replace soil roots with a leafy tank is an implied dimension of the genetic legacy bequeathed to all 12 descendant lineages by their common ancestor. This most ancient of the many lineages depicted—the one represented by the trunk of the tree—is envisaged as having possessed a rosette-type shoot readily modifiable to collect moisture and debris. Judging by the branching pattern of the tree, two of its daughter lineages experienced Darwinian selection that prompted realization of this potential.

Homoplasic traits can be deeply redundant or based on separate genetic foundations. The first possibility is exemplified by the way that certain dry-growing plants conserve moisture by taking up CO_2 at night, as described in Chapter 5 and depicted in shorthand in Figure 5.1. Many of the same genes mediate this mechanism among the taxonomically diverse species that benefit from its presence. Arrangements that conform to the second possibility represent more broadly convergent products of evolution (i.e., are not truly "homologous"). The ways in which a selection of distantly related epiphytes have become adapted to conduct photosynthesis while deeply embedded in dense forest illustrate nonhomologous-type homoplasy.

Figures 7.2B, 7.8C,E, 8.1D,F,G, and 9.10E show how one or more epiphytes within families Araceae, Cactaceae, and Orchidaceae, and the lycophyte genus *Huperzia* employ arching to pendent flat green organs to enhance their capacities to absorb shade light, which is scattered in addition to being weak. The cacti operate with naked, flattened stems (cladodes) and the orchid and lycophyte with two-dimensional, more or less vertically held leafy shoots. The aroid promotes light capture from multiple directions by dangling elongated narrow leaves. In essence, evolutionary accommodations by these disparate species to the diffuse energy supplies in dark living spaces involve structural convergence among organs whose identities vary by participant. Which organs could be modified was determined by phylogenetic constraints specific to four not very closely related lineages.

Conifers, legumes, and grasses, among other taxonomic groups, likely owe their minor occurrences or complete exclusion from aerial habitats to powerful phylogenetic constraints that exert their influences at different stages of the life cycle. Large seeds, massive overall stature, slow growth, relatively poor drought tolerance, and a host of additional characteristics top the list (Table 2.8). To what extent each trait impedes epiphytism probably varies by plant group and environmental context. Ericaceae and Melastomataceae exemplify families with numerous epiphytes but none that inhabit the canopies of other than moist, relatively cool tropical forests. Why being woody rather than herbaceous, which applies in both cases here, is so restricting is considered in Chapters 4 and 5.

Conceivably some of the adaptations that underlie epiphytism remain unrecognized, for instance, within family Gesneriaceae. For the most part, the hundreds of obligate epiphytes in the family lack features that visibly differentiate closely related arboreal from terrestrial species (see Chapter 8). Many additional families parallel the gesneriads in herbaceousness, pollination biology, seed dispersal mode, and tropical distribution, yet they harbor few if any epiphytes. Perhaps characteristics that alone would little affect lifestyle become more influential when associated with certain other attributes. I expect that relatively subtle differences in shoot architecture will turn out to be inordinately important.

Epiphytism and Speciation

Circumstantial evidence suggests that epiphytism is sufficiently conducive to speciation to have fostered numerous, exceptionally vigorous radiations (Table 2.7). Most of the arboreal gesneriads belong to just two of the five

Table 2.8. Comparison of epiphyte features

Features that over-occur among the epiphytes	Features rarely or never present in epiphytes
Perennial life cycle	Unusually long or short life cycle
Animal pollination	Wind pollination
Small, mobile propagules (seeds, fruits, spores)	Large seeds and fruits
Roots that emerge adventitiously over much of the shoot system	Discrete root system confined to base of shoot system
Herbaceous, small bodied, shoot growth indeterminate and often sympodial (see Figure 1.2C)	Body large, woody, unitary rather than comprising reiterating, semiautonomous units (ramets)
Distinctly xerophytic, more often drought tolerant (succulent, CAM-type photosynthesis) than drought avoiding (seasonally deciduous)	Root tubers (not stem tubers)
Moderate to slow-growing	
Structure that prolongs contact with precipitation (e.g., leafy impoundments, velamen-equipped roots)	
Mutualisms with ants	

subfamilies in that group and dominate many of its largest genera (e.g., *Aeschynanthus, Columnea, Drymonia*). Likewise, virtually all the epiphytic bromeliads belong to two of eight subfamilies (Bromelioideae and Tillandsioideae). For the orchids, it is just one of five subfamilies, and within Epidendroideae, predominantly epiphytic genera such as *Bulbophyllum* and *Pleurothallus* contain many hundreds to more than 1000 species each. Close to one-half of the more than 1500 peperomias of Piperaceae are epiphytic. Most of the epiphytic and hemi-epiphytic aroids belong to *Anthurium, Philodendron,* and *Raphidiophora*. Similar asymmetries prevail in Apocynaceae and Rubiaceae, among others.

Epiphytes tend to over-occur in Linnaean groups characterized by herbaceousness, small body size, modular architecture, adventitious roots, substantial drought tolerance, and highly mobile seeds (Table 2.8). Presuming that these traits predisposed terrestrial ancestors to generate arboreal descendants, it should come as no surprise that Orchidaceae exceeds every other group for engaging in this lifestyle. Additional similarly disposed clades well stocked with epiphytes include the modern ferns and the *homosporous* lycophytes along with Araceae, Bromeliaceae, and the other flowering plant families previously identified. Conversely, Fagaceae (the oaks and beeches) and Juglandaceae (the hickories and walnuts), like the other woody, large-seeded families, are seriously disadvantaged by these same measures and mostly lack arboreal members.

Epiphytism based on parasitism has a much narrower taxonomic base than the free-living kind. All but a handful of the branch-tapping parasites belong to closely allied families Loranthaceae and Santalaceae (Figure 5.6); moreover, the now robust DNA-based phylogeny of the mistletoes indicates that shoot parasitism evolved multiple times from root parasitism. All three members of Loranthaceae considered most primitive by flower structure are rather ordinary looking trees that attack similarly soil-rooted hosts below ground. Root-tappers overall are far more diverse by family affiliation than their arboreal counterparts, a point that accords with the fact that aboveground parasitism is the more challenging of these two physiologically equivalent ways for a plant to make its living.

Epiphytism remains an incompletely understood life strategy predicated on a less than fully characterized inventory of adaptations, no one of which is shared by all the species that grow this way. The epiphytes accommodate demanding growing conditions that differ among forest types and within the same woodland habitat and even inside the crowns of individual, free-standing phorophytes. Similar microclimates and equally unyielding substrates prevail elsewhere, so it is likely that some of the features that allow plants to use each other as substrates also explain their occurrences on media as unconventional as rocks and telephone wires (Figures 1.4, 1.5).

Finally, epiphytism is not the product of a single evolutionary event but has arisen time and again across the plant kingdom along with an undetermined number of adaptations that make this lifestyle possible. Characteristics as varied as leafy impoundments, ant houses, roots equipped with a velamen, and drought deciduousness have evolved more than once since the higher plants colonized land more than 400 million years ago. How many of these attributes emerged primarily to support soil-free existence above ground may never be known. We do know the ways in which they currently serve the plants to which this book is dedicated, and this is what Chapters 4 and 5 are all about.

3 Epiphytes in Communities and Ecosystems

Epiphytes are becoming increasingly popular choices for home, garden, and beyond. It's common these days to spot a specimen or two in a friend's home or brightening up a workplace. Professional displays are standard fare in airport concourses, shopping malls, and other public facilities. Encountering so many bromeliads, orchids, and others of their kind flourishing under such an array of artificial conditions can be misleading. Why so many of the epiphytes that you do not see are more challenging to grow should be evident after reading this chapter and the two that follow.

Unlike the cultigens that owe their most desirable qualities to human manipulation, the plants featured in this volume represent biological species. Being products of Darwinian evolution, they possess attributes attuned to nature, not to our fancy. Every bona fide species is unique in the ways its members reproduce, schedule other life cycle activities, obtain resources, respond to threats, and much more. All told, these characteristics amount to a species' *natural history*. Species also occupy *niches* defined by where and how their members live and what they do there. As a result, much about a plant's structure and function makes no sense except in light of the natural history and niche of its species.

The epiphytes warrant scientific inquiry if only because of the unusual ways they acquire moisture and nutrients, conduct photosynthesis, and interact with animals. How they affect their surroundings makes the case for serious study even stronger. Plants of this description can significantly alter ecosystem-wide processes like nutrient cycling and, if abundant enough, modify microclimates as well. Additionally, epiphytes sometimes adversely impact the welfare of their phorophytes. Because they are significant modifiers of environments, it is also worth noting that they create much of what they experience. The ways in which the epiphytes operate as members of communities and ecosystems and influence and are influenced by their surroundings are the subjects of this chapter.

The Nature of Aerial Habitats

Chapter 2 describes how the epiphytes are adapted to a broad array of growing conditions and substrates. Extraordinary variety is necessary because light intensity and temperature diminish downward through the canopies of dense forests, whereas humidity rises (Figure 3.1). Similar gradients often prevail within the crowns of individual, free-standing trees. A fourth variable concerns nutrients, which increase in abundance toward the ground. Consequently, shade challenges the deeply embedded epiphytes most, whereas those located higher above ground are likely to experience serious drought, potentially injurious exposure to intense sunlight, and more limited access to key substances like nitrogen and phosphorus.

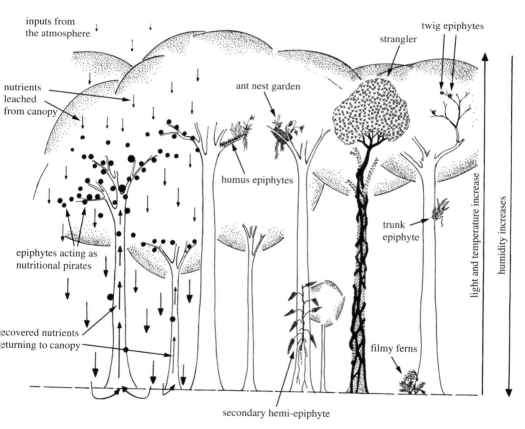

Figure 3.1. A forest with epiphytes and hemi-epiphytes with adaptive types identified. Also shown is the path followed by mineral nutrients as they enter and cycle within this woodland ecosystem.

Canopy habitats also incorporate multiple types of substrates, some suitable for many kinds of epiphytes and others to only a few specialists. Options are most diverse where high humidity encourages lichens and bryophytes to form mats thick enough to hold abundant moisture and insulate drought-vulnerable roots (Figure 3.2). Drier woodlands offer their users little more than naked bark. It is reasonable to consider these latter habitats aerial deserts complete with oases if water-retaining microsites such as knotholes are present to sustain scattered, drought-sensitive individuals among more xerophytic epiphytes.

Epiphyte-friendly anchorages differ by complexity and origin, unadorned bark being the simplest kind. Ants provide the most elaborate medium in the form of a composite material called *carton* that they manufacture to construct nests and covered runways (Figures 3.3, 6.2). Chewed plant material forms the basis of carton with the other components determined by availability and the architect's identity. A carton's suitability for epiphytes is based on its texture and composition. Least sustaining are mixtures composed primarily of plant fiber, because they incorporate few nutrients and retain little moisture. Cartons that include feces or terrestrial soil are far superior. Note how extensively the root systems of a colony of *Peperomia macrostachya* have penetrated the partially dissected ant nest illustrated in Figure 3.3.

Figure 3.2. An unidentified *Rhododendron* rooted on a mossy branch in Papua New Guinea.

Figure 3.3. Part of an Ecuadorian ant nest constructed of carton, illustrating its extensive exploitation by the roots of *Peperomia macrostachya.*

Other kinds of rooting media and plant-provided containments support still other types of epiphytes. Some of the orchids and pteridophytes habitually anchor in the thick mantles of aerial roots that clothe the trunks of certain tree ferns (Figure 9.11). Carnivorous *Utricularia humboltiana* favors moss-covered rocks and bark, but it also colonizes the water-impounding shoots of certain tank bromeliads in Venezuela and southeastern Brazil. Figure 2.7 shows a specimen in flower, with its elaborate tangle of shoots exposed to reveal the attached translucent traps. The primitive fern *Ophioglossum pendulum* roots mostly in the debris accumulated by the foliage of staghorn ferns (*Platycerium*) and bird's nest ferns (*Asplenium*) near Madang in Papua New Guinea (Figure 9.5).

Mineral Nutrients

Terrestrial plants obtain nutrients from the ground, and so do most of the epiphytes, although less directly. The latter also receive significant inputs from above ground in the form of aerosols and precipitation and the canopy washes created by heavy storms. Which vehicle is most important depends on the subject's mode of nutrition (its adaptive type), time of year, and a variety of additional factors such as a host's propensity to shed nutrients (Figure 3.1). The residents of cloud forests obtain much of what they need from mist and fog, two forms of *occult* or fine droplet precipitation that can exceed ordinary rain in nutrient content. The atmospheric bromeliad illustrated in Figure 1.4 depends primarily on dust and typical precipitation for nutrients, most of which in the second instance usually occur at concentrations well below one part per million (ppm).

Certain bacteria and electrical discharges during storms continue to inject plant-usable nitrogen into woodland ecosystems, just as they always have. It is the additional nitrogen originating from burning fossil fuels that is increasing baseline supplies. Forest fires are elevating airborne phosphorus and some of the other chemical elements as well, although more locally and not as much as with nitrogen. Rising inputs of the latter are already altering the mix of plant species in certain inherently infertile temperate zone ecosystems; whether the epiphytes are being affected yet is anyone's guess.

The soilborne nutrients that help sustain epiphytes reach their users by moving up the xylem vascular systems of the supporting vegetation (Figure 3.1). Mistletoes tap this supply en route, while the free-living types rely on physical processes or third parties to deliver what isn't diverted by parasites. Precipitation charged with useful substances leached from tree crowns, particularly from living foliage, plant parts shed as litter, and organic materials delivered by plant-feeding ants constitute three of the most significant of the indirect sources of soil nutrients for the nonparasitic epiphytes.

A number of studies have determined the amounts of nitrogen, phosphorus, and several additional nutrients that occur in tropical forest ecosystems, where they come from, and how they circulate after arrival. The few suspended soils that were examined turned out to be about as well provisioned with key nutrients as nearby terrestrial soils. Some of these same reports include data on the contents of the tanks of the local bromeliads. Even so, it is not yet possible to generalize about which sources of nutrients or plant adaptations promote epiphyte welfare the most or under what conditions.

Nitrogen is the best choice to probe more deeply into epiphyte nutrition for three reasons. First, it is the nutrient whose global abundance has already increased to troubling levels. Second is its preeminence as a governor of plant growth. Last, nitrogen can be tracked in nature by taking advantage of its occurrence in two stable isotopic forms that differ solely by atomic weight (^{14}N and ^{15}N). As luck would have it, the ratio of these two isotopes (the *isotopic signature* of nitrogen) varies by location in woodland ecosystems, including those populated by epiphytes.

Several investigations have provided insights into nitrogen nutrition, and one conducted at a site in Mexico is especially informative. The twig epiphytes growing there, more than the humus types anchored on the same trees, were subsisting primarily on nitrogen absorbed straight from the atmosphere. The same nutrient sequestered in the bodies of their supports assayed higher in ^{15}N than that obtained from the humus epiphytes, which in turn came close to those recorded in soil. Clearly, these two types of epiphytes exploit different sources of nitrogen, but the humus users are less discriminating.

Another study employing the same technology demonstrated how several bromeliads in the genera *Guzmania* and *Vriesea* shifted sources of nitrogen as their growing shoots became capable of collecting precipitation and litter. More than three-quarters of the nitrogen present in the bodies of juveniles too small to possess tanks had come from the atmosphere, but as development progressed, this figure fell to no more than a third, the balance having come from the ground via one of those indirect routes described earlier in this section.

Water

Except for those that inhabit the wettest forests, the epiphytes show unmistakable signs of preparedness for drought (Figure 4.1). At least modest succulence is common, and it can involve leaves, stems, or roots, or two or all three organs simultaneously. Capacity to store moisture far beyond a subject's immediate needs, plus additional, more subtle aspects of anatomy such as foliage equipped with thick cuticles, leave no doubt that aridity is the most powerful determinant of where the epiphytes grow. The ways in which these departures from more conventional form and physiology help stave off life-threatening desiccation are described in the next chapter.

Anatomy further indicates that epiphytes experience a kind of drought more characteristic of aerial than of terrestrial habitats. Soil-rooted xerophytes, for example, the desert-dwelling cacti and agaves, lack form, similar to the situation described in Chapter 4 for the aerial roots of orchids (Figures 2.2, 4.3). Also absent are the leafy tanks and moisture-absorbing foliar scales that serve the bromeliads and smaller numbers of epiphytes in several additional families (Figures 4.4, 4.5, 7.5B,C,E). All these features heighten the benefits of what above ground tend to be relatively fleeting contacts between a plant and its moisture supply. The mistletoes avoid this problem by tapping the water vascular systems of their soil-rooted hosts.

Being mostly drought adapted but to different degrees means that the free-living epiphytes should distribute across landscapes according to their capacities to rapidly absorb and store moisture and use it sparingly. This is exactly what they do. Figure 3.4 illustrates how the arboreal floras at five locations distributed across tropical America fall in number of species as well as number of families represented as annual rainfall diminishes. Epiphytes recorded along this humidity

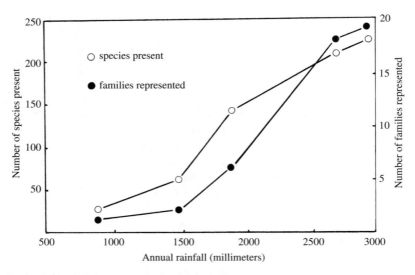

Figure 3.4. The relationship between annual rainfall and the diversity of epiphytes at five locations in tropical America (after Gentry and Dodson 1987).

gradient also occurred in greatest abundance and variety of adaptive types in ever-wet forests, particularly at elevations between about 500 and 2000 meters.

Data collected at three Ecuadorian sites, chosen because they support dry, moist, or rain forest, demonstrated that epiphytes react more adversely to drought than do co-occurring trees, shrubs, vines, and herbs (Table 3.1). Whereas arboreal species amounted to fully one-third of the total inventory of vascular plants at the most humid site, farther west where the dry season is most prolonged, their contribution fell to a mere 2%. Climbers were similarly affected but in the opposite direction. Trees were least sensitive to climate, with shrubs and herbs showing neither strong nor consistent trends.

Annual precipitation less reliably predicts epiphyte diversity than its distribution through the year. Species richness is greatest where at least 5 to 10 cm of rain fall monthly, but exceptions occur in both directions. A substantial number of anatomically desiccation-vulnerable species survive months of nearly rainless weather at Monteverde, Costa Rica, only because continuously humid air combined with moderate temperatures slow evaporation (transpiration). Conversely, many hot lowland sites that receive enough moisture to maintain wet forest still experience droughts severe enough to discourage colonization by any but hardy epiphytes.

Many of the epiphytes native to the most humid of tropical forests parallel their hosts in a way that demonstrates a basic principle of plant economics. Having access to more abundant and reliable supplies of moisture than most of their

Plate 1. Three pollination syndromes illustrated by members of the bromeliad genus *Billbergia*. **A.** Bird-pollinated *B. eloisiae*, photo by Phil Nelson **B.** Insect-pollinated *B. horrida*, photo by Phil Nelson **C.** Bat-pollinated *B. robert-readii*. Most distinguishing are the colors and sizes of the inflorescence bracts.

Plate 2. Orchids illustrating the unusual colors and shapes displayed by flowers borne by many members of their family. **A.** *Bulbophyllum phalaenopsis* **B.** *Bulbophyllum claptonense* **C.** *Dracula tubeana*. Photos by Phil Nelson. Mimicry is at work here. *Bulbophyllum phalaenopsis* emits a fetid odor that, combined with the deep purple, coarsely hairy floral parts, makes it a convincing simulator of rotting carrion. *Dracula tubeana* is probably a fungus mimic, especially the central portion of the flower, which induces egg-laying by fungus gnats. *Bulbophyllum claptonense* may be mimicking a territorial bee.

Plate 3. Three pollination syndromes illustrated by three bromeliads in subfamily Tillandsioideae. **A.** Spontaneously autogamous *Tillandsia recurvata,* photo by Bruce K. Holst; this flower is only about 5 millimeters long. **B.** Bird-pollinated *T. brachycaulis*, photo by Phil Nelson **C.** Moth-pollinated *T. usneoides*, photo by Bruce K. Holst. The bright red color of the foliage of *T. brachycaulis* is transitory, disappearing soon after the flowers wither.

A

C

Plate 4. Flowers and inflorescences of additional epiphytes. **A.** Night-blooming *Epiphyllum crenatum* (Cactaceae), photo by Phil Nelson **B.** Bird-pollinated *Macleania sleumeriana* (Ericaceae), photo by Phil Nelson **C.** Bat-pollinated *Merinthopodium neuranthum* (Solanaceae), photo by Linda Grashoff

B

Plate 5. Flowers and inflorescences of additional epiphytes, continued. **A.** Bat-pollinated *Hoya darwinii* (Apocynaceae), photo by Phil Nelson **B.** Cauliflorous *Medinilla* sp. 'Gregori Hambali' (Melastomataceae), photo by Phil Nelson **C.** Bird- or moth-pollinated *Marcgravia rectiflora* (Marcgraviaceae), photo by Bruce K. Holst

Plate 6. Flowers and inflorescences of additional epiphytes, continued. **A.** *Philodendron* sp. (Araceae), photo by Yuribia Vivas **B.** Pendent inflorescence of *Medinilla alata* (Melastomataceae), photo by Phil Nelson **C.** *Dieranopygium* sp. (Cyclanthaceae), photo by Bruce K. Holst. Note the characteristic aroid spathe-spadix–type inflorescence in B.

Plate 7. Ornamented foliage of epiphytes. **A.** *Columnea medicinalis* (Gesneriaceae), also illustrating the tubular, often bird-pollinated flowers produced by members of this highly evolved family, photo by Stephen Maciejewski **B.** *Vriesea splendens* (Bromeliaceae), photo by Kevin Swagel **C.** *Neoregelia chlorosticta* (Bromeliaceae), photo by Elton Leme

Plate 8. The brightly colored, fleshy fruits produced by epiphytes that belong to three families. **A.** *Aechmea brevicollis* (Bromeliaceae), photo by Phil Nelson **B.** *Anthurium gracile* (Araceae), photo by Phil Nelson **C.** *Sphyrospermum buxifolium* (Ericaceae). *Anthurium gracile* also illustrates the velamen-covered root of many epiphytic Araceae.

Table 3.1. Number of vascular plant species present in 3 types of forest in Ecuador differentiated by growth habit

Growth habit	Forest type		
	Wet	Moist	Dry
Epiphytes	35	8	2
Trees	31	38	28
Shrubs	11	10	6
Climbers	10	25	34
Herbs	14	11	29

Source: After Gentry and Dodson 1987

kind, they manage to conduct enough photosynthesis to support growth habits as shrubs and even small trees. Likewise, the high cost in water accompanying the manufacture of xylem tissue explains why the ratio of herbaceous to woody epiphytes rises so sharply along moisture gradients like the one surveyed in Ecuador.

Botanists still do not fully understand how the availabilities of water and nutrients influence the geographic or within-habitat distributions of epiphytes. Much additional information awaits discovery, judging by the performance of a handful of species that have already yielded to investigators armed with modern analytical instruments. These relatively well-studied bromeliads, ferns, and orchids tell us that just about every mechanism employed by higher plants to cope with drought is used by at least a few epiphytes (see Chapter 4).

Light

Figure 3.1 depicts the climatic gradients that exist above ground in a densely foliated tropical forest and illustrates why epiphytes experience growing conditions that range from bright and droughty to dangerously energy-poor but humid. Less than 1% of the solar radiation striking the top of such a forest reaches its base, and what filters through is more depleted in some wavelengths than in others. How are the epiphytes adapted to deal with this situation? More specifically, how do they respond to different intensities and qualities of sunlight?

Uneven absorption as it passes through foliage reduces the ratio of red to far-red radiation in sunlight, which in turn determines its capacity to influence the way a plant develops and conducts photosynthesis. (Far-red represents the less energetic portion of the entire red part of the electromagnetic [EM] spectrum.) Move a tank bromeliad from a fully exposed perch to a point deeper within a thick canopy, and its next offshoot (ramet) will display architecture better adapted to shade than to full sunlight. Note how the sun-grown individual illustrated in Figure 3.5 reduces its exposure to direct beam irradiation by holding its gray leaves stiffly upright, while its counterpart maintained in shade has droopier, thinner foliage, all the better to intercept scattered shade-type light (Figure 3.6). Too rapid a change in the opposite direction can spell disaster. Fell a tree in a dense forest, and the epiphytes anchored in the darker portions of its crown will likely die after experiencing unfiltered light too abruptly to avoid massive photoinjury.

Figure 5.2 illustrates the way two leaves, one adapted for dim and the other for unfiltered sunlight, respond to graded exposures. Note how the first organ achieves maximum output (becomes light-saturated) at a lower intensity. Higher exposure might have reduced its output even more than shown in this graph

Figure 3.5. Sun-grown *Tillandsia utriculata*.

Figure 3.6. Shade-grown *Tillandsia utriculata.*

(caused more photoinhibition). The same curves demonstrate that the amount of solar radiation required to balance respiration also differs, less being needed by the shade-adapted subject. Figure 5.2 further illustrates that a leaf prepared to perform most effectively in shade is less productive (compared on a leaf area basis) than its opposite kind while it is light-saturated.

More than a century ago, the pioneering German plant geographer A. F. W. Schimper described how the epiphytes he observed in South America differed depending on where they occurred along the gradients of light, humidity, and temperature shown in Figure 3.1. Today, ecologists understand the ways in which the two variables interact to help make tropical forests exceptionally nuanced living spaces capable of supporting record levels of botanical and zoological diversity. How the epiphytes have become adapted to exploit such a broad range of environmental conditions is covered in more detail in Chapters 4 and 5.

Given the environmentally mixed character of their habitats, it would be odd indeed if the epiphytes were anything less than adaptively diverse. Recall from Chapter 2 that individual species, arboreal or otherwise, occupy narrow physical niches, although how narrow varies. On balance, epiphytes tend to be more sensitive than trees, shrubs, vines, and understory herbs, all of which root in soil and so experience less rigorous challenges when it comes to securing vital resources (Table 3.1; Figure 3.4). More demanding conditions above ground have obliged more specialized ways of operating, and specialization promotes operational rigidity.

Much as for drought tolerance, certain structural and physiological attributes signal a plant's preparedness for shade as opposed to stronger sunlight. Biologist Collin Pittendrigh, while studying malaria in Trinidad during World War II, discovered that he could divide the bromeliads native to that Caribbean island into three light-related categories. His observations are particularly instructive because they reveal how aspects of leaf anatomy, particularly that of the foliar epidermis, and overall shoot architecture equip members of a collection of related epiphytes to exploit climatic mosaics.

Bromeliads confined to the darkest, wettest portions of the forests in which Pittendrigh worked possess shoots with lax, thin, wide leaves poorly equipped to store water within, or to impound more than modest amounts externally in leafy cups (Figure 5.4). At midcanopy, farther up the light gradient, his so-called sun types occur. These are the species with foliage capable of impounding more moisture relative to overall plant size. At the top, where sunlight is most intense and the air driest and warmest, reside Pittendrigh's so-called exposure bromeliads. Plants of this third description are even more compact bodied, and if they are impounders, they feature exceptionally deep narrow tanks that help minimize evaporative loss (Figure 7.5C). A second exposure type bears water-storing foliage covered with dense layers of absorbing, light-reflecting epidermal scales (Figures 4.5, 7.5D; Plate 3C).

Summarizing briefly, epiphytes vary greatly by adaptive type in ways that mirror the exceptional heterogeneity of their habitats. Forest canopies constitute deeply three-dimensional living spaces characterized by intersecting environmental gradients of humidity, light, nutrients, and temperature (Figure 3.1). Additionally, rooting media exist from the tops of the crowns of the tallest trees to just short of the forest floor, and their complexities have obliged much plant specialization, and for many an epiphyte, strict fidelity to a specific kind of substrate (Figure 6.2). Fauna have also been influential. Tropical forests are unparalleled for numbers and kinds of animals, no small portion of which partner with epiphytic plants in mutually beneficial relationships.

Epiphytes as Members of Communities

Ecologists describe organisms as "assembling" when they form "biological communities." What results can end abruptly, owing to a catastrophic fire or flood, or a community may simply dissipate as it exhausts some nonrenewable resource, as happens when scavenging insects consume a carcass. Occasionally, the physical system that supports a community fails, for example, when a broken branch causes the demise of a bromeliad along with the residents of its tanks. Even the most durable of communities changes over time as early occupants improve growing conditions for later arrivers capable of displacing them. More is made of this subject below.

The ways in which the founders of a community assemble is influenced by physical context. Forest canopies consist of scaffolds comprising trunks, branches, and twigs surrounded by intersecting gradients of moisture, nutrients, sunlight, and temperature (Figure 3.1). Should hemi-epiphytes be present, they augment this network with roots that further connect aerial and terrestrial living spaces. Options for anchorage range from naked bark to ant cartons to soil-like layers of suspended humus. The result is an intricately structured, deeply three-dimensional assemblage of interacting plants and animals.

Complementarity among residents further solidifies communities. Plants compete, but less than might be anticipated considering that all but the chlorophyll-free parasites require the same resources: light, moisture, and the same mineral nutrients. Antagonisms are less than shared needs and finite resources predict because every plant present within a community operates according to the unique life history and distinct niche of its species. Being organized in this fashion, mixed populations exploit universally required resources more effectively than if all present met their needs in the same ways.

A forest broadly exploited by diverse kinds of epiphytes includes individuals that process litter in tanks and others that depend on plant-feeding ants, or on nutrients extracted directly from precipitation and more. Virtually every kind of suspended substrate on site is hosting a green occupant. In effect, the local epiphytes "partition" shared living space and essential commodities, particularly light and nutrients, and perhaps most conspicuously, rooting media. They further promote community coherence by providing resources for other kinds of organisms, as described in Chapters 6 and 11.

Cooperation among unrelated organisms is a second community organizing force, as demonstrated by many flowering plants when they reproduce. If a given population of epiphytes happens to require visits from a certain kind of pollinator in April, it will not compete with another population that needs the same carrier in August. Additionally, by taking turns, the two maintain a common resource, one feeding said visitor while the other is doing something else such as ripening fruit. Benefits also tie in any third parties that happen to obtain goods or services from the same plant-dependent animals.

Epiphytes and animals further serve one another in ways that far exceed pollination for intimacy. The ant-fed species provide nesting space in return for nutrients and protection. The many shapes and sizes of the leaves and stems that serve as *myrmecodomatia* demonstrate one of the most striking examples of evolutionary convergence among the epiphytes (Figures 5.3, 7.2C, 7.5A,D, 8.3F,H,I, 8.4A,B,C,D,E, 9.4B,E). Likewise, these independently acquired, functionally equivalent organs attest to the advantage gained when arboreal ants act as proxies for roots. Such interspecies couplings qualify as *mutualisms,* and the free-living epiphytes probably hold the record for this kind of engagement, several examples of which are examined in Chapter 6.

It is also worth noting that the epiphytes are not equally important in communities and ecosystems. Some rarely or never significantly affect the welfare of other organisms, either because they are not common enough, are too small-bodied, or they fill relatively inconsequential niches. Other species contribute mightily, for example, those that provide food or nesting spaces for a variety of kinds of animals. Such *keystone* types decisively influence their ecosystems, often fostering much biodiversity, complexity, and stability, as described in Chapter 11. Many of the epiphytes and hemi-epiphytes, such as the large tank bromeliads and the strangling figs, warrant this designation.

Random Factors Also Structure Communities

Factors in addition to the growth requirements and tolerances that differentiate species help shape the structure and composition of communities of epiphytes. Random events such as where a seed lands or a branch breaks contribute as well. Should occurrences of the second kind take place with appropriate frequency, the sum of their impacts can be quite influential. Rather than destroying a community, localized disturbances can promote species richness, the simplest measure of biodiversity. Why this is so is addressed by the intermediate disturbance hypothesis.

Figure 3.7 illustrates how small-scale accidents that randomly eliminate individuals, or several near-neighbors, influence the number of kinds of plants that can live together. Disturbance of this nature acts by reducing antagonisms among co-occurring populations whose needs, particularly for rooting media, overlap. As disturbance decreases, competition for the safe sites (i.e., germination sites) that every population requires to maintain its numbers stiffens as the more aggressive players increasingly co-opt more than their share at the expense of less vigorous residents. Ratchet up disturbance, and populations also disappear. According to the intermediate disturbance hypothesis, species richness peaks when the rate of disturbance falls midway between these two extremes.

Plant communities whose composition reflects the regulatory power of intermediate disturbance host species that produce mobile seeds or spores, and in large numbers, two attributes of epiphytes. So equipped, every contender can recruit for its kind enough of the spaces freed by accidents to avoid what ecologists label *competitive exclusion*. Intermediate disturbance, acting in purely lottery-like fashion, eliminates individuals and makes room for replacements irrespective of their prowess as competitors. Postulating that intermediate disturbance promotes species richness among the epiphytes implies that their communities include populations with overlapping requirements.

Animal communities whose members stay in one place or confine their movements to small territories—barnacles and coral reef fish being classic examples—often owe their high species counts partly to intermediate disturbance. Epiphytes have not yet received this sort of scrutiny, although promising candidates abound. Among the better possibilities are the orchids that occur by the dozens of species per hectare in the canopies of certain mid-elevation rain forests in places like Andean Colombia and the central mountains of New Guinea. If these mostly small-bodied plants share substrates as freely as their fine-scale distributions suggest, it is difficult to imagine a more plausible explanation for the occurrence of so many kinds in such dense aggregations.

Too little data are available at this juncture to more than speculate about the degree of influence of the rates at which trees fall, branches break, and bark sloughs off on the number of kinds of epiphytes that a forest can support. However, enough is known about plant physiology and tree crown environments to cite drought and nutrient scarcity as influential relative to the effects of disturbance. Both agencies slow photosynthesis and accordingly growth and reproduction, so they should reduce competition among co-occurring epiphytes in all but the most resource-rich, stable environments. At this point, it seems reasonable to assume that if disturbance helps determine the ways in which woodland communities regulate their inventories of epiphytes, its impact is most telling where climates are most humid.

Disturbance may also explain the unusual anatomy demonstrated by the most structurally abbreviated of the free-living epiphytes. Forest canopies characterized by pronounced drought, fragmented substrates, and also perhaps intense

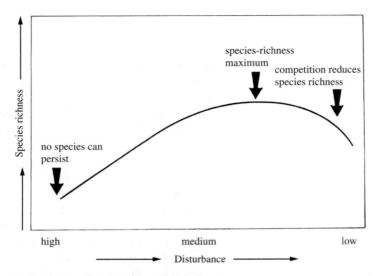

Figure 3.7. The intermediate disturbance hypothesis.

small-scale disturbance have long subjected their botanical inhabitants to powerful Darwinian selection. Conceivably the bodies of the most streamlined of the bromeliads and orchids are fitness-elevating consequences of extended histories of environmental hardship. Why would *Tillandsia usneoides* no longer produce roots, or the shootless orchids have dispensed with expanded leaves and long internodes if not to heighten material economy in resource-scarce habitats (Figures 2.2, 7.6)?

Ecological Succession

Damage a community of organisms and it soon begins to regenerate; destroy it outright, and the space left behind inevitably refills. Recovery in both instances, especially the second, tends to follow a staged process called *ecological succession*. The first plants to colonize an emptied substrate are called pioneers, and they in turn yield to longer-lived, later-stage types that require conditions provided by their predecessors. What began as a modest collection of loosely organized pioneers matures into a community characterized by greater coherence, diversity, and stability.

Continuous growth combined with branches that break and mats of suspended humus and flora that lose their grip make tree crowns precariously unstable habitats for epiphytes, especially those that grow slowly. Moreover, substrates that turn over at such high rates relative to the life spans of their users seem unlikely to endure long enough to support multistaged successions comparable to those documented for terrestrial plants that exploit sand dunes, fallow crop fields, or burned-over forests.

Something resembling ecological succession occurs when other kinds of epiphytes colonize the debris accumulated by the urn-shaped shoot of a large tank bromeliad, a bird's nest *Anthurium,* or a staghorn fern (Figure 9.5). The thousands of humus-type epiphytes illustrate a more widely occurring candidate for this process by requiring bark that has been "conditioned"—essentially overgrown by lichens and mosses acting as quasi pioneers. Finally, some of the carton specialists that populate the more elaborate Amazonian ant nest-gardens may arrive in some as yet unrecognized sequence.

Another arrangement that looks like succession operates at a more elevated level of organization: phorophytes generally harbor increasingly diverse communities of epiphytes as they age. Whether such progressions develop more or less randomly, with seeds and spores being scarce and their delivery often haphazard, or if plants adapted for early arrival prepare sites for others that return the favor by displacing them remains to be seen. What looks like succession may be no more than slow growers yielding to more precocious companions, the prevailing order being determined by time of arrival rather than by hostile interactions among different kinds of residents.

An important aspect of forest ecology that undoubtedly influences the ways in which communities of epiphytes assemble, and perhaps also the way they undergo succession, is not shown in Figure 3.1. Studies conducted at sites where epiphytes are plentiful and diverse and their phorophytes densely foliated agree on one point: aerial habitats, especially those represented by the crowns of isolated trees, are zoned for different kinds of occupants. Epiphytes that grow on the centermost, thickest branches are not the same as those that anchor on the finer branches and twigs making up the crown periphery.

Several investigators claim that a third living space exists between the first two, and that its growing conditions are distinct enough to favor a third combination of epiphytes. Should humidity, light, and substrate quality vary enough to partition a tree crown in this manner, what happens to its community of epiphytes as its diameter increases? Do the shade-tolerant, drought-sensitive types deepest in the community progressively displace their neighbors, and, if so, is this ecological succession? What happens when a tree reaches the end of its normal life span, its crown already having been in decline for years? Do its epiphytes respond by disappearing in some predictable order? Do any take advantage of their host's moribund condition?

What Makes a Tree a Host for Epiphytes?

Despite growing within easy range, thousands of kinds of trees and shrubs seldom or never host epiphytes. Such species are labeled *axenic* to recognize their evident hostility to would-be users. This observation plus the fact that few of the more accommodating types welcome every potential colonizer persuaded several influential early twentieth-century botanists to speculate that fidelity runs high, that most of the epiphytes have but one, or at most, only a few kinds of phorophytes. Broader surveys conducted since then have shown that only the occasional mistletoe and even fewer of the free-living species fit this description.

What is known about the workings of the epiphyte-host relationship concerns mostly users rather than providers, and many worthwhile questions remain unanswered. For example, is axeny usually based on relatively simple factors such as the possession of smooth or unstable bark? How often are toxic secretions involved (allelopathy)? Why do so many kinds of trees support only a fraction of the epiphytes that share their habitats? At this juncture, host-epiphyte compatibility seems to hinge on a variety of factors, some imposed by the environment and others by attributes inherent in the participants.

None of the orchids or mistletoes that anchor exclusively on one kind of support operate in this fashion for reasons known to science. Parasites are the most likely candidates for compatibility based on physiology. Seeds that require invasion by a fungus to germinate might explain why some of the members of Orchidaceae rival the most exacting of the mistletoes for host specificity (see Chapter 7; Figure 7.2 upper left corner). Perhaps the distributions of these microorganisms determine where the choosiest of free-living epiphytes grow.

Use by a certain kind of epiphyte can require that a tree possess certain measurable qualities. Propensities to form knotholes, or to hold dead limbs aloft longer than usual, or to support mantles of suspended humus make some phorophytes hospitable to specific kinds of users (see Chapter 2); conversely, smooth-surfaced trees and those with unstable bark deny all comers secure anchorage. Natural history can be just as decisive. Fast-growing, short-lived woodland pioneers like the members of genus *Cecropia* seldom host vascular epiphytes, whereas the most heavily exploited supports are usually old members of more durable species.

Phorophytes also differ in their utility for epiphytes according to the transparencies of their crowns and perhaps also how abundantly they shed key nutrients. Which potential users are the better disposed to benefit from these opposing conditions depends on their needs and tolerances. Sun-loving epiphytes well prepared to resist dehydration that also can subsist on dilute canopy washes are well suited for supports characterized by thinly foliated, infertile crowns. The more shade-tolerant, drought-vulnerable types, which generally mature faster and feed more heavily, should fare better on hosts that lose more nutrients from leafier crowns.

Tillandsia paucifolia in southern Florida behaves in a way that supports the "canopy quality" hypothesis. Some of its most heavily burdened hosts are cypress trees stunted by shallow, infertile soils perched atop marine limestone. For this stout-bodied, high-light–requiring bromeliad, a relatively transparent canopy is mandatory. Better-nourished individuals rooted in deeper substrates nearby produce more fertile bark and stem-flow, but their crowns cast denser shade and support fewer although more robust *T. paucifolia* specimens. Low concentrations of tissue nitrogen and phosphorus accord with this bromeliad's capacity to flourish under conditions that more conventional plants would experience as substantial impoverishment.

More remote factors including third parties further influence where certain kinds of epiphytes grow. Some of the hemi-epiphytic *Ficus* species over-occur on trees that attract birds that favor fleshy fruits. Different, but otherwise similar phorophytes growing nearby support many fewer of the same kinds of plants in their crowns, or they remain barren, probably because what they offer holds less allure for animals bent on supplementing earlier meals of ripe figs.

Epiphytes that belong to the ant nest-garden category grow at the pleasure of their insect guardians (Figure 6.2). Which phorophytes get colonized is influenced by enticements like the sugary secretions produced by many tropical woody species to secure the services of ant guards. Other associations may hinge on nothing more elaborate than a tree's suitability to accommodate the sap-sucking aphids and scale insects farmed by many of the carton-building, nest-gardening ants (see Chapter 6).

Finally, the serviceability of a tree for epiphytes can be conditional, less, for instance, at an upland site compared with another closer to a pond or river. Vulnerability during a single life stage could make all the difference. Modestly higher atmospheric humidity during the dry season might render one location more suitable for germination or seedling survival than another. One or more remote factors may also contribute, perhaps a higher incidence of crown-scorching fires where conditions are drier or fuel more abundant. Greater exposure to frost as a consequence of a more open canopy or local topography is another possibility.

How Epiphytes Can Impact Their Hosts

Residing above ground on a taller plant comes with certain advantages such as the ability to escape terrestrial herbivores. It also reduces the probability of starving for lack of adequate light or of suffocating under a layer of fallen litter. But what goes on with the phorophyte? If it experiences neither benefit nor harm, then its uninvited guests are engaging in a type of symbiosis known as *commensalism*. If they materially diminish its capacity to reproduce (reduce its *fitness*), and do so routinely, then over time, qualities that promote axeny might emerge. So far no one has made a convincing case for plant attributes adopted primarily to discourage colonization by epiphytes.

Precisely how might large numbers of modest-sized, nonparasitic plants sufficiently disadvantage their much larger woody supports to prompt a Darwinian response? More, it turns out, than meets the eye. The possibilities range from conspicuous to subtle and their impacts from negligible to lethal. Which outcome prevails depends on the identities of the participants and certain site-specific circumstances. A rather obscure process, but one with potentially major consequences for plants and whole ecosystems ranks high because of the ways in which epiphytes influence the paths that nutrients follow as they circulate within woodland ecosystems.

No site can support more vegetation than its stocks of growth-limiting resources permit. Nutrient supplementation experiments have shown that the supplies of several key elements in tropical forests commonly prevail at levels well below what the local flora can use. Artificially augment what is already present (the baseline supply), and photosynthesis quickens, with vigor increasing close behind. In time, however, much of the added nitrogen or phosphorus migrates from the plants that initially absorbed it out into the rest of the ecosystem. In effect, what was artificially added joins what was naturally already on site by also moving atom by atom around the system in a process called *biogeochemical cycling* (Figure 3.1).

Much of the nitrogen and phosphorus that normally circulates within a mature forest ecosystem occurs at any instant within its vegetation, while smaller fractions reside in the bodies of the other residents. The balance is distributed among the nonliving as opposed to the living "compartments," principally in the soil and dissolved in ground water, and in any streams or ponds present. Residence times vary depending on location (i.e., compartment) within the ecosystem and the chemical element in question: movement into and out of plants is relatively rapid; passage through soil takes longer, especially for phosphorus, which for reasons of its chemistry is relatively immobile in this medium.

Competition among plants for required chemical elements in tropical forests can be stiff. Where infertility is especially pronounced, phosphorus in particular cycles faster than most of the other mineral nutrients. Manganese, magnesium, and iron, to name just three that behave otherwise, turn over far more slowly, but this slower turnover rarely poses problems because these elements typically occur in overabundance relative to biological demand. Shortages just don't develop. Elements like phosphorus cycle rapidly largely because they are so scarce.

When the root of a tree absorbs an atom of phosphorus, that atom moves from a nonliving compartment (the soil) into a living compartment within the hosting ecosystem. The energy required to make this transfer comes from the sun courtesy of photosynthesis. Uptake also occurs against a steep concentration gradient, with phosphorus (like most other nutrients) being more abundant in living plant tissues than in most soils. An herbivore mediates the next step by consuming that part of the tree containing the absorbed phosphorus atom. A carnivore acts next by eating the herbivore. Later, microbial decomposers complete the biogeochemical cycle by returning to the soil the minerals (including the phosphorus atom) contained in their food, which is dead biomass, the remains of a predator in this instance. Phosphorus shed in litter takes a shortcut by skipping the two animal compartments.

The fact that much of the phosphorus added to our hypothetical ecosystem entered its flora only to exit soon after to circulate among its other compartments is central to the point about to be made. Such behavior is normal yet problematic. Because they are long-lived perennials, trees cannot avoid losing nutrients as they shed spent foliage and other relatively short-lived organs. This kind of leakiness is sustainable only if what gets lost is mostly recovered. Vulnerability stemming from this phenomenon positions the free-living epiphytes to seriously diminish the health of their hosts.

Nutritional Piracy

The free-living epiphytes, as opposed to mistletoes, "pirate" rather than extract by parasitism what they need from a living host. Despite being more gentle and less direct, they still reduce the capacities of phorophytes to recover the nutrients shed in litter and lost to the leaching effects of flowing precipitation. The impounding epiphytes exploit both sources, but the crucial point here is not how a transfer occurs but its consequences for the loser. Whether the mechanism is piracy or parasitism, one player deprives another of vital resources. Mode of action becomes even less relevant when the impacts concern entire ecosystems rather than individual trees.

Epiphytes in abundance also should increase the capacity of a forest ecosystem to accumulate nutrients, and a simple analogy illustrates why. When a nitrogen or phosphorus salt is dissolved in water and poured onto an impermeable surface like a concrete sidewalk, it flows away. Not so when the target is a forest. Most of what arrives in this second case, especially if locally scarce, will be quickly absorbed by vegetation, after which it begins to circulate through the broader ecosystem, as described above. In nature, inputs to a forest ecosystem from the atmosphere balance losses in runoff and by other routes. A kind of nutritional "steady state" prevails, meaning what comes in more or less balances what goes out.

It stands to reason that epiphytes help forests trap nutrients. Tree foliage can extract the same substances from precipitation, but the epiphytes do it better. Being on average relatively slow growers as well, they also tend to hold longer what they remove from circulation. Being perched in the crowns of trees further assures their potential as major players in the nutritional affairs of their neighbors. Being rooted above ground may increase a plant's exposure to drought, but at the same time it grants direct access to the most heavily traveled of the highways plied by nutrients as they cycle between the two largest compartments in forest ecosystems: the dominant vegetation and the supporting soil (Figures 3.1, 3.8).

Epiphytes will not make much difference to adjacent flora, at least not to their mineral nutrition, unless they remove from circulation enough of the local stocks of key chemical elements to seriously deprive them. If the hosting ecosystem is liberally supplied with nitrogen, phosphorus, and so on—if the pools of these potentially growth-limiting nutrients are sizable relative to biological demand—nothing nutritionally adverse will materialize as a consequence of epiphytes being present. Should the site be more impoverished, however, the balance of its plant life could end up being more debilitated as a consequence.

When a dense infestation of free-living epiphytes appears to be inflicting damage suggestive of parasitism, nutritional piracy should be the suspected cause. Symptoms can include sparsely foliated crowns, the presence of many dead and dying branches, and pale, yellowish leaves. Despite being passive actors compared with the mistletoes, dense colonies of free-living epiphytes accumulate large quantities of key elements that would otherwise be cycling more

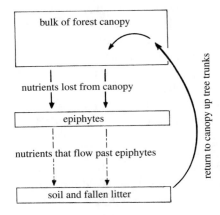

Figure 3.8. Nutritional piracy. The arrows indicate the movements of nutrients among the major compartments (rectangles) within a forest ecosystem that includes epiphytes.

rapidly between the resident woody vegetation and the underlying soil. Were no epiphytes on site, some of these nutrients would be supporting tree photosynthesis and the additional organisms that indirectly depend on it.

Additional Ways That Epiphytes Harm Their Hosts

The free-living epiphytes can harm their hosts by means other than nutritional piracy, casting shade being a second mechanism. Effects will vary depending on the victim's energy requirement and certain aspects of the habitat. Atmospheric conditions that reduce sunlight much of the year may render cloud forest trees more sensitive than most. Interestingly, these are the same cool, hyperhumid ecosystems that support the densest populations of epiphytes, which, including the local lichens and mosses, often add up to multiple metric tons of biomass per hectare (Figure 3.2).

Epiphytes can cast growth-suppressing shade at sunnier sites as well. It's hard to imagine that a host as densely festooned with Spanish moss as the subject pictured in Figure 1.3 is unaffected by its burden. And why else would so many similarly infested trees and shrubs across Florida's natural and built landscapes feature so many dead and dying branches? It is not easy, of course, to determine which came first, dense colonization by this exceptionally prolific bromeliad, or crown dieback prompted by something else. Only extended observation will tell whether Spanish moss is capable of inflicting this kind of injury, or if its target must first decline for another reason and only then becomes a candidate for such massive exploitation.

Trauma is another route to host injury. Stroll through any epiphyte-rich forest, and it won't take long to appreciate how frequently overburdened twigs and branches fall to the ground. Less clear is any harm that epiphytes might inflect by encouraging the kinds of pathogens that attack woody plants. The thick layers of mosses and vascular plants that envelop old branches and trunks in wet tropical forests may shelter potentially virulent or wood-rotting bacteria and fungi (Figures 2.4, 3.2).

Chemical warfare is yet another possibility, in this case perpetrated not by phorophytes to ward off epiphytes, but the other way around. Several reports from South America describe how certain sun-loving members of genus *Tillandsia* of family Bromeliaceae appear to chemically defoliate the canopies of their living supports, coincidentally, or perhaps adaptively, improving living conditions for themselves. No toxins were characterized or mode of delivery identified.

It's a good bet that combinations of conditions and actions account for the capacities of the free-living epiphytes to injure their supports, but how often this occurs and how severely, no one can say. They definitely break off heavily laden twigs and branches, intercept light that would otherwise fall on host foliage, and limit opportunities to recycle scarce nutrients. The free-living epiphytes may also secrete poisons and promote disease; however, it is the co-option of key nutrients and the casting of shade that provide the basis for what likely rank among the epiphyte's most pervasive influences on forested ecosystems.

Manifold Effects on Ecosystems

Most of the plant material present in a forest belongs to its mature trees, which usually also conduct the bulk of its photosynthesis. The smaller flora contribute less biomass but at the same time may exert unanticipated influence. Under the right circumstances, they can set the pace for food manufacture, occasionally even exceeding the forest dominants as producers. This chapter concludes by describing how epiphytes, as powerful mediators of biogeochemical cycles and competitors for light, can affect whole-system performance beyond what their numbers and mass might suggest.

The distributions of key nutrients within an ecosystem help determine which of its residents contribute more or less to its dynamics. Epiphytes can rank high in this respect. A survey of a wet forest in Southwestern Taiwan, for example, revealed that 18–43% of the foliage-associated calcium, magnesium, nitrogen, phosphorus, and potassium was sequestered by its canopy-based vegetation. In other words, trees accounted for most of the local biomass, but not the part most heavily provisioned with nutrients: foliage. It is the most nitrogen-enriched of the botanical components within an ecosystem that most powerfully influences its energetics; however, some mitigating circumstances complicate this picture somewhat, one of which concerns the basic principles that govern the performance of leaves.

Chapter 4 discusses the reasons the kind of foliage borne by typical natives of arid environments use water more economically than the foliage type adapted to operate where moisture is more plentiful. In essence, the dry growers must conduct photosynthesis slowly to achieve the high water-use efficiencies mandated by drought. Owing to this functional tradeoff, the leaves of xerophytes must live longer to pay back their relatively high costs of construction with time left over to make a profit (Figure 4.2). Conversely, leaves that serve plants better supplied with moisture are cheaper to manufacture and die sooner, but they necessarily expend more water to make a given amount of sugar.

Most trees produce more drought-vulnerable and productive but shorter-lived foliage than a majority of the epiphytes. Being terrestrial ensures the former access to more plentiful supplies of moisture than are available to the epiphytes, except for those that possess water-collecting tanks or the ability to tap some other similarly abundant aerial supply. As a result, the photosynthetic output of a forest should diminish to the extent that epiphyte replaces phorophyte foliage. This outcome is inevitable where relatively active leaves give way to others that cannot manufacture food at the same or higher rates.

In the final analysis, when epiphytes of the more typical kind are abundant enough to seriously shade or massively displace host foliage, then whole system photosynthesis should suffer. However, if an otherwise equivalent ecosystem supports epiphytes capable of more active photosynthesis than that of the average local tree, it should use light more effectively and be more productive. Conceivably, such an arrangement would also promote more efficient employment of nutrients and moisture and better support animal life.

4 Water Management

Introductory biology students often complain about having to cram their heads full of imminently forgettable facts. A few facts, however, aren't so easily put aside, like the ones about water. Water makes up the bulk of our bodies, so the lesson goes, the actual number falling somewhere around 90–95%. The deeper message is certainly memorable: life for animals wouldn't be possible were it not for this vital substance. Less often is it noted that the same lesson applies to plants.

The land plants face countless challenges, but most threatening is the ever-present possibility of lethal desiccation. This is much of the reason why our planet's terrestrial landscapes remained barren for billions of years while the oceans teemed with life. Drought continues to limit plant activity more than shortages of any of the other required commodities, including nitrogen and CO_2. This limitation is especially true for the epiphytes, and it explains why some of the most stress-tolerant of their kind have already attracted substantial scientific inquiry.

Variations on Basic Themes

Every beginning botany text describes how green plants use sunlight to convert CO_2 and water into sugar with oxygen as a byproduct. How they absorb and use mineral nutrients such as phosphorus and potassium is another standard entry. Next comes the subject of water: How is it acquired, transported through xylem tissue, and expended during photosynthesis? Plants are portrayed as able to perform all these vital tasks in ways that match the conditions under which they grow in nature.

The fact that plants differ according to the ways in which they make food, acquire minerals, and manage water has momentous consequences. Were these and the other basic plant processes conducted more uniformly, biodiversity would be but a small fraction of its current magnitude. Planet Earth would not be supporting anything close to its current inventory of some 300,000 species of higher plants and many times more animals. Likewise, forests would be far less epiphyte rich. Most assuredly, our world would be a less interesting place in which to study botany or zoology.

Every green plant manufactures sugar by using energy provided by the sun, CO_2, and water, according to the biochemical pathway shown in abbreviated form in the upper left box of Figure 5.1. They also use chlorophyll to harness sunlight and the same master enzyme to catalyze the assimilation of CO_2 into glucose. The molecular machinery that converts solar radiation into the chemical energy needed to drive carbon fixation is similarly ubiquitous. But other aspects of this most fundamental of biological mechanisms vary, as do the ways that plants expend water to acquire CO_2 (Table 5.1).

How the green plants conduct photosynthesis and manage their supplies of water influence numerous aspects of their biology, including where they fit into communities and ecosystems. Variations in both processes help explain why species thrive only within certain temperature ranges, require bright light or shade, and need more or less water or some nutrient like nitrogen. Nonuniformity in the ways resources are acquired and used also provides insight into why specific kinds of plants grow fast or slow and whether their leaves have short, medium, or long life spans.

Because environmental physiology so profoundly influences where plants occur and how they grow, it has to be part of our treatment of epiphytism. What follows does just this: it describes the peculiarities of physiology and anatomy that make life above ground possible. A brief look at a universal principle of biology comes first, followed by a discussion of water management. Photosynthesis and mineral nutrition are the subjects of Chapter 5.

How Biological Structure Relates to Function

The shape and size of a plant and those of its component parts, particularly the way its leaves are constructed and how long they live, say much about its performance, needs, and tolerances. This is true because all these attributes influence the ways in which water and mineral nutrients are acquired and used and food is produced. These factors also have a lot to do with where a plant grows and how it interacts with its neighbors (see Chapters 3 and 6).

The sympodial body plan illustrated in Figure 1.2C, which characterizes more of the epiphytes than any other, is well suited for life above ground for two reasons. First, it allows long-lived, small perennials to thrive in cramped quarters, for instance, tucked into the crotch of a tree, or rooted along one of its slender branches. Second, only modest evolutionary adjustments need occur to render this arrangement serviceable under a variety of additional growing conditions such as different degrees of humidity and exposure to sun.

The monopodial epiphytes are better structured for vining, sprawling, and hanging than for making effective use of confined substrates (Figure 1.2D). Several families have taken advantage of this second kind of architecture as they underwent substantial radiations in aerial habitats. Especially notable are the hundreds of hemi-epiphytic aroids and the variously canopy-adapted members of *Hoya* and *Dischidia* of family Apocynaceae (e.g., Figures 8.3I, 8.4D). Quite a few of the ferns creep through the crowns of trees in similar fashion (Figures 9.3B, 9.4A,B,C,E,F,G,H). Monopodial form is also widespread among the canopy-dwelling orchids.

Leaves, roots, and stems have evolved a variety of special features in response to growing conditions peculiar to certain kinds of aerial habitats. The strangler-type lifestyle pursued by the hemi-epiphytic figs requires roots capable of substantial thickening and auto-fusion (Figure 2.8). Stem tubers are widespread as well, owing to their owners' need to store moisture and nutrients, especially where dry seasons are extended. Among the most unusual specializations are those that equip the stems and foliage of many of the epiphytes to house colonies of ants that feed and protect plants (Figures 5.3, 7.2C, 8.3F,H,I, 8.4A,B,C,D,E, 9.4B,E).

Leaves are the most versatile of the epiphyte's vegetative organs, sometimes conducting important functions in addition to or instead of photosynthesis. These added tasks include prey capture and processing, holdfast, as illustrated by the gripping foliage of some of the bromeliads, ant exploitation, as just mentioned, predator deterrence where spines occur, water and nutrient absorption through special epidermal hairs, and, finally, the attraction of pollinators and seed dispersers (e.g., Plate 3B). Leaf shape, size, texture, and longevity also vary in ways that help the epiphytes fix CO_2 into sugar in challenging environments.

Water Management

The land plants face a life-threatening dilemma: in order to manufacture food from CO_2 drawn from the atmosphere, they must expend water through a process called *transpiration*. Minute organs called *stomata* located on the surfaces of leaves and a waxy cuticle that seals the rest of the epidermis provide substantial capacity to regulate gas exchange between themselves and the environment, but not enough to eliminate the possibility of lethal dehydration (Figure 4.1). Despite being more than 400 million years removed from their aquatic

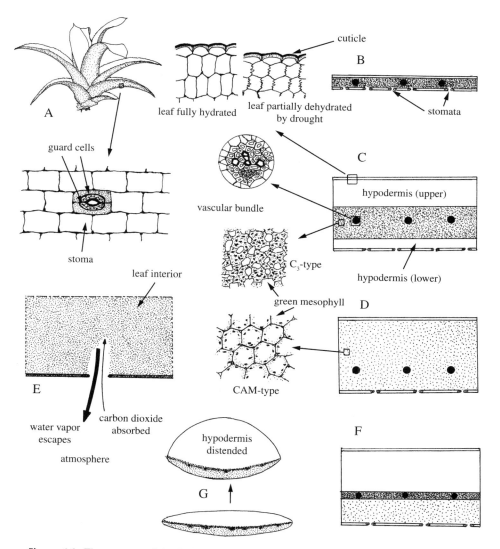

cuticle

B

leaf fully hydrated

leaf partially dehydrated by drought

stomata

A

guard cells

C

vascular bundle

hypodermis (upper)

stoma

leaf interior

C_3-type

hypodermis (lower)

green mesophyll

D

CAM-type

E

water vapor escapes

carbon dioxide absorbed

atmosphere

hypodermis distended

F

G

Figure 4.1. The anatomy of the foliage of diverse epiphytes, illustrating some of the structural adaptations that enhance drought performance and the paths followed by water vapor and CO_2 during photosynthesis. **A.** Stoma on the underside of a leaf of a tank bromeliad **B.** Cross-section of a drought-deciduous–type leaf **C.** Cross-section of an evergreen-type leaf equipped with well-developed hypodermal layers, the upper of which is shown in partially dehydrated and fully engorged conditions **D.** Cross-section of a succulent CAM-type leaf **E.** Gas exchange between the interior of a leaf and the adjacent atmosphere illustrating why land plants necessarily expend large amounts of moisture as they acquire CO_2 for photosynthesis **F.** Cross-section of a leaf that performs a mixed syndrome type of photosynthesis **G.** Cross-section of a balloon leaf of *Codonanthe digna* (Gesneriaceae) showing normal and greatly water-distended hypodermal layers.

beginnings, they still have not evolved a way to deal more effectively with the powerful capacity of air to evaporate water. Nor is water vapor in humid air available for plant use before returning to liquid form as dew or precipitation.

Each stoma (singular for stomata) consists of two bean-shaped *guard cells* surrounded by a larger number of *subsidiary cells* that fit together like the parts of a jigsaw puzzle (Figure 4.1A). Ventilation occurs through a pore that opens and closes as the guard cells on either side alternately swell and shrink by exchanging certain ions and moisture with their subsidiary cell neighbors. Little water vapor can transpire from a leaf, or CO_2 enter, while its stomata are closed. The situation boils down to an all or nothing proposition: make food and court disaster by desiccation, or remain watertight and curtail photosynthesis by shutting off access to one of its raw materials.

Plants adapted to survive drought expend less moisture to make a given amount of sugar than do their counterparts suited to grow under better-watered conditions. In other words, the dry-growing types achieve higher *water use efficiencies.* Scientists quantify this aspect of botanical performance as the weight of the water sacrificed during photosynthesis relative to the weight of the CO_2 assimilated over the same interval, a relationship called the transpiration ratio. How efficiently a plant uses water varies as its physiological status and certain aspects of its circumstances change, particularly the relative humidity of the adjacent air mass.

All but the epiphytes native to the wettest forests probably operate with better than average water use efficiencies, meaning with transpiration ratios less than about 500:1. The most impressively drought-adapted bromeliads and orchids do much better, giving up as little as 20–30 grams of water for every gram of dry organic matter produced. Numerous ferns fall at the opposite end of the spectrum, but a full assessment of their vulnerabilities to drought has not been made. It can be said that some of the filmy types dry out to brittleness within hours following removal from their typically hyper humid, forest understory habitats (Figure 9.7).

The performances just described raise an interesting question: If effective management of water is so crucial to a land plant, why don't the relatively profligate types use water as economically as their more conservative counterparts? Why don't they rival the exceptionally competent bromeliads and orchids in this respect? The reason is survival; they don't operate this way because if they did, they could not grow as fast as competitors that use water less efficiently. High water-use economy comes at a cost—an unsustainable one where moisture is abundant.

The dry-growing epiphytes and similarly adapted terrestrial plants convert CO_2 into sugar relatively slowly because the same robust leaf anatomy that conserves moisture by reducing transpiration slows the rate at which CO_2 can diffuse inward to fuel photosynthesis (Figure 4.1). Such couplings of positive and negative outcomes represent what biologists call *adaptive trade-offs.* The existence of this particular trade-off confirms that the vascular plants continue to pay a price for leaving the relative safety of their ancestral aquatic habitat. Recall that Chapter 3 describes another functional trade-off in the way leaves adapted to operate in deep shade or full sunlight perform poorly or fail under opposing conditions (Figure 5.2).

Comparing an atmospheric bromeliad to a tomato plant puts the vigor for water economy trade-off in clearer perspective. It also illustrates the way in which context can render one plant characteristic indispensable and another unworkable. Conditions where most of the epiphytes grow ensure that they benefit more from being drought tolerant than from being high-performance competitors. A tomato plant can make food faster and invest more resources in its offspring, but only if heavily fertilized and irrigated, as occurs in culture. How successful could it be compared with the bromeliad if both were anchored and left unattended in the same tree crown?

How Epiphytes Cope with Drought

The dry-growing epiphytes cope with drought in three ways. One collection of species stores enough moisture in thickened organs to survive months of rainless weather. Members of a second group dodge lethal desiccation by timely jettisoning their most desiccation-prone parts, which happen to be leaves. The few exceptions that make up the third group lack even modest capacities to retain or store moisture, but they incur no permanent injury when severely desiccated. The first and third types are said to "endure" drought, whereas those that practice the second option survive by avoiding it.

Drought endurance of the type associated with succulence is practiced by more of the epiphytes than by those equipped to operate according to the other two strategies combined. Moisture destined for uncommonly economical expenditure during photosynthesis is most often sequestered in thick foliage, the arboreal cacti with their often robust green stems being the most notable of the exceptions (Figures 8.1A,B,C,E, 8.2). Many of the epiphytic ferns possess fleshy rhizomes, but the record for versatility belongs to the orchids, whose roots and stems, in addition to its leaves, often store abundant reserves (Figures 7.2A, C,D,F, 9.4C,D,F,G).

Succulent leaves are not anatomically uniform. Much of their thickness may be due to the presence of a *hypodermis* that consists of densely packed, large, colorless and collapsible thin-walled cells positioned immediately under the epidermis. If two are present, which is usually the case, the upper one is better developed (Figure 4.1C). Sandwiched between is a zone consisting of smaller loosely packed cells devoted to photosynthesis and supplied by bundles of phloem and xylem tissue.

The succulent leaves of members of *Codonanthe* (family Gesneriaceae) and *Peperomia* of Piperaceae illustrate a second arrangement. Beginning just below the upper epidermis, they feature a robust hypodermis, then a much thinner, deep green vein-bearing zone, and finally a somewhat thicker, paler green layer beneath this (Figure 4.1F,G). The third pattern is the least structurally complex, the leaf interior consisting entirely of densely packed, pale green, relatively large cells supplied by the usual arc of vascular bundles (Figure 4.1D).

Epiphytes in at least five families accumulate extraordinarily large quantities of water in so-called balloon leaves. Only the upper hypodermis expands, after which at some point its contents flow into nearby younger foliage. Organ thickness can increase up to fivefold in *Codonanthe digna* (Figure 4.1G), but entirely through cell enlargement rather than division. Leaves equipped with the more standard type of hypodermal layer shrink and swell as wet and dry conditions alternate. Much of the moisture stored there is transferred during drought to help maintain the vitality of the adjacent layer of more desiccation-sensitive green cells (Figure 4.1C).

The second version of drought tolerance is common among the mosses and lichens, but rare for a vascular epiphyte. Species that employ this "resurrection" strategy are labeled *poikilohydrous,* because the water contents of their bodies fluctuate according to the weather. The fronds of the North American epiphyte *Pleopeltis polypodioides* curl, turn brown, and lose up to 98% of their moisture even during short bouts of rainless weather (Figure 9.3B). Wetted by precipitation, they plump up and turn green within hours, simultaneously resuming photosynthesis.

By contrast, the water contents of the *homiohydrous* drought tolerators of the first group are more stable, owing to their superior capacity to regulate transpiration. On the other hand, having less permeable foliage means that they cannot match the poikilohydrous types for speedy elimination of moisture deficits. Desiccation, more than drought tolerance, accurately describes the remarkable dry-weather performances of the resurrection-type epiphytes. Greater reliance on foliage than on roots for water absorption is another hallmark of these unusual plants.

Pleopeltis polypodioides is also frost hardy enough to range northward into central Kentucky, where except for a mistletoe or two, low winter temperatures exclude all the other North American epiphytes. Along with several members of its genus, it also ranges into dry forests in tropical South America. Some of the most heavily colonized sites experience nightly mists followed by sunny days that assure the kind of wet-dry cycling normally experienced by some additional poikilohydric ferns and lycophytes that grow on the ground.

Drought Avoidance

The drought-avoiding epiphytes anticipate the driest months of the year by shedding their leaves from typically succulent stems (Figures 2.6, 7.2A, 7.7B). Many of these same species flower soon thereafter, perhaps being better prepared to attract pollinators while leafless. Shifting photoperiod, which compared with weather is the more reliable indicator of time of year, probably cues both these activities and the flushes of new leaves and roots that occur as the dry season closes.

Rather than the thick, durable leaves borne by the water-storing, drought-enduring epiphytes, the drought avoiders produce flimsy, more ephemeral organs, as illustrated by the *Catasetum* orchid in Figures 4.1B and 7.2A. Were its foliage more robustly constructed to slow transpiration, the coupled reduction of photosynthetic capacity would jeopardize its ability to make enough food for the entire year during a single wet season. Note the distinct abscission zone located at the summit of each leaf base.

Most of the drought-avoiding ferns possess extensive root systems, and the usually thick layers of accompanying rhizome scales assist them (Figures 9.4C,H, 9.6). Being dead, but absorptive, they promote deeper hydration by passively sponging up precipitation, thereby prolonging for the plant what otherwise would be even more transitory contacts between its intermittent supply of moisture and its roots. The trash basket orchids operate similarly, except that assistance is provided by masses of upright, lifeless roots instead of by rhizomes covered with wettable scales (Figures 2.6, 4.3).

That fewer opportunities exist in aerial habitats for drought avoidance compared with drought tolerance is witnessed by the fact that relatively few epiphytes employ the first option. Substrates may partially explain this asymmetry. The *Cyrtopodium* featured in Figure 2.6 and others of its kind tend to maintain preparedness for the occasional wet season drought by penetrating rotten wood or pockets of moist humus with at least a few of their longer-lived, nontrash basket–type roots. Twig use is out of the question for obvious reasons. Modest numbers of bromeliads and ferns, and a somewhat larger contingent of orchids, account for virtually all the seasonally deciduous epiphytes (Figures 7.2A, 7.7B, 9.6).

Leaf Economics

Leaf anatomy, longevity, and performance indicate the environmental conditions to which plants, whether arboreal or terrestrial, are adapted. This is true for two reasons: photosynthetic organisms have experienced substantial incentive to evolve economical operations, and where moisture is concerned the possibilities for doing so are quite limited. Why else would the many thousands of dry-growing epiphytes representing such a disparate array of taxonomic groups deal with drought in only three ways? Thinking more like an economist than a biologist helps address this question. It also explains why plants function as they do in many additional respects.

Step 1 requires equating a growing plant with a growing human enterprise. Development in both cases involves acquiring raw materials (water, nitrogen, and so on for the plant and whatever for the factory) to make products (roots and leaves versus fabricated items). What gets produced early on allows for acquisition of more raw materials to make more products as the plant matures and the factory expands. The ultimate goals are progeny for the plant and profitability for the business. Step 2 involves monetization. The costs of leaves and roots are fixed; those of the raw materials needed for their production vary according to the amount available relative to the amount required.

Just as a factory operates to make a profit, a plant grows (mindlessly of course) to propagate its genes into the next generation by way of its offspring. Both achieve their goals by creating value-added products from resources that require investments to secure. For a plant to maximize its reproductive success, it must accumulate the stuff needed to make progeny. To realize this outcome cost-effectively, it must "choose" how many of each kind of resource-acquiring organs are required as it allocates limited resources during the process of becoming large enough to be a parent. The same imperative applies to a factory facing a stiff market as it does for a plant surrounded by competitors.

A plant, like the manager of a successful factory, decides which mix of investment vehicles (kinds of resource-capturing organs) is most cost effective for reproducing under a particular set of environmental circumstances. For example, if a plant finds itself growing in a nitrogen-deficient, but sunny habitat, it should allocate more of its accumulated resources to the production of roots than to leaves. If the scarcest commodity is sunlight, the emphasis should be reversed. It is this kind of flexibility that allows a plant to operate like a well-managed factory.

Economic analysis further explains why leaf anatomy, performance, and longevity occur in so few of the many possible combinations among the epiphytes (Figure 4.2). It says that the robust-type foliage exemplified by the drought-enduring orchids and bromeliads must operate (i.e., conduct photosynthesis) longer than the kind that serves the natives of wetter habitats. *Xeromorphic* leaves such as these cost a great deal to manufacture, and, being only modestly productive, their cost is recouped slowly. The same logic explains why, being shorter-lived, the foliage of the drought avoiders needs to be cheaply constructed and capable of vigorous food-making (while well supplied with moisture).

Plants also operate economically when they allocate scarce resources for different functions within the same organs. A shade-grown plant, for instance, favors

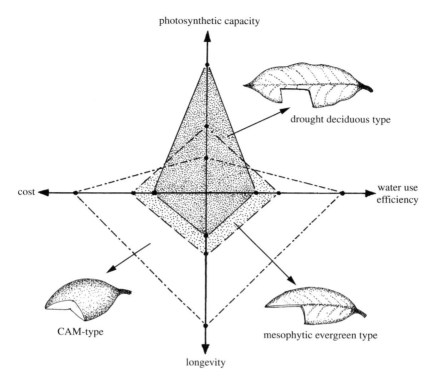

Figure 4.2. The relationship of foliar structure and longevity to leaf performance, specifically, to its water use efficiency and capacity to conduct photosynthesis.

its light-harvesting apparatus. Cultivated in brighter light, proportionally more of the same commodities—nitrogen, glucose, and so on—will be committed to building the enzymes and such needed to convert that absorbed CO_2 into sugar. Here again, necessity determined by supply relative to demand prompts a factory-like (i.e., economical) response. Reverse this pattern, and the plant would possess excess ability to harvest energy in the first instance, and in the second, be endowed with more capacity to fix CO_2 than with energy to use it.

Roots

A large majority of the epiphytes employ roots to absorb moisture and nutrients, but a substantial minority have switched to foliage. Which arrangement prevails depends on the subject's taxonomic affiliation; roots suffice for the arboreal aroids, orchids, cacti, and many more. Most of the bromeliads, some ferns, and certain members of the lily complex, plus a scattering of others rely on leaves. The record for specialized roots belongs to the orchids; for foliage, it is the bromeliads.

The highly specialized aerial root of an orchid demonstrates particularly well the tight association between plant structure and function. Note in the anatomical cross section provided in Figure 4.3 that it consists of five layers of tissue; three of these are unconventional, modified to operate above rather than embedded in the ground. Starting at the surface, the first and second layers are the *velamen* and *exodermis;* the third is the *cortex,* and the fourth and fifth constitute the more conventionally organized root core.

Unlike the epidermis of one cell thickness that serves the more typical vascular plants, the velamen is multilayered and composed entirely of dead light-reflective cells. The exodermis is single layered, and each of its three kinds of cells is dedicated to one of three distinct functions. Most common are the impermeable *barrier* cells, readily identifiable by their thin outer and much more robust inner and lateral walls. The more delicately constructed *passage* cells are many fewer, and the empty *aeration* cells are more scattered yet.

Passage or *transfer* cells, consistent with their names and dense living contents, represent portals through which nutrients and moisture pass from the velamen en route to sites deeper inside the root, and from there upward into the adjoining shoot. Gatekeeping is the role of the aeration cells as well, but in this case for oxygen needed from the atmosphere to support root respiration and for CO_2 to supply the photosynthetic apparatus. Stomata are not an option because they occur only on shoots, this condition being one of the few immutable rules of plant anatomy.

The aerial root illustrated in Figure 4.3 operates in the following manner. When moistened with precipitation, what was an empty light-reflecting velamen quickly engorges, after which its liquid contents move much more slowly into the cortex by way of the passage cells. Flow proceeds as long as rain continues to fall and for a time afterward because the velamen represents a miniature reservoir. As such it increases the time available for uptake after which its role shifts from acquisition to moisture retention.

While empty, the velamen retards evaporation from the root interior by sequestering a layer of stagnate, humid air. Because the living interior of the root is separated in this manner from the usually drier atmosphere, less water vapor will diffuse out than would be the case were the same organ equipped with a more conventional single-layered epidermis. Without the velamen, the distance that water molecules would have to travel to escape would be shorter and the time required correspondingly less. In effect, the orchid root "rectifies" moisture exchange: it allows water to flow inward at a much higher rate than it can move in the opposite direction.

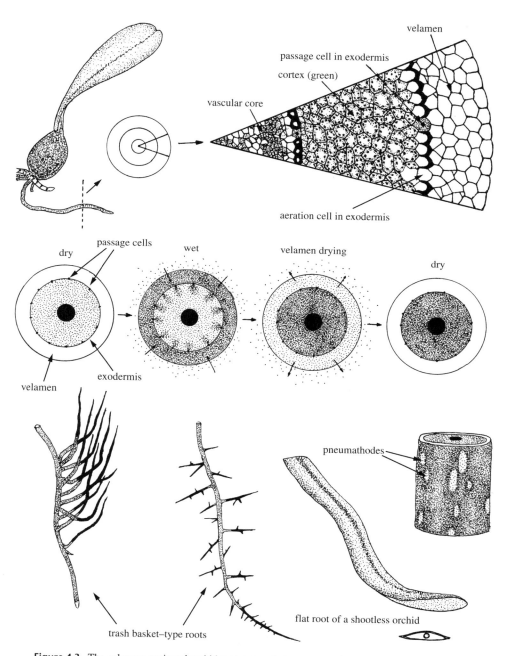

Figure 4.3. The velamen-equipped orchid root: internal structure, uptake and retention of moisture, and structural modifications that enhance litter collection and light capture for photosynthesis.

The cells of the cortex of a typical aerial orchid root contain *chloroplasts* like those present in the green cells within foliage (Figure 7.8E). Organs serving the shootless orchids, such as the *Harisella filiformis* specimen illustrated in Figure 2.2, conduct enough photosynthesis to meet the plant's entire energy budget. Roots of the leafy orchids assimilate CO_2 less vigorously, so their outputs constitute supplements, and comparatively modest ones at that.

As so often occurs when plants adopt special features to counter extreme challenges, the benefit of having a velamen obliges a functional trade-off. Orchid roots adapted to operate in air suffocate in overly humid environments. Water-repelling regions in the velamen called *pneumathodes* mitigate this problem somewhat, but not enough to head off failure should a normally dry-growing specimen be potted in a mixture that holds too much moisture.

Pneumathodes are evident as circular to oval-shaped light gray patches visible against the underlying green cortex that elsewhere shows through the velamen while it contains water (Figure 4.3). Located in the exodermis immediately below each pneumathode is one or more of the thin-walled aeration cells described above that allow diffusing gases to enter and exit the green-celled cortex.

The roots of three non-orchid epiphytes, one a member of genus *Epiphyllum,* another of *Rhipsalis* (Cactaceae), and the third a species of *Hoya* (Apocynaceae), operate like those of a tested terrestrial barrel cactus and a single member of *Agave* (a century plant). Drying consistently caused the cortex to partially collapse and a waxy substance called *suberin* to impregnate the surrounding layer of cells. Neither change was reversible, but together they substantially retarded further dehydration. Even so, partially dried roots had regained full pretreatment capacity to absorb moisture only a few days following rewetting.

The need to repeatedly use organs damaged by drought is relaxed for many of the desert dwellers because they renew their fine root systems annually. None of the epiphytes seems to engage in this costly behavior, except perhaps some of the deciduous orchids. Whatever the case, it seems that the kind of hydraulic rectification conducted by the velamen-exodermis complex does not require similar degrees of anatomical specialization among many of the non-orchid epiphytes.

Leaves as Proxies for Roots

Epiphytes substitute foliage for roots in three ways: by creating litter and moisture-impounding tanks, chambers for plant-feeding ants, or by employing leaves covered with absorptive hairs (Figures 4.4, 4.5, 5.5, 7.5E, 10.3). More than 1500 bromeliads operate according to the first or second options, or both. Dozens more species combine the second and third options (Figures 5.3, 7.5A).

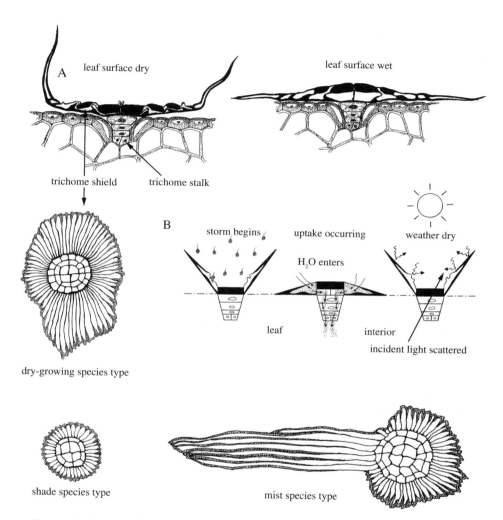

Figure 4.4. The bromeliad trichome. **A.** Cross-section of the type of appendage borne by the atmospheric-type species in moist and dry configurations **B.** Schematic depiction of the effects of wetting and drying on the shape of the shield, its capacity to reflect light, and the path followed by water as it moves from the surface of a leaf through a trichome into the leaf interior. Also shown are trichome shields characteristic of bromeliads (subfamily Tillandsioideae) native to humid, shady (lower left corner) and cool, misty habitats (lower right corner).

About 25 members of family Apocynaceae house ant nests inside or under their leaves (Figures 8.3F,H,I, 8.4D). Another group dominated by aroids and ferns collects useful substances with funnel-shaped arrays of leaves augmented with tangled aerial roots (Figures 2.5, 7.7F).

The absorptive trichomes of Bromeliaceae occur in multiple versions, each adapted to operate under somewhat different circumstances. Those located on the bases of the leaves of the tank-forming species tap the contents of watery impoundments. It is a different story for the atmospheric members of subfamily Tillandsioideae. Here the same appendages exhibit more elaborate construction and provide photoprotection and slow water loss, in addition to acting as roots (Figures 1.3, 4.4, 4.5, 7.6).

The atmospheric-type trichome consists of a single-layered platelike *shield* or cap composed exclusively of dead cells attached to the epidermis proper by a

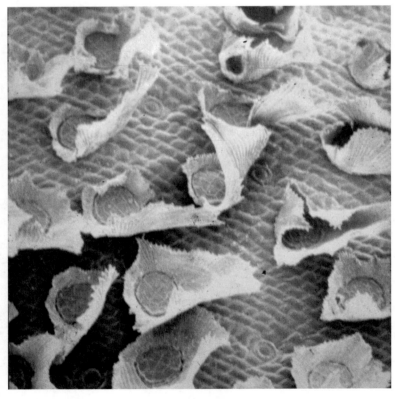

Figure 4.5. A scanning electron micrograph showing trichomes on the leaves of the atmospheric bromeliad *Tillandsia ionantha.*

living multicelled stalk (Figure 4.4A). Centermost within the shield and directly above the stalk are four equal-sized empty cells, each of which possesses thick stiff upper and substantially thinner, more flexible lateral and lower walls. Several additional rings, each containing twice as many cells as the one immediately within, surround the four central cells.

Fringing the shield is a *wing* that contains more than twice as many, more elongated cells than present in the outermost ring. Thin pliable upper cell walls cause one or more of the rings to operate as a soft hinge, allowing the wing to flex upward, which increases its capacity to scatter light (Figures 4.4A,B, 4.5). The natives of cloud forests bear trichomes with markedly asymmetrical shields (Figure 4.4 lower right). Those borne on the tank-forming members of subfamily Tillandsioideae possess narrower, more rigid, nonreflective caps (Figure 4.4 lower left).

Rather than beading up, drops of rain falling on a leaf invested with atmospheric-type trichomes rapidly spread from shield to adjacent shield. Moisture from the resulting film surges inward, causing the shields to swell and flatten formerly upright, light-scattering wings against the leaf surface. Flow continues into the stalks and from there into the leaf interior. Much the same occurs when water

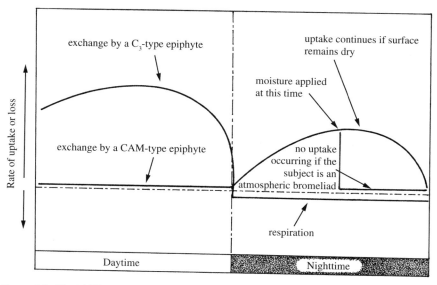

Figure 4.6. The inhibitory effects of wetting the leaf surfaces of an atmospheric bromeliad and the patterns of CO_2 gain and loss exhibited by CAM versus C_3-type plants. Note that the day-night patterns of CO_2 exchange by the two subjects are reversed, the CAM-type absorbing CO_2 mostly after sundown. Uptake by the atmospheric bromeliad (a CAM performer) ceased abruptly when it was moistened midway through the night.

moves from an engorged velamen through the underlying passage cells on its way to the core of an orchid root (Figure 4.3).

As the leaf surface dries, the four cells that make up the centers of the trichome shields settle back, reestablishing their pluglike configurations while the wings flex upright to resume reflecting light. Once again the leaf is protected against evaporation other than through its stomata. Had the central disks failed to collapse, water could wick back out into the atmosphere through the living stalks. Similarly, were the wings to remain prostrate, they could not help the plant avoid photoinjury. Like the velamen with its underlying exodermis, the trichome shield and stalk operate in tandem as a "hydraulic rectifier."

The functional trade-off faced by the velamen-equipped orchids similarly complicates life for the atmospheric bromeliads. While wet, the densely trichome-covered leaf cannot exchange gases through what during this interval are stomata occluded by a barrier of moisture-saturated shields (Figure 4.6). Should this condition persist long enough, death by suffocation results, much as for the overwatered orchids. Growers soon realize that the typical atmospheric bromeliad requires fairly frequent irrigation but enough turbulent air for its surface to remain dry most of the time.

Quite a few ferns, including *Pleopeltis polypoidoides,* bear trichomes with the same umbrella shape modeled by Bromeliaceae, but their powers of absorption remain little studied (Figure 9.3B). Because they lack movable parts, it is unlikely that they rival their counterparts among the bromeliads. Similarly overlooked are the appendages that line the tanks of the impounding astelias (Figure 10.3). It's also worth mentioning that the shields of the trichomes borne by some of the tillandsias that inhabit cloud forests repel rather than absorb moisture (Figure 4.4 lower right). Clearly, additional investigation of this tiny but versatile appendage is warranted.

5 Photosynthesis and Mineral Nutrition

Almost every kind of land-based habitat is at least moderately deficient in one or more of the resources that plants require. Drought has already been identified as the most pervasive of these challenges and especially for the epiphytes. Shade and shortages of key nutrients rank second and third. Plants are not uniformly prepared to deal with these environmental shortcomings, and not a single species can be described as superbly equipped to counter all three.

The ways in which the epiphytes that experience arid conditions avoid serious dehydration, or minimize injury when they cannot, are described in Chapter 4. Members of a second subset of species that lack equal drought-hardiness thrive in dim light. Adaptations of both kinds occur widely among the terrestrial plants as well; however, when it comes to securing nitrogen and phosphorus, many of the subjects featured in this book rival or exceed for novelty just about everything else in the plant kingdom. Having already dealt with drought, we now move on to photosynthesis and then mineral nutrition.

The Photosynthetic Syndromes

The shorthand employed by physiologists to summarize how plants use CO_2 to make glucose says nothing about how this process differs among species, let alone why it does. Table 5.1 and Figure 5.1 address this deficiency by comparing two of what are known as *photosynthetic syndromes*. Botanists apply the term *syndrome* here much as it is used in medical science. Just as pathological conditions among humans tend to have complex causes and multiple presentations, the photosynthetic syndromes also possess both structural and functional dimensions, and their external manifestations are diverse.

Leaf structure and longevity, how stomata behave, and the biochemistry abbreviated in Figure 5.1 distinguish the vascular plants relative to how they manufacture food. Which of the three basic photosynthetic syndromes is

Table 5.1. Modes of photosynthesis and water usage by nonparasitic epiphytes

Mode of photosynthesis	Water balance strategy	Maximum rate of photosynthesis	Water use efficiency (transpiration ratio)
C_3 syndrome	A. Desiccation-sensitive and evergreen	Moderate	Moderate
	B. Desiccation-tolerant and evergreen	Low to moderate	Poor
	C. Drought avoiding (seasonally deciduous)	Moderate to high	Moderate
CAM syndrome	Drought enduring	Low to moderate	High

Notes: Comparison of how photosynthesis is conducted and water is used by the nonparasitic epiphytes depending on whether they operate according to the C_3 or CAM mechanism (syndrome), and in the first case, among species that belong to the two drought-enduring and the drought-avoiding types.

employed in turn influences how efficiently a subject uses water, how fast it grows, and how it survives drought and several additional threats (Table 5.1). Taken together, these attributes go a long way in governing where and under what circumstances the members of different species thrive.

Only two of the three fundamental photosynthetic syndromes occur among the epiphytes (Figure 5.1). The succulent-bodied, drought-enduring types described in Chapter 4 fix CO_2 by a biochemical pathway known as *Crassulacean acid metabolism* (CAM). In other words, they perform CAM-type photosynthesis. The drought-avoiders are C_3-types, as are the desiccation-tolerant ferns and the mistletoes that produce some of their own food (the hemi-parasites). Epiphytes (the hygrophytes and mesophytes, Table 2.4) that grow where moisture is plentiful year-round also belong to the C_3 category. While close to nine-tenths of the vascular plants operate in this mode, fewer than half of the epiphytes do.

Biologists have yet to discover everything worth knowing about the ways in which the photosynthetic syndromes influence plant welfare. Water use efficiency is definitely an issue, but so probably is the economy with which leaf nitrogen is utilized and photoinjury avoided. It can be said that being equipped with a particular syndrome does not limit a plant to a specific kind of habitat. Most assuredly, these syndromes are neither geographically nor ecologically exclusive. Nor is their occurrence uniform among close relatives such as the members of a single genus (e.g., *Tillandsia* of Bromeliaceae).

It is not uncommon to see C_3-type, drought-deciduous orchids and CAM-equipped, atmospheric bromeliads growing side by side in tropical America, but they need to tap different sources of moisture to do so. Water sequestered in litter lodged among a trash basket–type root system or drawn from a moisture-retaining anchorage represents the relatively durable supply necessary to sustain the orchid, whereas the bromeliad gets by solely on the precipitation that periodically courses over its trichome-covered foliage (Figures 1.3, 2.6). Being leafless rather than foliated during the driest months of the year also makes a difference.

C₃ versus CAM-type Photosynthesis

C_3-type plants take up CO_2 from the atmosphere during daylight hours and assimilate it into glucose using the one-step, light-driven process summarized by the chemical equation provided in the lower left corner of Figure 5.1 (upper box). Fixation occurs immediately following diffusion through open stomata into the leaf's green interior (Figure 4.1A). When darkness falls and photosynthesis cannot continue, the stomata close and transpiration slows to a near standstill until the next morning.

CAM plants open their stomata for business beginning late in the day until early the next morning, so CO_2 enters their typically succulent green leaves or stems when glucose cannot be produced. Instead it is consumed via an alternative, less energy dependent metabolic pathway that operates through the night and yields large quantities of malic acid (Figure 5.1, lower box). Fixing CO_2 into malic acid expends reserves, usually starch, built up during previous bouts of photosynthesis. CAM makes sense economically because less energy is required to synthesize malic acid than glucose, the difference eventually being used to fuel growth and reproduction.

Around dawn, after a CAM-type plant has buttoned up its stomata, it begins to degrade the malic acid accumulated the previous night. The CO_2 thus regenerated cannot escape through what by day is a nearly gas-tight epidermis. At this point the same cells that harvested CO_2 from the atmosphere the night before reprocess it into sugar using sunlight and the C_3 pathway. CAM is a more complicated and energy-expensive process than strict C_3-type photosynthesis, but under appropriate circumstances it is the superior option.

A closer look at CAM, particularly the timing of its two-step fixation mechanism, explains why its operation promotes water-use economy. Plants that employ this syndrome expend moisture more sparingly than their C_3-type counterparts because evaporation slows after sundown, night air being cooler, although no less humid in the absolute sense than it was during the day. This being the case, it possesses less drying power, in other words, its relative humidity, although not its absolute water content, is higher after sundown. As for the other gas involved, the rate at which CO_2 will diffuse into a plant remains much the same all the time.

CAM-type photosynthesis represents the most effective way to make food if water, of all the commodities needed by green plants, is the one in shortest supply. Arid habitats tend to be sparsely vegetated, so they challenge their residents

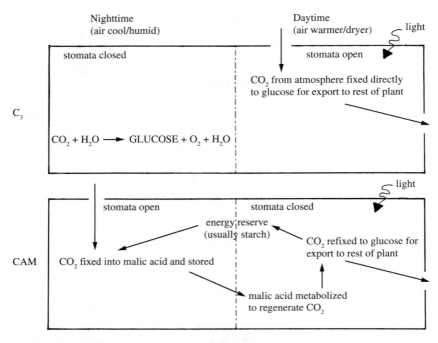

Figure 5.1. The way in which carbon derived from CO_2 obtained from the atmosphere is processed into glucose by plants equipped with the two photosynthetic syndromes (the CAM and C_3 pathways) that occur among the epiphytes.

more by drought than by shade. Consequently, securing enough solar energy to power photosynthesis presents no problem; remaining adequately hydrated does. Simply put, a C_3-type plant versus a CAM-type would have to expend considerably more water to make the same amount of sugar were both operating in the same arid environment.

Although C_3-type photosynthesis can support more robust growth than is usually possible for a CAM plant, conditions that favor its presence tend to be less common in aerial than in ground-based habitats. Accordingly, the latter types are proportionally more abundant in the canopy. What we see operating here is the functional tradeoff described in Chapter 4: grow fast and heighten the risk of desiccation, or use water more sparingly and increase the chance of being overwhelmed by competitors. The third (C_4) photosynthetic syndrome remains unreported among the epiphytes.

Figure 5.1 graphically illustrates how C_3-type plants use only the second of the two carbon fixation reactions employed by the CAM-equipped species to accomplish the same outcome. It is this second step that represents the more primitive of the two in addition to being the indispensable one. The initial fixation of CO_2 is supplemental to the essential step, its presence providing benefit only by allowing stomata to remain closed during the day. Evolution added fixation number 1 because CO_2 cannot be stored; its accumulation in plant cells requires its incorporation into a molecule such as malic acid.

Although malic acid contains too little energy to fuel plant growth, it is workable as an intermediary along the synthetic pathway that yields a final product that can: sugar. Why the CAM mechanism incorporates such circuitous biochemistry boils down to the fact that different amounts of useful energy exist in the chemical bonds tying carbon atoms together in different kinds of molecules. The carbon in glucose is a rich source of biologically usable energy; in CO_2 it is not. The carbon contained in malic acid falls between these two values, and this particular chemical compound can be massively sequestered overnight in cells capable of performing CAM-type photosynthesis.

Light and Adaptive Growth

Chapter 3 describes how different kinds of epiphytes segregate along the steep environmental gradients characteristic of dense tropical forests (Figure 3.1). According to Collin Pittendrigh's now 60-year old survey conducted in Trinidad, the bromeliads native to that island nation behave this way owing to their mixed tolerances and requirements for light and humidity. What underlies this behavior had to remain obscure until photosynthesis and water relations were better understood.

Epiphytes require species-specific exposures much like they need wet versus drier and warm versus cooler growing conditions. Moreover, these light-related *set points* are decided by anatomy and physiology, and being adapted for a specific intensity obliges a functional tradeoff that parallels the arrangement introduced in Chapter 4 that pits vigorous growth against high water-use economy. This time the opposing conditions are shade tolerance versus susceptibility to photoinjury. Figure 5.2 illustrates how shade- and sun-adapted leaves respond to different light intensities. Before exploring this issue further, it is worth considering what adaptation is all about.

Plants are well served by altering their form and function over short and longer terms because it keeps them compatible with growing conditions that change daily, seasonally, year to year, and beyond. "Short term" for this discussion means within the lifetime of an individual: change over multiple generations better fits the generally held notion of what constitutes evolution, but this is illusionary. Capacity for short-term adaptation is no less an evolved trait, but exploring why would take us well off-point.

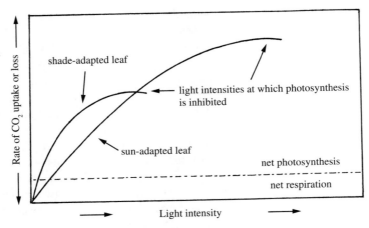

Figure 5.2. Photosynthesis by sun- and shade-adapted leaves subjected to a range of light intensities. Note that the shade leaf achieves net CO_2 uptake at lower exposures than its sun-adapted counterpart and also photosaturates in dimmer light; however, the sun-type organ is capable of more vigorous photosynthesis.

Adjustments that occur within weeks to months amount to *phenotypic* or developmental plasticity. Epiphytic *Guzmania monostachia* of Bromeliaceae demonstrates this kind of change by switching between CAM and C_3-type photosynthesis in response to seasonally fluctuating moisture supplies. *Tillandsia utriculata* can tolerate widely diverse exposures, in part owing to the light-directed, developmental plasticity of its shoot (Figures 3.5, 3.6). Drought stress induces the first kind of change, whereas the ratio of red to near far-red radiation in shade versus unscreened sunlight cues the second (see Chapter 3).

Bromeliads, more than the members of most other families of flowering plants, also illustrate plasticity that involves the ubiquitous red to purple pigments known as *anthocyanins*. These are the same compounds that color fruits and petals and convert the entire flowering shoots of many of the family's epiphytes into beacons for avian pollinators (Plate 3B). Expose any number of bromeliads to unscreened light, and their foliage turns bright red to orange, illustrating both the photoresponsiveness of anthocyanin synthesis and the utility of the product for photoprotection.

Chlorophyll is the principal player in yet another short-term response to exposure. Vegetation habituated to deep shade usually displays darker green foliage than when grown in full sun. High concentrations of this pigment increase a leaf's capacity to harvest the scattered photons that mostly make up shade light. Conversely, intense irradiation dissipates chlorophyll and promotes the accumulation of certain orange to yellow *carotenoids* that help an overexposed leaf dispose of excess absorbed energy, thus protecting the delicate light-harvesting part of its photosynthetic apparatus.

Some of the hemi-epiphytes use light quality to adaptively mold the architecture of their shoots. Differences between sun and shade forms can far exceed the variation demonstrated by *Tillandsia utriculata,* and the same individual may exhibit both conditions at the same time (Figures 3.5, 3.6, 7.7D). Many philodendrons and other aroids employ *heteroblasty* to discriminate between patches of well-illuminated and intervening darker spaces as they wander vine-like through light-dappled forest understory habitats.

Hemi-epiphytes that switch between shade-induced, spindly shoots bearing unexpanded leaves on widely separated nodes and stouter, more telescoped systems equipped with fully developed foliage benefit by growing this way (Figure 7.7D). Doing so allows them to pack energy-rich spaces with green tissue, and at the same time husband resources while traversing less rewarding, darker regions between. This is another example of how plants operate economically, as described in Chapter 4. Other species exhibit more rigidly programmed dimorphism. Shade-friendly architecture persists as the young individual ascends through the canopy, after which it produces more robust, adult-type leaves followed soon after by flowers.

Most plants benefit from *phototropism,* the mechanism that causes a shaded shoot to grow toward brighter light. Numerous vines and secondary hemi-epiphytes native to rain forests do just the opposite. They improve their chances of becoming more fully illuminated later by practicing *skototrophism.* Growing toward rather than away from a shadow cast by a tree trunk helps them locate routes to brighter futures. While this kind of behavior reduces a young plant's opportunity to modestly increase photosynthesis early on, it elevates the likelihood of gaining a host-assisted chance to harvest more energy later.

Mineral Nutrition

Published reports about epiphyte nutrition concern mostly fertilizers and their commercial applications. Many fewer deal with wild plants, and these that do tend to describe arcane phenomena such as which substances a certain bromeliad absorbed from its leafy tank or an ant-fed type obtained by way of a modified stem or leaf (myrmecodomatium). Absorptive scales and velamen-equipped roots have received some attention as well. More studies like those described in Chapter 3 that identified the sources and tracked the movements of nitrogen would be useful.

More than plants generally, the epiphytes enlist helpers, both casual and symbiotic, to obtain nutrients. Their partners include ants, *detritivores* (invertebrate animals that consume dead organic matter), frogs and salamanders, and several kinds of microbes (Figure 7.5E). Chapter 7 describes the relationship with fungi required by all orchids to germinate. The root-inhabiting *mycorrhizal* types that enhance life-long mineral nutrition for most terrestrial flora are probably less important above ground. Not so the bacteria that help decompose impounded litter or fix nitrogen for the tank-bearing epiphytes.

The shape of an epiphyte and where it grows usually indicate where its nutrients come from and how it absorbs them. The twig users look like the consummate scavengers they actually are (Figure 2.2). Being so small, they cannot impound litter or house any but the smallest of ant colonies. Instead, they rely on special devices such as foliar scales and velamen-bearing roots, plus the cost-saving, streamlined architectures described below. Impounding shoots and trash basket root systems need no further airing here.

The atmospheric bromeliads possess remarkable capacities to accumulate nutrients from dilute sources and some additional substances of interest as well. The ability of Spanish moss and several of its close relatives to sequester high concentrations of toxic metals, including chromium, lead, and mercury, has encouraged their use as inexpensive air quality monitors. Tracers added to fertilizer have pinpointed the foliar trichome as the device responsible for this exceptional performance.

The ant-fed epiphytes exploit their six-legged benefactors in two ways. The relatively small-bodied, more taxonomically diverse ant-house types employ cavity-forming stems or leaves to entice ant queens searching for nest sites (Figures 7.2C, 7.5A, 8.3F,H,I, 8.4A,B,C,D,E, 9.4B,E). Within weeks a queen's initial brood of workers are busily importing nutrient-rich materials from well beyond the host plant's most extended roots. A second, smaller subset of epiphytes produces alluring seeds that certain arboreal ants obligingly incorporate into the walls of their manufactured nests (see Chapter 6; Figure 8.3B).

Experiments have confirmed that the ant-houses provided by members of families Apocynaceae, Bromeliaceae, Orchidaceae, Rubiaceae, and a diverse collection of ferns are effective proxies for roots. Within days, radioactive calcium and glucose that had been placed inside these organs had become distributed throughout the bodies of the treated subjects (Figure 5.3). Similarly, tagged glucose set out near specimens of actively ant-inhabited *Myrmecodia* (Rubiaceae) experienced the same fate.

None of the ant nest-garden epiphytes has received as much attention as several of the ant-house species, which is not surprising because it is obvious where their nutrients come from (Figure 3.3). More interesting is the possibility that they benefit from unusual substances present in carton. Conceivably, one or both of the ant-fed types can metabolize nitrogenous substances that are not as abundantly available to plants that root in most other kinds of substrates.

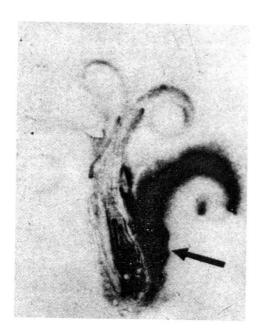

Figure 5.3. An autoradiograph illustrating how radioactive calcium applied to the inner surface of a single leaf base (arrow) of an intact *Tillandsia caput-medusae* specimen had been absorbed and transported throughout much of the shoot after 10 days. This image was produced by pressing both halves of a bisected specimen against a sheet of X-ray film.

The humus-rich soil substitutes created by thousands of epiphytes with impounding leaves or roots, or both, were mentioned in the preceding section on water relations. Nutrients are obtained from the same sources, and the way this is accomplished involves some interesting plant refinements. The trash basket orchids produce two kinds of roots, one for anchorage and the other for intercepting falling litter (Figure 2.6). Those that do the collecting grow upright rather than penetrate the substrate. The exposed roots of *Gramatophyllum speciosum* go one step further by bearing short, spinelike lateral branches, perhaps to better secure litter or deter herbivores (Figure 4.3 lower left).

The leafy tank is a more versatile device for enhancing plant nutrition above ground than a system of aerial roots. A single shoot of a large tank bromeliad can hold up to multi-liter quantities of soil-like material, which can sustain a host of beneficial animals and microbes (Figures 5.4, 7.5E). Foliage marked with purple to deep green horizontal bands alternating with paler zones and even more colorful mottlings conceivably help dozens of mostly medium-sized species camouflage the detritus feeders upon which they depend (Plates 1A, 7A,B). Dark brown leaf bases might serve the same purpose. Shoot shape also varies, no doubt much to the advantage of certain users in addition to the epiphyte.

Narrowly tubular architecture makes some of the water-collecting bromeliads especially inviting for amphibians and reptiles that require secure, humid

Figure 5.4. A shoot of the tank-forming bromeliad *Guzmania monostachia* in south Florida dissected to reveal the impounded, partially degraded litter.

refuges (Figures 6.3, 6.4, 7.5C). Occupied plants receive nutrients in return. Foliage produced by *Aechmea bracteata* and its structurally comparable relatives perform double duty by intercepting moisture and litter among the bases of some leaves while providing dry spaces for ant colonies and termites in others (see Chapter 6; Figure 7.5E).

Catopsis berteroniana alone among the hundreds of water-impounding bromeliads uses its vase-shaped, unusually yellowish shoots to recruit prey (Figure 5.5). Pivotal to this performance is a thick layer of loose wax that coats the lower third or so of each of its tank-forming leaves. Being highly light reflective, the wax renders the upright shoot invisible against open sky. Being slippery as well, it prevents colliding insects from climbing out of water-filled leaf bases.

It is odd that only two of the bromeliads, terrestrial *Brocchinia reducta* being the other, alone in their respective genera are carnivorous. Every other prey user is either the sole member of its genus or it has close relatives, all of which make their living the same way. None belongs to a genus that includes carnivorous and conventional feeders, yet the memberships of *Catopsis* and *Brocchinia* exceed 20 species each.

Figure 5.5. The carnivorous, tank-forming bromeliad *Catopsis berteroniana* growing well exposed in the crown of a shrubby phorophyte in south Florida. Note the powdery wax covering the bases of its leaves.

Experiments conducted to determine what sorts of nutrients the noncarnivorous bromeliads can absorb from their tanks suggests capacities to use amino acids and other small nitrogen-containing molecules and perhaps even certain proteins. Decomposing biomass, whether captured prey or intercepted litter, yields a complex mixture of soluble organic byproducts, including some of those already tested. At this point, it looks as though the nutrition of the tank bromeliads, whether carnivorous or otherwise, may be extraordinary in more ways than reported so far.

How the members of genus *Nepenthes* trap and digest prey is better understood than for *Catopsis berteroniana,* but only about six members of this

Australasian to South Asian genus are regularly epiphytic (Figure 10.1C). A few more species in a third carnivorous family also live above ground. Two members of *Pinguicula* and a dozen or so utricularias (both groups representing family Lentibulariaceae) grow on bark, but only where high humidity encourages dense, water-retaining growths of leafy liverworts and mosses. Several members of the second genus also colonize bromeliad tanks (Figure 2.7).

So far, this discussion and the brief allusions to epiphyte nutrition in Chapters 2 and 3 have emphasized sources and uptake rather than demand and use. Precedents elsewhere suggest that the requirements for phosphorus and several additional key nutrients by many of the epiphytes are relatively modest, as befits vegetation adapted for impoverished habitats. What in nature are normally nutrient-deprived plants grow slowly even when lavishly fertilized. Inherently slow growth signals fixed, modest demand. It's just this simple if the underlying physiology is ignored.

Abbreviated anatomy is another avenue to resource economy. Reductions in the complexity of the vegetative body epitomized by Spanish moss and the shootless orchids not only relax material demand, they also shorten the time required to achieve maturity, which benefits plants that depend on relatively ephemeral perches (Figures 2.2, 7.6F). Why the orchids have emphasized one organ system to achieve this outcome while the bromeliads have opted for another is considered in Chapter 7. Either way, scarce resources that more conventionally built plants apportion more evenly between roots and shoots are freed up for other purposes such as reproduction.

The Mistletoes

The mistletoes enjoy advantages and face challenges unlike those experienced by their free-living counterparts. On the positive side, they tap richer and more plentiful sources of moisture and nutrients than most of those utilized by the nonparasites, and this occurs unassisted by impoundments, myrmecodomatia, velamentous roots, absorptive scales, and other such embellishments. At most, the mistletoes possess moderately succulent foliage borne on shoots that otherwise exhibit no obvious specializations for life above ground (Figure 5.6).

Birds pollinate and disperse the vast majority of the mistletoes just as they do many of their nonparasitic, arboreal companions; however, once deposited on the surface of a compatible shrub or tree, a mistletoe seed faces a unique challenge. It must forge a lifelong physical connection to its host as it germinates. It is this phenomenon plus the physiology that comes with its odd way of acquiring resources that most decidedly sets a branch parasite apart from the epiphyte that uses the same kind of support primarily for mechanical anchorage.

Figure 5.6. The mistletoe *Phorodendron flavescens* parasitic on *Fraxinus caroliniana* in central Florida. The swollen region at the point of attachment of the seedling indicates the presence of reaction wood caused by its haustorium. Also shown is a detached, fruit-bearing branch obtained from a nearby adult. Photo by Linda Grashoff

Mistletoes make their vital attachments by employing an invasive organ called a *haustorium*. Its emergence, which is the first visible sign of germination, is followed by enzyme-assisted penetration of host bark. Depending on the assailant's identity, the resulting infection remains confined or spreads. Haustoria that extend considerable distances within a parasitized branch or snake over its surface often produce secondary shoots up to meters beyond where germination took place.

Host and mistletoe xylem, but not the corresponding phloem tissues, make direct contact. Even so, whenever traceable CO_2 has been fed to the foliage of an infected tree, a significant amount of radioactivity has ended up in its parasites. Nutritional dependence varies, with even the leafiest of the "xylem-tapping" types receiving at least some carbohydrates across haustorial bridges. Conversely, the "dwarfed" mistletoes are wholly host-dependent (holo- rather than hemi-parasitic). What evolution has conserved of their greatly abbreviated and mostly bark-embedded bodies more closely resembles a wood rotting fungus than any part of a typical higher plant.

Unusually leaky stomata assure that the mistletoes are profligate water users, as they must be because heavy transpiration is crucial for parasitism. In no other way could enough host xylem sap be diverted to satisfy the needs of a plant

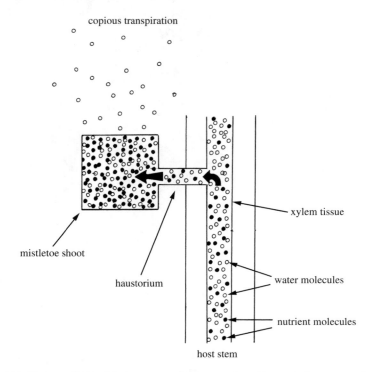

Figure 5.7. The osmotically driven pump mechanism employed by a mistletoe to tap the xylem vascular system of its host.

parasite. Hydraulically subjugating a victim's water-conducting system is impossible without first accumulating quantities of osmotically active material that only a heavy draw on a host-provided supply can deliver.

Mistletoes need 5–10-fold greater concentrations of calcium, magnesium, and potassium among other inorganic ions in their bodies to generate the tensions (negative pressures) necessary to overwhelm what their living supports maintain to drive their own water transport systems. A large quantity of xylem sap also assures that the parasite acquires enough nitrogen to meet its needs for growth and reproduction. Figure 5.7 illustrates how the mistletoes tap their hosts by operating as osmotically energized pumps.

Mistletoes seldom kill, although they can retard tree growth and diminish its commercial value by causing massive proliferations of tumor-like "reaction" wood around infection sites. Lumber quality can suffer enough to warrant expensive interventions. The dwarfed mistletoes of genus *Arcethobium* are especially troublesome in northern coniferous forests. Removal by pruning is a common orchard practice in many other parts of the world. Parasite-inflected water stress can pose a serious threat to arid land hosts.

Much remains for botanists to learn about the mistletoes. Plenty of questions worth someone's time await answers. Preliminary evidence suggests, for example, that infection by one mistletoe can grant immunity against attack by others that arrive later. Host specificity, which can be high, probably also has a physiological dimension. Another issue concerns mimicry and involves a group of Australian mistletoes that look like their hosts. If herbivory is in fact responsible for these remarkable examples of convergent leaf color and structure, then how did they come about? Were the agents surviving arboreal marsupials or among the many species extirpated since humans arrived on that continent more than 50,000 years ago?

6   Reproduction and Other Interactions with Animals

Evolution is a concerted process: when one group of organisms achieves a major adaptive breakthrough, others follow. Habitats suitable for air-breathing animals, for instance, could not exist until the higher plants had become well enough established on land to support them. Countless species have come and gone since this momentous event, but fauna still depend on flora for food and shelter.

Over the course of the past 400 million years, the vascular plants and terrestrial animals have been forging increasingly complex interactions, many of which are not one sided the way herbivory is. Some benefit both participants, whereas others favor plants over animals. It is these younger associations insofar as they involve epiphytes that serve as the subjects for this chapter.

Pollination

Most of what is known about the ways in which the epiphytes exchange pollen to reproduce can be summarized in three statements. Animals make the deliveries except for the few peperomias that appear to rely on wind (see Chapter 10). The fauna involved range from insects to birds and bats, and some of the most elaborate and species specific of the plant-pollinator relationships occur among the epiphytes (Plates 1–6). Claims about *breeding systems*—the mechanisms and devices that influence mate choice—and several additional aspects of epiphyte reproduction range from weakly supported by evidence to unmitigated speculation.

A number of authors have suggested that the epiphytes, more often than their terrestrial counterparts, produce seeds with self-pollen (are self-pollinated). *Self-compatibility* is indeed widespread and perhaps over-occurs among some of the more specialized groups like the ant-nest users; however, *self-incompatibility* is anything but rare. Whether underrepresented or otherwise among the epiphytes, it is a mechanism that assures failure for pollen that ends up on the stigmas of the plants that shed it. Consequently, every sexually produced member of a self-incompatible species has two parents.

Opposing this notion about mate choice is a second proposal to the effect that, more than plants in general, the epiphytes produce showy flowers that offer energy-rich rewards. This condition is necessary, the argument continues, in order to attract the long-range visitors that tend to foster cross-pollination, which leads to what geneticists label *allogamy,* as opposed to *autogamy.* Strong fliers are supposedly essential because the individuals making up the populations of many epiphytes are more widely scattered than usual. So far, this assertion lacks compelling support.

Many of the self-compatible epiphytes promote outcrossing with flowers that release and accept pollen sequentially over two successive days, or their stamens and stigmas are positioned far enough apart to discourage autogamy. Fail-safe mechanisms include stamens that flex over time, assuring that flowers that have not recruited outcrossed pollen after a certain period following anthesis (bud opening) at least receive self-pollen. It seems likely that just about all the mechanisms employed by plants to secure the benefits of outcrossing short of sacrificing reproductive potential (fecundity) occur somewhere among the epiphytes.

The ways flowers behave and are presented to pollinators further subdivide the epiphytes by reproductive mode. Some of the arboreal gesneriads (e.g., many *Codonanthe*) bloom almost continuously. "Big bang"–type displays are abrupt, short lived, and achieved with multiple flowers that open simultaneously on a single inflorescence (Plates 1A, 5A). Sequential flowering can extend opportunity to set fruits for weeks to months (e.g., *Merinthopodium neuranthum,* Plate 4C). The one to a few blossoms per shoot (ramet) produced by some of the orchids exceed just about all others in floral longevity (Plate 2C).

Plates 1 to 6 and Figures 9.2, 9.10, and 10.1A illustrate the substantial diversity that characterizes the reproductive organs of epiphytes. At one extreme are the peperomias, featuring small spike-type inflorescences that bear numerous, densely packed, minute *florets* (Figure 10.1A). The agents that convey their pollen remain largely undetermined, but long-distance fliers, and particularly birds, are not likely candidates. Such large, active animals would starve were their foraging restricted to plants that offer such meager rewards. Other epiphytes bear flowers far better suited to satisfy visitors with steep metabolic demands. The spore-bearing organs of the pteridophytes exhibit far less complexity and variety, which is not surprising considering that no pollinators are required (Figures 9.2–9.4, 9.10A,B,C).

Many of the arboreal orchids rely on floral deception and offer no food (Plate 2A,B,C). Some attract predatory insects by simulating prey. More often, the model is a flower produced by some non-orchid that continues to invest in the usual sugary rewards. Members of a third group of tropical American natives enjoy near celebrity status among botanists for blossoms that emit species-specific mixtures of powerful perfumes that male euglossine or "metallic" bees use to attract mates. These typically one-on-one relationships have promoted much speciation in numerous genera (see Chapter 7). Still other orchid flowers resemble nest sites, edible fungi, or territorial insects.

Birds move pollen for more than their share of the members of many of the most heavily epiphytic families, particularly Bromeliaceae, Ericaceae, Loranthaceae, and Gesneriacae (Plates 1A, 3B, 4B, 7A). Abundant nectar is the standard reward; edible pollen may also be present or substitute where the targeted visitors are bats. Bat and bird flowers presented individually are sizable (Plate 4C); when small, they occur in large numbers on densely packed inflorescences (Plates 4B, 5A). The bat attractors emit strong, unpleasant odors and mostly at night. The bird-dependent types lack fragrances, and their stamens and stigmas protrude beyond long, stout, tubular corollas (Plate 3B). Brightly colored foliage can strengthens the visual signal (Plates 3B, 7A). Some of the bird-mediated relationships among the mistletoes involve intricate floral structure and behavior, including tension-loaded parts that explode when probed. Table 6.1 summarizes the attributes that distinguish the major pollination syndromes among the epiphytes.

Clusters of closely related epiphytes demonstrate which aspects of the reproductive apparatus most often change as one pollination syndrome evolves to become another. Plate 1A,B,C illustrates how three members of the bromeliad genus *Billbergia* manipulate three kinds of animals. Note how the sizes, shapes, and colors of the prominent floral bracts and smaller petals vary, whereas basic floral design remains unaffected. Odors range from nil for bird-pollinated *(ornithophilous) B. eloisiae* to pleasant for insect-pollinated *(entomophilous) B. horrida,* to rank for bat-pollinated *(chiropterphilous) B. robert-readii.* Plate 3A,B,C illustrates a moth flower (C), a bird-attracting type (B), and a third autogamous arrangement (A), again all drawn from family Bromeliaceae.

Closely related epiphytes also demonstrate how rapidly breeding systems can change. Dioecious populations, meaning those whose members bear either female *(pistillate)* or male *(staminate)* flowers, sometimes belong to genera that also include species that retain the more primitive bisexual or *perfect* arrangement (e.g., *Aechmea* and *Catopsis* of Bromeliaceae). *Catopsis nutans* of the same family includes populations comprising entirely single-gendered individuals and others of plants that produce both functional stamens and pistils, although not necessarily compatible pollen and pistils. Members that make up small *disjunct* (geographically isolated) populations within more broadly distributed species do tend to produce single-parented seeds irrespective of how their relatives operate.

Table 6.1. Characteristics of the flowers associated with the most common of the pollination syndromes that occur among the epiphytes

Method of pollination	Flower characteristic				
	Color	Fragrance	Reward	Shape and size	Time of opening
Bat	Dark maroon or cream white	Strong, unpleasant	Copious nectar and/or pollen	If solitary, flowers large; if small, many in dense clusters	Night
Bees and wasps	Pastels	Pleasant	Nectar and/or pollen or none when mimicry is involved	Small-medium, many shapes	Day
Hawk moths and other evening-active types of insects	Light pastel or white	Pleasant	Nectar	Medium-large, long tubular corolla	Evening-night
Birds	Red-orange or other bright colors or white	None	Copious nectar	Medium-large, long tubular corolla	Day
Autogamous	Greenish and dull	None	None	Small, especially the petals	Day and night or never open

Blossoms markedly smaller than those borne by close relatives often set fruits whether or not visited by pollinators. Nature's penchant for material economy is evident in the minimalist flowers of the bromeliad *Tillandsia recurvata* (Plate 3A). Being spontaneously autogamous, this species would waste resources were it to produce larger petals or secrete fragrance or nectar. This small-bodied, highly prolific epiphyte may well owe its exceptional distribution and dense local populations largely to its fail-safe reproductive apparatus. Closely related, but allogamous, *T. usneoides* occupies even more territory, but probably because of the readiness of its festoons of much-reduced shoots to break into wind-dispersible fragments (Figure 1.3).

Fruits and Seeds

Identifying the type of fruit that works best for the epiphytes is no easier than determining the most propitious way to exchange pollen to determine the parentage of offspring. Here as well, multiple means yield acceptable results. The capsule-type fruit is the most widely occurring arrangement, but only because orchids make up more than half the arboreal species (Table 2.7; Figure 7.2 upper left corner). Switch from tallying species to families, and top contender shifts to a small berry usually provisioned with numerous modest-sized to tiny seeds (Figures 8.1C, 8.3B, 8.4A; Plate 8A,B,C).

The numerical dominance of the epiphytes by one family assures that the bias that applies to fruit type extends to the seed. The so-called microsperm characteristic of Orchidaceae is not associated with epiphytism in any other family, only with root parasitism (see Chapter 7; Figures 7.2 upper left corner, 7.3). In fact, the variety of kinds of seeds associated with living above ground is extensive. Canopy users in Apocynaceae, Bromeliaceae (subfamily Tillandsioideae), and certain members of Ericaceae and Gesneriaceae also bear capsules, but they release wind-dispersed seeds orders of magnitude heavier than the orchid microsperm (Figure 8.3E,G). Hairs more often than wings account for their air worthiness.

Size and shape are only two among the many factors that influence seed success. Others are seed longevity, physiological state upon dispersal, and which of several environmental conditions triggers germination. What little is known about the seeds of the epiphytes suggests that they tend to be short lived and nondormant, and that exposure to light often activates growth. All three of these qualities also occur widely among terrestrial plants. *Vivipary* (germination prior to dispersal) may be more narrowly associated with epiphytism, although the best-known examples of this condition occur among the mangroves.

A number of fleshy-fruited aroids, bromeliads, cacti, and gesneriads appear to be viviparous. Seeds produced by some of the white-berried anthuriums (Araceae) and aechmeas (Bromeliaceae) have already begun to green up by the time the enclosing fruit is ripe. Those of *Epiphyllum phyllanthus* (Cactaceae) vary on this point, only some germinating prematurely. Presumably, getting off to a head start is the main advantage of vivipary and, if so, likely a beneficial characteristic in aerial habitats with thin substrates and droughty conditions. Tides and waves that threaten seedling establishment probably explain the over-occurrence of vivipary among the mangroves.

Whereas weight and shape determine the mobility of the wind-dispersed seeds, the enclosing fruit wall is influential where animals are involved. Fleshy fruits, and probably the seeds inside, match their conveyors. Family Bromeliaceae once again is instructive. Several billbergias advertise their comparatively large berries with odors reminiscent of rotten fruit and reflective surfaces that increase visibility at night. Note how the white-coated fruits illustrated in Figure 6.1 further enhance the brightness of the inflorescence of bat-pollinated *Billbergia robert-readii*. Over-occurrences in knotholes, the persistent bases of palm leaves, and similar sorts of cavities accord with bats as frequent seed dispersers.

Rather than the dull gray brown to silvery fruits produced by the billbergias, members of *Aechmea* and more than a dozen related bromeliad genera display scentless, smaller red, white, blue, or maroon berries much favored by birds. Similar arrangements occur in other families (Plate 8B,C). Dispersal probably occurs in two ways. Bill wiping is pivotal for one mode, practiced perhaps to spare the animal problems caused by swallowing seeds that ought to be rejected. Transferring a seed from a fleshy fruit to the surface of a host by the second route requires safe passage through somebody's gut.

The berries produced by many of the epiphytic aroids, cacti, and members of additional families, like those of the fleshy-fruited bromeliads, tend to extrude portions of their contents upon harvest (Figures 7.7G, 8.1C). Firmer but otherwise similar types are more likely adapted for consumption intact. Seed characteristics may vary accordingly. Layers of sticky mucilage or attached fibers could encourage beneficial bill wiping. The seed coat might be another distinguishing feature, being thicker as required where dispersal includes contact with corrosive digestive fluids.

The flowerpeckers (genus *Dicaeum,* particularly *D. hirundinaceum,* the mistletoe bird) of Australia and nearby islands are especially well disposed gutwise to disperse berry-fruited epiphytes, particularly the mistletoes, owing to the coatless condition of their seeds (Figure 8.1I). Passage through these animals occurs in record time, with enough adhering mucilage remaining to allow defecated seeds

Figure 6.1. Light-reflecting berries of *Billbergia* sp. (Bromeliaceae).

to stick to bark. Berries produced by the mistletoe cacti resemble those of their parasitic namesakes, but how faithfully is not clear. Cactus fruits definitely differ by containing dozens of small rather than one larger seed (Figure 8.1C). Instances of fruit mimicry probably exist elsewhere among the epiphytes.

A third subset of fleshy-fruited bromeliads, along with some members of half a dozen more families, employ the fragrance-based mechanism described later in this chapter to encourage carriage by ants. Still other bromeliads rely on semifleshy capsules that burst to disperse their contents (e.g., the bromeliad

Rhonnbergia explodans). The most impressive species on this score are the dwarfed mistletoes of genus *Arcethobium,* whose "ballistic" seeds travel up to a meter distant from fruits that remain attached to the parent.

Plants that produce fruits or seeds adapted to cling to animals root mostly on the ground, often in forest understories or along edge communities located where tall and shorter vegetation meet. Such species typically grow no more than about a meter tall with a couple of the exceptions being epiphytes. The small single-seeded fruits of *Peperomia* are adapted to disperse by virtue of the sticky contents of minute, readily ruptured papillae arrayed over the fruits, or parts of them (Figure 10.1A). Insects attracted to the viscous pulp discharged from the soft-walled capsules produced by certain *Vanilla* orchids take away some of the many thousands of tiny embedded seeds.

Asexual Reproduction

Epiphytes, being mostly long-lived, herbaceous perennials, typically propagate by vegetative in addition to sexual means. The thousands of species with compact sympodial bodies exemplified by most of the bromeliads and a majority of the arboreal orchids routinely fragment as the rhizomes connecting their quasi-autonomous ramets decay (Figures 1.2C, 7.2D). The isolated plantlets that result, being genetically identical, represent members of *clones.* Progressive dieback causes the monopodial types to proliferate asexually as well, although less extensively. Many of the creeping ferns multiply the same way.

A few of the tillandsias of Bromeliaceae and some orchids (e.g., *Phalaenopsis*) clone in more orderly fashion by way of offsets that develop on spent or sterile inflorescences. Occasional axillary buds located on the senescing pseudobulbs of some of the deciduous orchids (e.g., catasetums and dendrobiums, Figure 7.2A) generate rooted lateral shoots in cultivation, but how often in nature remains undetermined. Only rarely do new individuals begin as buds on roots. Sometimes the flower acts as a cryptic asexual device. At least one bromeliad and more orchids ripen pseudoseeds containing what behave like true embryos but are not the products of fertilized eggs.

Everything considered, it is fair to say that beyond some odd manipulations of pollinators and flowers weird enough to make this possible, the epiphytes are not particularly noteworthy for the ways they multiply. Fruit types, pollination syndromes, modes of floral and fruit display, and breeding systems more or less parallel what occur among plants that root in the ground. At this point, it looks as though no earthshaking changes in reproduction occurred as the vascular plants acquired the wherewithal to use each other as substrates.

Plant Defenses

Luck cannot explain why the land plants are still around after being food for predators and hosts for pathogens for more than 400 million years. Such persistence is entirely attributable to the presence of a bewildering array of mechanical deterrents, toxins, and evasive behaviors. In no other way could vegetation of any description have avoided being overwhelmed by legions of herbivores and microbes. Quite a few species, including many of the epiphytes, go a step further by augmenting these more conventional defenses with the services of ant guards, as described in the next section.

Judging by the myriad agents that plague the epiphytes, tree crowns offer no escape from the usual enemies of plants, with one notable exception. Few of the species that root above ground brandish armature that even approaches the standard set by the desert-dwelling cacti and their thorny, shrubby companions, and no doubt because few large-bodied grazers can climb trees. The epiphytes that deploy sturdy spines along the margins of their foliage (e.g., *Aechmea bracteata,* Figure 7.5E) are usually either facultative canopy users, or they have close, similarly equipped, terrestrial relatives.

Whether the epiphytes are victims of more or less herbivory than otherwise comparable ground-based flora, they engage in an exceptionally broad array of mutually beneficial partnerships with animals. Most common are the associations that result in pollination and seed dispersal. Plant protection is another positive outcome. Still other combinations, especially those that enhance plant nutrition, if not unique to the epiphytes, are better developed among these plants than in just about any other. It is here that the ants truly reign supreme.

Ants and Epiphytes

Three reasons explain why the epiphytes receive more than their share of the services that ants provide plants. One is geographic: both ants and epiphytes densely populate the canopies of many of the same humid tropical forests. Epiphytes also rank high as providers of nesting sites, and they and ants partner in additional, although somewhat less intimate ways. Finally, lacking roots that reach the ground, the epiphytes are better positioned than most other flora to benefit from ant-enhanced nutrition.

Ants in turn are exceptionally well suited to assist plants, especially those kinds characterized by durable colonies. Pairings can last for as long as the botanical member survives, which may be decades for a particularly long-lived *Hydnophytum* or *Myrmecodia* specimen (Figure 8.4A,B,C,E). Additional aspects of ant biology that determine the ways in which an associated plant can benefit include diet, behavior, colony size and social cast structure, and whether queens prefer ready-made cavities or nests constructed from scratch.

The kinds of ants that partner with epiphytes range from nomads seeking chambered leaves and stems to house a few dozen individuals, to others that construct vegetated carton nests populated by tens of thousands of residents. Workers representing the second type conduct diverse tasks, three of which (seed collection, plant feeding, and protection) serve what are known as the ant nest-garden epiphytes. This second kind of mutualism makes ant-supported plants major players in woodland affairs. A study conducted in Amazonian Peru determined that 40% of the canopy of a local forest was actively patrolled by ants that cultivate epiphytes (Figure 3.1).

The two aspects of an ant's biology that most powerfully determine its capacity to promote epiphyte nutrition are its diet—how nitrogen-rich—and its foraging behavior. Workers that search widely for food for queens, nest-bound workers, and young can deliver significant inputs from locations well beyond reach of the root systems of even the largest of their botanical partners. How this source is tapped differs depending on whether the plant involved is anchored in a carton or houses a nest inside its body. Proof that transfer occurs from ants to ant-house epiphytes is provided in Chapter 5 (Figure 5.3).

Not much is known about the chemistry of ant carton, but its utility for epiphytes varies and, as a consequence, for the architects as well. Constructions that support the most luxuriant gardens often become so thoroughly penetrated by roots that little space remains to accommodate workers and brood (Figure 3.3). Others remain barren or nearly so, although not necessarily for reasons of infertility or poor water-holding capacity. Gardens vary in floristic composition in part because different ants prefer different kinds of seeds to include among the materials they use to construct covered runways and nests (Figure 6.2; see Chapter 8).

All that an ant-house epiphyte need do to secure ant-provided nutrients is offer an attractive cavity capable of absorbing what its tenants deliver. Like the ant-gardened species, what is brought to the plant has not been identified, but its significance must be substantial. More than a dozen angiosperm families and several groups of ferns include one or more ant-house or ant-garden epiphytes, or both, proof that feeding by both routes has evolved repeatedly (Figures 3.3, 5.3, 6.2, 7.2C, 7.5A, 8.3F,H,I, 8.4A,B,C,D,E, 9.4B,E). Of course, it is possible that reduced pressure from herbivores has been more instrumental in promoting this outcome than ant-enhanced nutrition.

Ant-houses are not equally inviting to ants or comparable in cost to the plant. Members of family Rubiaceae offer the most elaborately structured and probably the most hospitable of the many versions of the myrmecodomatium. Shape and size differ depending on the species, but the interiors of the swollen stems

Figure 6.2. *Codonanthe* sp. rooted in a carton-covered arboreal ant trail on the trunk of a rain forest tree in southern Venezuela.

provided always include labyrinthine cavities vented to the outside through spontaneously formed ports that sometimes resemble miniature lunar impact craters (Figure 8.4B,C). *Myrmecodia, Hydnophytum,* and the members of three smaller satellite genera field more than 150 species equipped in this manner.

The chambers within the myrmecodomatia of some of the rubiaceous epiphytes come in two versions, one supposedly better equipped to absorb nutrients than the other. Somehow their users sense this distinction or some related difference and select the first kind as repositories for debris and body waste. This is a fortunate choice for the plant, given the stubby roots lining the inner walls. Ant brood is maintained exclusively within the smoother-walled cavities that presumably lack equivalent capacity to take up beneficial substances.

Most of the ants that nest in the bodies of epiphytes are not particularly reliable. The rubiaceous species fare best, usually attracting the same one or a few longer-term, more faithful residents. Epiphytes that produce lower-grade shelters experience uneven occupancy involving more kinds of ants. Often it does not seem to matter to parents or caretakers whether young are reared in cavities provided by plants or in something else. All the ants obtained from a sampling of native Florida bromeliads qualified as "weedy" types, some being introduced aliens in that part of the world.

A third party may benefit when an especially predatory ant partners with an epiphyte. Such was the case recorded in the crowns of swamp forest trees surveyed in southeastern Mexico. Host foliage was nearly free of damage up to about a meter distant from each of a number of ant-inhabited *Aechmea bracteata* specimens, whereas many of the leaves farther removed were well chewed by beetles (Figure 7.5E). Ants that had taken up residence in a colony of Mexican ant-house orchids (*Myrmecophila*) (Figure 7.2C) acted quite differently, choosing to flee rather than mount even feeble attempts to fend off intruders, which in this case were a couple of curious biologists.

The nest-garden epiphytes reward their insect keepers in three ways. Well-rooted occupants help maintain the physical integrity of a densely colonized nest and also provide a sump-pump–like service. Shorn of vegetation at a site in Amazonian Peru, tested cartons became so sodden with precipitation that their ants departed, leaving the abandoned nests to collapse. Nest-gardens also serve as pastures for ant-tended aphids and scale insects. How the botanical members fare in this three-way proposition depends on whether any larger herbivores deterred by the ants would have inflicted more damage than the smaller types being farmed.

Some of the most aggressive ants (e.g., members of the carpenter ant genus *Camponotus*) create carton nests that support diverse combinations of the aroids, bromeliads, cacti, ferns, orchids, and so on that grow nowhere else. Ant behavior suggests why these gardens can become so lush. Even a slight nudge will elicit a roiling mass of hundreds of stinging, biting workers, many agitated enough to leap into the air to attack their tormentor. The smaller ants (frequently members of *Crematogaster* and *Solenopsis*) that often share the same cartons are seldom seen during these incidents.

Phloem sap allows the nest-gardening ants to be so numerous and influential, but accessing this sugar-rich, relatively nitrogen-poor food requires piercing mouthparts that ants lack. Many hundreds of temperate-zone and tropical species compensate by relying on the parasitic insects just mentioned to pierce the tough vascular bundles coursing through stems and foliage. Unlike their protectors, these slow-moving "plant lice" feed exclusively on the contents of phloem tissue (sieve tube elements, Figure 1.2B) and necessarily in large volumes to obtain enough nitrogen. The excess sugar is excreted in a liquid, ant-usable form called *honeydew*.

The ant nest-garden epiphytes were once thought to colonize developing cartons by offering soft-walled, colorful fruits to birds that obliged by delivering the contained seeds to what amount to widely scattered locations (Figure 8.3B). Now we know otherwise. About a dozen ant-garden species from almost as many families produce seeds laced with the volatile chemical methyl-6-methylsalicylate as a means to distribute their offspring among isolated patches of rooting medium. Why only the nest-gardening types find seeds provisioned with this compound desirable for carton building is not known. The bright yellow arils attached to the seeds of *Codonanthe crassifolia* further contribute to its association with ant nests (Figure 8.3B).

Seeds produced by the tropical American ant nest-garden endemic *Peperomia macrostachys* contain at least five chemicals that when present together attract workers of *Camponotus femoratus*. Some of these substances elicit different responses from other ants, several of which produce the same compounds in their mandibular and other glands, possibly to control pathogenic fungi or communicate with nest mates. In any case, it is pretty clear that the Amazonian ant nest-garden mutualism is mediated primarily by signaling molecules rather than by food.

Ants rely on olfaction more than sight to negotiate their miniature worlds. The question now is, which of the numerous chemically elicited ant behaviors do the nest-garden epiphytes manipulate to benefit their offspring? Unlike most of the terrestrial ant-dispersed species, many of the nest-garden specialists, especially those native to the Paleotropics (e.g., *Aeschynanthus*, *Dischidia*, Figure 8.3E,G) produce dry, wind-dispersed seeds poorly suited to incorporate food for dispersers or to sequester volatile lures. Mimicking ant pupae is another possibility that in some instances accords with seed size and shape (e.g., *Codonanthe* spp., Figure 8.3B). Whatever the enticement, once a seed ends up deposited in a proper carton, it has reached one of the most hospitable of all the many kinds of rooting media available to an epiphyte.

Termites

A number of termites combine bits of plant material, feces, and saliva to construct carton trails and nests in the canopies of tropical forests. Few of the epiphytes root in this typically hard medium, and probably none use it on anything even close to a regular basis. Two additional pairings bring epiphytes and termites together, neither of which seems likely to benefit the botanical partners. Diets based on wood and similarly nitrogen-poor litter, plus indifference to herbivores rule out termites as serious contributors to either plant nutrition or security.

Two Mexican investigators observed the usually epiphytic orchids *Brassavola nodosa* and *Myrmecophila grandiflora* rooted on covered trails built by *Nasutitermes nigriceps* on low-growing *Bursera fragaroides* trees at a site in Vera Cruz state. All were small, and the few adults present were terrestrial, apparently having fallen to the ground after beginning life on cartons. I have seen occasional specimens of an unidentified bird's nest–type *Anthurium* growing in termite-provided media in moist lowland forests in southwestern Costa Rica. It is quite possible that the plants had arrived first.

Carton-covered trails leading to sizable tank bromeliads provide the only clue that a relationship of the second kind is under way. So far, its occurrence has been documented on only a few small Caribbean islands and at a single study site in Minas Gerais state in southeastern Brazil. None of the specimens examined bore the kind of damage expected if their users had been seeking food. Water was the scarcer of the two commodities locally and probably in higher demand. Greater vulnerability to dehydration makes carton manufacture a more moisture-demanding activity for termites than for ants.

Relationships of the third kind, although probably more common than either of the other two, are not much better understood. In the single case described in print, termites were living among the dry outer leaves of large *Aechmea bracteata* specimens anchored in the canopies of the same seasonally inundated, Mexican swamp forest mentioned above (Figure 7.5E). Again, the absence of damaged tissue indicated that termite nutrition was not the incentive for occupying these plants. The same cannot be said for all the many additional residents, some of which were ants known to favor termites as prey.

Where the occupants of these shoots chose to reside reflected their needs and tolerances. Those with aquatic lifestyles and others that require moist but better-aerated surroundings were confined to the water-filled and wet-surfaced spaces among the inflated bases of the youngest to intermediate-aged leaves (Figure 7.5E). Additional air breathers making up a mixed collection of predators and prey that need still drier surroundings were living among the more loosely overlapped, moribund and dead foliage.

In the final analysis, the densely foliated, tank-forming bromeliads act as something akin to botanical apartment complexes filled with residents with disparate needs and mixed compatibilities, some potentially antagonistic, others possibly mutualistic. Information on how such diverse users manage to cohabit and perhaps even cooperate could be interesting. Also worth pursuing are experiments designed to address the question of whether any occupants of these or other kinds of epiphytes receive benefits not provided by identically configured and provisioned vessels constructed of an inert material such as glass or plastic.

Leafy Tanks and Phytotelms

Nearly two centuries have passed since naturalists first reported how the water-filled cavities called *phytotelms* characterizing certain kinds of plants often harbor complex biological communities (Figures 6.3, 6.4, 7.5B,C,E). Today, hundreds of publications confirm that these wetland *microcosms,* which range from the contents of tree holes to bromeliad tanks, are exceptionally accommodating for invertebrates and higher animal forms alike. Largely ignored is the possibility that some of the epiphytes providing these accommodations embellish them in ways that benefit providers and users alike.

The vast majority of the microbes, worms, and arthropods reported as residents of tank-forming bromeliads are opportunists because they also frequent other kinds of wet habitats. Members of a second category associate more faithfully, but only to secure temporary shelter, moisture, or food. Obligate dependence prevails when an animal breeds or spends another of its life stages nowhere else. Many of these most dedicated of the tank users, the majority

Figure 6.3. Brazilian frog residing in the center of a tank bromeliad, using its rounded bony head to discourage predators and avoid desiccation. Note how the color and texture of the top of the head with eyes closed suggests a phytotelm clogged with debris rather than the presence of an amphibian.

being insects, salamanders, and frogs, exhibit shapes, colors, and behaviors that indicate long associations with botanical partners (Figures 6.3, 6.4).

Little evidence suggests that the bromeliads coevolved with the animals that occupy their shoots. Nevertheless, this is a possibility worth pursuing. Many of the tank formers possess highly ornamented foliage, and shoot architecture ranges widely, as described in Chapter 5 (Plate 7BC; Figure 7.5B,C,E). Species that maintain leafy reservoirs exhibit forms that tend to parallel local climates, as discussed in Chapter 4, but this does not exclude additional modifications adapted to promote mutualism. Perhaps different groups of animals helped fine-tune the broadly utilitarian quality of the tank-forming shoot, improving its performance, much as flowers evolved a variety of syndromes to more effectively exploit specific kinds of pollinators (Table 6.1).

Bromeliads that maintain heavily populated phytotelms create biodiversity *hotspots* within woodland ecosystems. Invertebrates have been recorded at abundances and diversities well above those observed across much of the rest of

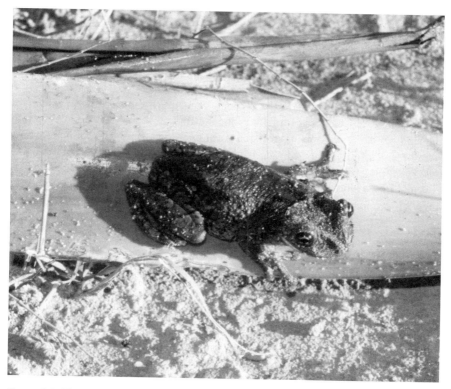

Figure 6.4. The same frog illustrated in Figure 6.3 fully exposed.

the same aerial habitats. Only the occasional water-filled tree hole and perhaps some of the arboreal ant nest-gardens and the most inviting of the myrmecodomatia approach the tanks of large bromeliads as support systems for complex, dynamic biological communities.

The suitability of a tank shoot for its users depends on a variety of factors, the most influential being the amount of moisture present and its permanence. Many phytotelms dry out for several months each year, whereas those associated with plants native to regions with more uniformly distributed precipitation are continuously aquatic. Leaf shape, size, and orientation determine the capacity of a shoot to collect litter and moisture and how much light reaches any green organisms living inside. Architectures that result in multiple small chambers rather than fewer, larger ones favor residents obliged to share quarters with predators (Figure 7.5BC).

The character of a living space provided by a tank-forming epiphyte changes over time. The suitability of a single leaf base, and ultimately the entire shoot, for specific kinds of occupants shifts as its capacity to hold water lessens and the litter within decays. Shoots of the more leafy species around midlife feature compartments ranging from wet to dry and from litter free to clogged with the same material reduced to fine particle humus, as previously described for *Aechmea bracteata* (Figures 5.4, 7.5E). Long-established individuals consisting of multiple ramets of mixed maturities provide the most heterogeneous support systems of all.

Several recent reports describe a group of primarily marine crabs that raise their young exclusively in bromeliad shoots. More attention has been devoted to the salamanders and frogs that display similar behaviors in the same quarters. Members of a third group of organisms, to which most of the obligate tank users belong, although individually less spectacular, contribute more to epiphyte success and forest biodiversity. All these animals benefit from their epiphytic hosts; a few even improve the services received.

Case Studies

Metopaulias depressus resembles the Atlantic blue crab we prize so highly as food, but its ecology deviates from that of the more primitive members of its fundamentally marine genus. Much of its existence is spent foraging through the crowns of trees and shrubs along tropical coastlines. When the time comes to reproduce, bromeliads top the list of choices, but often what they offer needs improvement. Crab young, being hypersensitive to water chemistry and vulnerable to predators, require interventions that only a dutiful parent can provide.

Metopaulias depressus manipulates the aquatic environments it chooses for its eggs and larvae by adding fragments of snail shells to reduce its acidity and boost often unacceptably low calcium ion content. Gravid females also remove much of the litter present, thereby eliminating a source of humic acid and food for microbes that if allowed to multiply might consume dangerous amounts of dissolved oxygen. The adult further nurtures its young by destroying any damselfly nymphs that happen to be lurking in its arboreal nursery (Figure 6.5).

The *Metopaulias* story is also interesting for what it says about the tempo of an adaptive radiation—in this instance, about how long ago the transition from salt to fresh water occurred among the secondarily arboreal members of its genus. Comparisons of DNA from all seven tree-climbing species, plus a number of the more primitively marine types, indicate that ocean habitats were abandoned no more than four million years ago. Quite likely, water-impounding bromeliads played a role in this transition, although not an active one.

Whereas much crab behavior, in addition to physiology, had to change to permit bromeliad use, the botanical side of the partnership was already poised to benefit from the attentions and products of formerly seagoing crustaceans. No adjustments, for example, were necessary to make use of the wastes produced by adults and crab larvae, because other aquatic arthropods that almost certainly long before lived in bromeliad shoots excreted the same nitrogenous substances.

Conversely, salamanders and frogs, being fundamentally freshwater creatures, had no need to adjust their physiology to adopt bromeliads as vessels for breeding. Body shape and some key aspects of reproduction are another matter. Tank-dwelling salamanders in particular possess markedly thinner trunks and limbs than their closest terrestrial relatives, probably to ease difficulties caused by having to negotiate the narrow spaces created by tightly overlapped leaf bases (Figure 7.5B,C).

Compared with the tree-dwelling salamanders, the arboreal frogs are more diverse, range across the tropics, and occupy more kinds of habitats. It should come as no surprise, then, to learn that they exceed the salamanders as specialized tank users, and that they exploit them in a greater variety of ways. Almost everywhere that water-impounding epiphytes occur, frogs of some description can be found using their phytotelms at least as daytime refuges. Nighttime foraging often ends with these relatively casual users returning to the same bromeliads, sometimes even the same leaf bases.

One anatomical feature that unequivocally prepares a frog for prolonged use of a bromeliad occurs among certain species endemic to regions visited annually by pronounced dry seasons. Skin tightly co-ossified to the upper skull equips a number of members of several genera, including *Gastrotheca* and

Figure 6.5. Adult damselfly recently emerged from a bromeliad tank in southeastern Brazil.

Trachycephalus, to wait out unfavorable conditions in the centers of tank shoots tightly sealed inside by their firm, rounded heads. Dislodging the animal illustrated in Figures 6.3 and 6.4 required vigorous shaking; its slow movements afterward made it easy pickings for watchful predators.

Frogs that breed in bromeliad shoots scale their reproductive efforts to match confined quarters. Clutch sizes, meaning the numbers of eggs laid per batch, are lower among the tank users than among those that exploit larger, more permanent bodies of water. Also, the tails of their larvae tend to be oversized to enhance gas exchange, should dissolved oxygen become scarce (Figure 7.5E). Metamorphosis from tadpole to frog is precocious, beginning with eggs containing more than the usual amounts of yoke to compensate for the usually thin rations in bromeliad tanks. The larvae of the most specialized species lack functional digestive tracts altogether.

Some of the frogs that reproduce using bromeliad tanks tend their young. *Dendrobates pumilio* exhibits the most impressive post egg-laying behavior reported so far. Despite being terrestrial except during the breeding season, the female demonstrates incredible powers of recall and navigation above ground. One by one, tadpoles hatched on the forest floor dutifully climb aboard her back to be deposited in nursery plants accompanied by an unfertilized egg added as food. Rearing involves repeated visits to the same bromeliads and more sacrificial eggs. The mother's persistence is exceeded only by her uncanny ability to service her scattered offspring.

The tank bromeliads that offer the most austere accommodations grow where long dry seasons select for shoots featuring relatively few leaves that form a single deep phytotelm (e.g., *Aechmea nudicaulis* and several billbergias, Figure 7.5C). Being so narrowly constructed reduces interception capacity, but then the thin crowns of arid land hosts tend to shed relatively modest amounts of litter anyway. Dissected shoots also often reveal few aquatic invertebrates, in part also because their architecture does not favor coexistence between antagonistic occupants. It is the flatter, leafier shoots that exhibit the bright ornamentations that horticulturalists and perhaps certain tank users find more appealing (Plate 7B,C).

Tank-forming epiphytes also represent important resources for arboreal mammals. Foraging by monkeys and marmosets for frogs and other sizable prey in bromeliad shoots occurs through much of tropical America. Considerable nontank-dwelling fauna benefit less directly owing to the capacities of these plants to modify intracanopy climate. One estimate for a cloud forest in northern Colombia cites bromeliads as responsible for suspending approximately 5000 liters of water per hectare above ground. Imagine the importance of this resource for desiccation-sensitive insects like mosquitoes during protracted rainless weather. Opportunities for breeding follow suit. Dozens of mosquito species, including some that vector human disease, regularly pass their larval stages in bromeliad tanks.

Experiments have demonstrated that some of the mosquitoes that use phytotelms provided by epiphytes choose among the possibilities by cuing on leaf color and possibly the shape of the container. Bromeliads growing in shaded locations, and individuals that for other reasons also appear unlikely to dry out before any larvae present can mature, attract the most egg laying. Evidence also suggests that the quantity of debris a tank shoot contains influences the amount of attention it receives from gravid females.

7 The Epiphytic Monocots

It is impossible to know how often epiphytism has evolved, but without doubt only a few of what presumably were many such events account for most of the living arboreal species. Fully two-thirds of the 28,000 modern epiphytes belong to a mere three families—all *monocot*-type angiosperms (Table 2.7; Figure 7.1). Ferns and lycophytes make up a sizable fraction of the rest, and what remains unassigned consists of non-monocot flowering plants augmented by just five gymnosperms.

Why are the monocotyledonous families Araceae, Bromeliaceae, and especially Orchidaceae so inordinately successful in aerial habitats? Is this bias a statistical aberration—simply a consequence of one family's exceptional propensity to proliferate species, most of which just happen to be epiphytes? If so, then why do two additional families that belong to the same Linnaean class, both of which differ from the orchids and from each other, include so many of the remaining canopy-dwelling species? It is more likely that something basic about being a monocot is at work here.

The monocots, contrary to the rest of the angiosperm complex, are predominantly herbs equipped with bodies comprising repeating, semiautonomous ramets abundantly supplied with adventitious roots (Figures 1.2C, 7.2A,C,D). Some of the same and similar characteristics probably predisposed the ferns and lycophytes for aerial life as well (Table 2.8). It is also significant that only the orchids, along with the spore-bearing ferns and lycophytes, produce immense numbers of tiny, highly mobile offspring (Figures 7.2 upper left corner, 7.3).

Inexpensive, nonwoody construction and body plans that foster opportunistic growth almost certainly favored multiple adoptions of epiphytism within the monocot assemblage. The groupwide occurrence of these attributes does not tell the whole story, however, particularly why its epiphytic membership is so varied in other important respects, such as reliance on leafy tanks and absorptive hairs versus velamentous roots in Bromeliaceae and Orchidaceae, respectively. The conclusion that monocot-type epiphytism evolved repeatedly from what was already a well-differentiated terrestrial ancestral stock is inescapable.

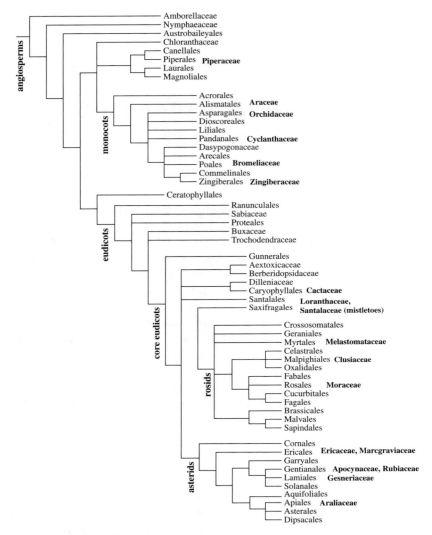

Figure 7.1. Angiosperm phylogeny illustrating which of the families and orders contain most of the flower-producing epiphytes (adapted from Angiosperm Phylogeny Group 2003).

What follows in this first chapter of a four-part survey of the epiphytes are treatments of the three families just identified, plus those assigned to Liliales, an order that includes Amaryllidaceae and additional smaller families erected to accommodate species removed from what formerly was a more inclusive lily family (Liliaceae). Descriptions of additional monocot families are reserved for Chapter 10.

Orchidaceae

Orchidaceae is the appropriate place to begin comparing the vascular epiphytes. In addition to sharing top billing with Asteraceae as one of the two most species-rich families, more than two-thirds of its members grow above ground. Additionally, only the bromeliads and the ferns rival the orchids for adaptive variety. Orchidaceae also argues most convincingly that conditions in aerial habitats foster exuberant speciation. It is difficult otherwise to explain the predominance of epiphytism in so many of its largest genera (e.g., *Bulbophyllum, Dendrobium, Encyclia,* and *Epidendrum*).

Two facts indicate that the kind of epiphytism exhibited by the orchids is relatively young and not the first version of this lifestyle to have evolved among the flowering plants. No fossils more than a few tens of millions of years old can be unequivocally assigned to the family, and most of its canopy users belong to its phylogenetically most recently emerged tribes (see Chapter 2; Figure 2.1). At the same time, it is important to recognize that small soft-bodied organisms make poor candidates for preservation in sediments. Finally, divining how any plant lived from ancient, fragmentary remains is difficult.

The existence of the many adaptive types described below helps explain why the orchids are numerically so superior in aerial habitats. Versatility relative to climate is another factor. No matter how hot or cold, dry or wet, sunny or shady the location, if vascular epiphytes are present, at least one is almost certain to be an orchid. Orchidaceae, with its terrestrials included, contributes heavily to virtually all the tropical biodiversity hotspots.

What else about the orchids might explain their overrepresentation among the epiphytes and the impressive size of their family? It would not be prudent at this juncture to claim anything as certain, but some novel biology suggests a possibility worth exploring. To fully appreciate this hypothesis requires familiarity with a suite of orchid traits that individually do not shed much light on why one family among the numerous contenders has become nearly omnipresent in aerial habitats that host vascular epiphytes.

The Vegetative Body

Chapter 4 describes how the epiphytic orchids employ specialized, velamen-equipped roots to maximize access to the intermittent and often scarce supplies of moisture and mineral nutrients that characterize many of their habitats (Figure 4.3). Those that serve the shootless species also conduct enough photosynthesis to compensate for what has become vestigial foliage (Figure 2.2). Roots that serve the less specialized leafy orchids make less food, and some lack this capacity altogether.

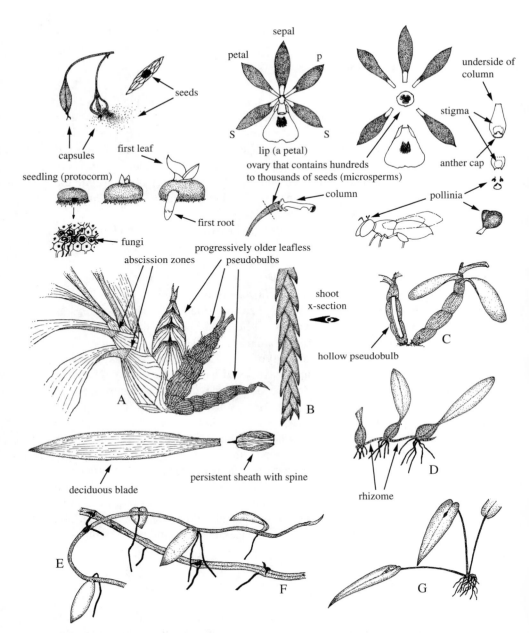

Figure 7.2. Orchid seeds (microsperms), seedlings, and adult vegetative morphology. Also shown are the reproductive organs drawn to emphasize aspects of orchid biology that are central to the rapid speciation hypothesis. **A.** Drought-deciduous *Catasetum incurvum* with ramets in different stages of development and senescence **B.** The leaflike two-dimensional shoot of *Lockhartia* sp. **C.** *Myrmecophila* sp. with a pseudobulb cut away to reveal its chambered interior that frequently houses ant nests **D.** Pseudobulbous ramets of *Bulbophyllym* sp. connected by relatively long rhizomes **E.** Leafy *Vanilla bahiana* **F.** Leafless *Vanilla madagascariensis* **G.** *Pleurothallus isthmica* illustrating ramets that lack pseudobulbs.

The orchid leaf varies in structure, physiology, and longevity, and much to the advantage of its bearers (Figure 7.2A). Foliage produced by the drought-deciduous species exemplified by members of *Catasetum* and *Cyrtopodium* is cheaply constructed, capable of high rates of photosynthesis, and short lived, functioning only through a single wet season (Figures 2.6, 4.2). Many times more orchids bear more robust, CAM-equipped foliage that expends water most economically and operates longer, in some cases for several years.

Orchid stems come in myriad shapes and perform different functions for different species. The leafless vanillas are wholly dependent on green stems for photosynthesis (Figure 7.2F). A majority of the sympodial orchids possess *pseudobulbs* that represent swollen segments of determinate shoots (ramets), which are solid except where modified to house nesting ants (Figure 7.2C). Only one internode is involved in many instances; for other species, the number of phytomeres is higher and ramets are more elongated (Figure 7.2A,C,D).

Ramets produced by the sympodial orchids often evolve more slowly than other parts of the body. The bulbophyllums, for example, despite their dizzying floral diversity, feature pseudobulbs dominated by a single internode topped by one or two evergreen leaves (Plate 2A,B; Figure 7.2D). The catasetums produce cigar-shaped, multinoded ramets equipped with deciduous foliage borne in two opposing ranks (Figure 7.2A). Short rhizomes often tie series of pseudobulbs into tight clusters whereas those of other species are much longer.

Thousands of additional orchids belong to the monopodial category. For them, shoot growth is more open ended (indeterminate). Species with the least rigidly programmed architecture include the vine-producing to hemi-epiphytic members of *Vanilla* (Figure 7.2E,F). Horticulturally popular genera such as *Phalaenopsis* and *Vanda,* and their shootless relatives even more, possess relatively compact versions of this same, less regularly branching body plan (Figure 2.2).

Reproduction and Speciation

How the orchids reproduce and where the majority grow may explain why their species are so numerous. Particularly noteworthy is the seed, which being miniscule and rudimentary, can develop by the thousands to millions inside a single capsule-type fruit (Figures 7.2 top left, 7.3). Each appropriately named *microsperm* consists of nothing more than an undifferentiated embryo, which along with some empty space is enclosed inside a membranous coat (Figure 7.3). Dump on a flat surface what's inside a ripe fruit, and you get what looks like a pile of dust; breathe too heavily, and it just as readily goes airborne.

Microsperm can be so minute because the food that allows the embryo of a more typical plant to become a self-sufficient seedling is not present in the seed.

Orchid parents obviate this expenditure by dispersing seeds that depend on invasion by a fungus to germinate. Rather than yielding as it would if attacked by a competent pathogen, the young seedling, activated by its assailant, uses that same organism to compensate for its parent's negligence. In no other way could the orchids achieve the economy necessary to produce so many offspring. Likewise, in no other way could the family proliferate so many species according to the hypothesis about to be presented.

Some of the fungi that induce the orchid microsperm to germinate are virulent pathogens to other plants. Other so-called orchid fungi are *saprophytes* because they normally subsist on dead tissue. Either way, the infected embryo digests portions of the invading fungus and obtains the nutrients from it that its seed parent failed to provide (Figure 7.2 upper left corner). Rather than being *mycorrhizal,* hence by definition a mutually beneficial relationship, the orchid-fungus association amounts to predation, with the fungus being the prey.

How the orchid fungi induce germination and feed the resulting seedlings has attracted numerous investigators interested in the physiology of symbiosis. The

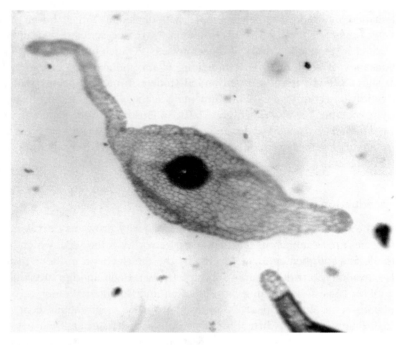

Figure 7.3. A single microsperm produced by the epiphytic orchid *Encyclia tampensis.* The small object in its center surrounded by empty space is the poorly differentiated embryo unaccompanied by food reserve tissue (endosperm). The greatest dimension of this seed is less than 0.5 millimeter.

manner in which this odd relationship might affect a more global aspect of orchid biology has not been as well appreciated. What follows is a plausible explanation of the ways in which a disparate mix of plant attributes, including seed biology, have helped Orchidaceae outstrip all but possibly one other family (Asteraceae) as a botanical engine for making species.

Two additional parts of the orchid reproductive apparatus figure prominently in what hereafter will be called the rapid speciation hypothesis. Both parts are as necessary for achieving the high numbers of seeds that an orchid flower can produce as the microsperm's minute size and fungus-dependent germination and subsequent growth of the embryo. Additional aspects of the orchid flower and the ways it attracts and manipulates visitors address the speciation question as well.

Except for part of family Apocynaceae, only the orchids package their pollen in detachable delivery devices called *pollinia* (Figure 7.2 top right). A single pollinium contains enough grains to fertilize all the *ovules* (unfertilized seeds) present in an orchid flower's three-parted hyperovulate ovary. Because the contents of these male and female organs, respectively, are numerically matched, a single pollination can yield up to millions of seeds. Numerous flowers and a correspondingly high number of pollinations would be necessary for a more conventional plant to achieve the same reproductive outcome.

Several centuries ago, naturalists began reporting that some of the orchids attract unusual pollinators despite offering no food. They also noted how fruit set could be just as inexplicably low. Charles Darwin was sufficiently inspired by these phenomena to devote an entire book to what he called the unusual contrivances by which the orchids reproduce. In it he describes some of the most exclusive of the relationships between orchids and their insect visitors, some of the latter as unlikely as the males of certain parasitic wasps.

According to the rapid speciation hypothesis, Orchidaceae ranks highest among families for pollen exchange among members in ways that can foster prolific speciation. Fundamental to this phenomenon is the orchid family's uniquely enabling combination of pollinia, hyperovulate ovaries, and juveniles capable of obtaining nutrients from fungi. Important as well are intricately constructed flowers that allow their owners to exploit animals capable of acting as exclusive albeit sometimes patently inept pollinators (Plate 2A,B,C).

The rapid speciation hypothesis posits that the combination of orchid characteristics just listed has sped up multiplications of species by relaxing constraints on seed production and the dependency of progeny on parents for early-stage nutrition. Being equipped to avoid reproductive failure by possessing a sexual apparatus capable of yielding with a single pollination thousands or more seeds containing predatory embryos is crucial. So endowed, the orchids have been free to adopt pollinators that, by their visitation behavior, tend to fragment gene pools, and this in turn sets the stage for speciation. Forging the necessary plant-animal relationships required evolving all manner of floral embellishments, many of which contribute by deceiving pollinators.

Rather than employing nectar and floral platforms accessible to a variety of pollinators, many orchids rely on chemicals, shapes, and colors that only one or a few species of animals deem worth their attention. Targeted are such unlikely candidates for transporting pollen as fungus gnats and fruit flies, in addition to predatory wasps. No other family so effectively employs floral mimicry to exploit insects that normally do not concern themselves with flowers, but seek shelter, food, and mates using cues that orchids have duplicated.

According to the rapid speciation hypothesis, the orchids tend to employ pollinators prone to break into genetically isolated fragments populations of sexually compatible individuals. Qualified animals, rather than being generalist-type foragers, discriminate by cuing on heritable flower characteristics such as fragrance chemistry and petal shape and color. In essence, they target floral *phenotypes* distinguished by these traits; being a good pollinator is not necessary. How often a visit yields a fruit is less important than sticking to one kind of blossom.

Any change in the flowers produced by a population of orchids that dampens the interest of one of these exclusive-type pollinators can set in motion its proliferation. Should such an event transpire, the bearers of the altered floral phenotype find themselves reproductively isolated, thereafter unable to mate with individuals that retain the original or *wild type* condition. What had been a single gene pool has become split into two smaller gene pools.

If the individuals equipped with the derived phenotype (and its underlying new "genotype") subsequently replace their former with a new pollinator, they become a second, in this case, *derived* gene pool. Provided enough time and the right circumstances, their group (now also a separate lineage, see Figure 2.1) will survive to evolve further, perhaps enough to become a new species. Should the wild type gene pool persist as well, it too might evolve, and in due time neither linage will resemble its shared ancestor or each other (Figure 2.1).

Orchid proliferation likely has had an ecologically driven in addition to a pollinator-driven dimension. This is where epiphytism completes the story. It is common to encounter dozens of kinds of orchids growing in close proximity, many apparently undifferentiated by rooting medium or any other requirement for growth (see Chapter 3; Figure 3.7). Combine a mechanism that vigorously proliferates species capable of sharing a widely available, relatively empty living space, and a picture emerges of how modern Orchidaceae may have achieved its record size and unparalleled prominence in aerial habitats.

The Adaptive Types

Although Orchidaceae is numerically preeminent in tree crown habitats, epiphytes representing other groups exceed them in several other respects. None of the orchids utilize litter as a source of nutrients as effectively as a large tank-forming bromeliad. Nor do any orchids parallel the atmospheric types for employing foliage covered with absorptive trichomes, or rival the poikilohydric ferns for tolerating desiccation. Members of Orchidaceae are peerless, however, when it comes to versatile roots, and it is this part of the plant that above all differentiates the family into its many types of epiphytes.

Dozens of reports describe how this or that orchid fixes CO_2 at night or otherwise copes with drought. It was recently confirmed that CAM-type photosynthesis has evolved repeatedly in the family. Several additional phenomena related to orchid epiphytism have not received as much attention. Why, for instance, do the nest-garden species root exclusively in ant cartons? How do their microsperms, being so small and thin walled, attract carton-building ants and survive their attentions? Is a food reward involved? Are alluring chemicals part of the mechanism, as described in Chapters 6 and 8 for the larger-seeded species that share the same substrates?

Members of Orchidaceae that provide nest sites for ants are not nearly as well prepared as similarly equipped epiphytes in several other families. Rather than the elaborately appointed myrmecodomatia provided by the ant-fed members of Rubiaceae (Figure 8.4), those produced by orchids amount to ordinary pseudobulbs hollowed out and fitted with a single slit-shaped entrance (Figure 7.2C). Extrafloral nectaries that encourage pugnacious ants to patrol young inflorescences are another matter, being quite common and often unusually generous with their secretions.

The orchids widely exceed the bromeliads and ferns for exclusive rooting media, consistent with possession of multifunctional, highly specialized roots. In addition to the obligate ant nest-garden users, others grow mostly in knotholes or on rotten wood. For reasons that remain obscure, still other species never mature on axes more than about a centimeter thick (the twig epiphytes). The trash basket orchids benefit from litter impounded by tangles of aerial roots (Figure 2.6), and a number of vine-bodied types operate as secondary hemi-epiphytes (Figure 7.2E,F). Finally, some of the CAM-equipped orchids exploit under-resourced habitats every bit as successfully as the members of any other family.

Bromeliaceae

Anyone looking for appealing subjects to stock a constructed aerial garden is well advised to emphasize Bromeliaceae. Its tank formers come in just about every shape and size, and many display brightly dappled or banded foliage (Figure 7.5; Plate 7B,C). Species that fit this description also impart a Neotropical aspect should it be desired because few Old World epiphytes match the bromeliads for distinctive silhouettes (Figure 7.4).

Figure 7.4. Atlantic rain forest in southeastern Brazil populated by abundant epiphytes, and most conspicuously by large tank bromeliads.

Only Cactaceae among the other medium-sized flowering plant families is as exclusively New World as Bromeliaceae in its geographic distribution and geologic youth. The same cannot be said for adaptive variety or biological importance, as the cacti trail far behind the bromeliads by both measures. Whereas Cactaceae contains fewer than 1500 species, only about 10% of which grow on other plants, the equivalent numbers for Bromeliaceae are about 50% of a membership that exceeds 3000.

Bromeliads versus Orchids

Despite the overwhelming superiority of the orchids in number of species in aerial habitats, the bromeliads equal and occasionally surpass them in several other respects. Most notable are ecological variety, stress tolerance, biomass, and especially value as resources for other organisms. Arboreal members of both families range from sea level to locations high enough to subject their floras to brief hard frosts. Likewise, many survive severe drought with adaptations that range from CAM-type photosynthesis to seasonally deciduous foliage.

Both families achieve their greatest diversities and abundances where plentiful moisture and thick mats of mosses and lichens create exceptionally favorable conditions for epiphytes (Figures 2.4, 3.2). Shared as well are nutritional modes based on ant use and the exploitation of litter, although the bromeliads far surpass the orchids by this second consideration (Figures 2.6, 5.4, 7.5). To be so comparable relative to adaptive variety and ecological breadth seems odd considering that the canopy-dwelling orchids range worldwide and exceed by tenfold their number in Bromeliaceae. But then the bromeliads lack those aspects of reproductive biology that prompt the rapid speciation hypothesis.

Bromeliaceae and Orchidaceae definitely part company when it comes to impacts on forest communities and ecosystems, especially regarding their significance to plant-dependent animals. Chapter 6 describes how the bromeliads with tanks far outstrip the orchids as providers of food and housing, especially for invertebrates with aquatic larvae (Figure 7.5E). The bromeliads also contribute more biomass to the canopies of woodland ecosystems, ranking second only to the bryophytes.

Adaptations for Epiphytism

Three attributes go a long way in explaining why Bromeliaceae perform so well in aerial habitats. Particularly influential is CAM-type photosynthesis (Figure 5.1). The desert-dwelling cacti and agaves, along with many additional arid land flora, likewise owe their capacity to cope with drought in large measure to this mechanism. The second and third adaptations, the absorptive foliar

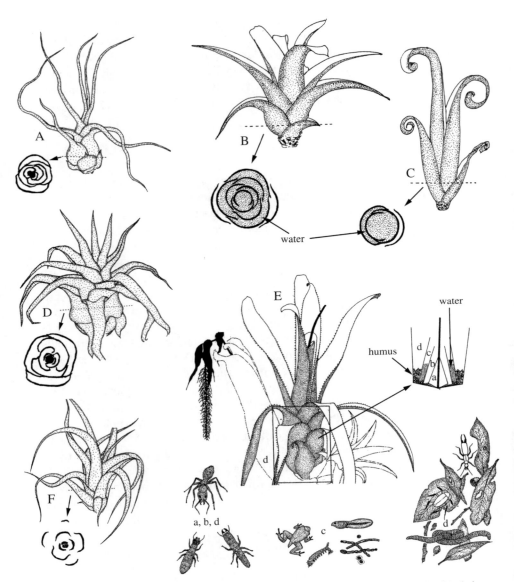

Figure 7.5. The shapes of bromeliad shoots and the interfoliar cavities within. **A**. *Tillandsia bulbosa* with dry leaf chambers that often harbor ants **B**. Tank shoot with multiple water-impounding leaf bases **C**. A more tubular-shaped tank shoot with essentially one centrally located water impoundment **D**. *Tillandsia streptophylla* with dry leaf chambers that are often occupied by ants **E**. *Aechmea bracteata* showing its multiple leaf base chambers and samples of their contents, which include litter, diverse invertebrates, and a tadpole **F**. *Tillandsia flexuosa* with dry leaf chambers that are too loosely overlapped to attract nesting ants.

trichome and the tank-equipped shoot, are more narrowly associated with epi-phytism and more impressively in Bromeliaceae than in any other family.

The absorbing trichome is the most distinctive of the adaptations associ-ated with bromeliad-type epiphytism (Figures 4.4, 4.5). In addition to its contribution to the family's spectacular success above ground, its adoption made possible an unprecedented evolutionary accomplishment: a massive structural makeover that culminated in a body comprising a highly special-ized, multifunctional shoot accompanied by a substantially diminished root system (Figure 7.6).

Two of the three adaptations largely responsible for bromeliad epiphytism and several additional, more minor ones have emerged repeatedly in the family. Leafy tanks evolved on at least three occasions, which should not be surprising

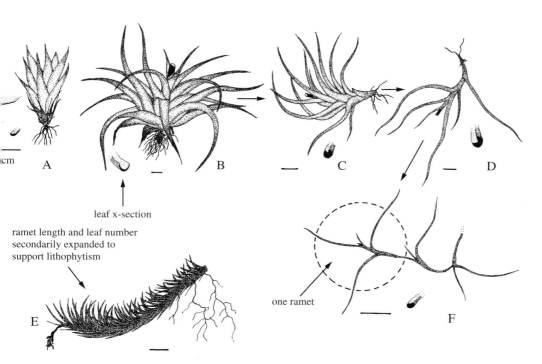

Figure 7.6 Proposed heterochronic evolution in subfamily Tillandsioideae of Bromeliaceae. **A.** A 1-year-old seedling and a 3 to 4-year-old juvenile of a typical tank-bearing species of *Tillandsia* showing the abrupt transition from the production of juvenile to tank-forming foliage **B.** *Tillandsia hondurensis* **C.** *Tillandsia schiedeana* **D.** *Tillandsia recurvata* **E.** Lithophytic and caulescent *Til-landsia arujii* **F.** *Tillandsia usneoides*.

considering the high probability that its ancestors possessed shoots consisting of typical, monocot-type, strap-shaped leaves borne in spirals on short stems (see Chapter 2, Figure 2.1). Crafting a device capable of impounding a substitute for soil required little more than additional telescoping of some internodes and inflating a corresponding number of overlapping leaf bases (Figure 5.5).

Ant housing is another arrangement that occurs across much of Bromeliaceae, and again probably because not much had to change to craft a bulb-shaped shoot equipped with enclosed (hence dry), leaf base chambers (Figures 5.3, 7.5A,D). The ant nest-garden species are fewer and exclusively members of subfamily Bromelioideae. Dry fruits and seeds and root systems better suited for mechanical anchorage than acquiring resources probably explain why none of the other epiphytic bromeliads use ants in this manner.

CAM-type photosynthesis provides yet another example of evolutionary redundancy, arising independently at least four times in four of the eight currently recognized subfamilies. DNA analysis indicates that the most recent common ancestors of Bromeliaceae were C_3 types, and that they rooted in well-watered, infertile soils in savanna-type ecosystems in what is now northern South America. Some of their descendants evidently adopted this less water-expensive way to make food as they penetrated drier regions or adopted epiphytism during just the past 10–15 million years.

The most advanced version of the bromeliad trichome that allows roots to be downgraded to anchors or eliminated has a different history (Figures 4.4, 4.5). It occurs only in subfamily Tillandsioideae, and when present at high densities allows its atmospheric-type bearers to scavenge key nutrients from exceptionally dilute sources and protect foliage by reflecting excess light. Less structurally refined trichomes with more modest powers of absorption occur in two additional subfamilies (Brocchinioideae and Bromelioideae). How they relate to those that serve the dry-growing members of subfamily Tillandsioideae (the atmospherics) remains undetermined.

Hemi-epiphytism

A modest number of bromeliads deviate from the family's basic rosette-style shoot architecture (Figure 7.5). Several members of the predominantly terrestrial genus *Pitcairnia,* plus a larger contingent of mostly tillandsias produce elongate or *caulescent* shoots with which they scramble up taller neighbors, or as lithophytes, creep along or hang from rocky perches (Figures 7.6E, 7.7A). Because they die from the rear forward in typical monocot fashion, the pitcairnias that ascend hosts are well disposed to be secondary hemi-epiphytes.

Pitcairnia riparia demonstrates how little evolution was necessary to modify a well-entrenched body plan and shift from a terrestrial to a quasi-epiphytic

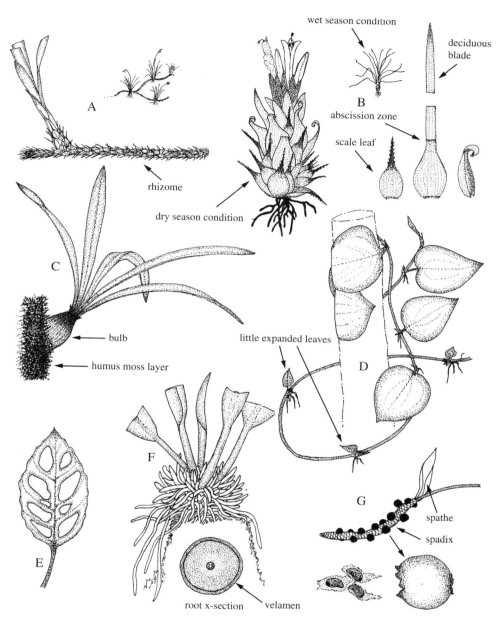

Figure 7.7. Miscellaneous monocots. **A.** Sometimes hemi-epiphytic *Pitcairnia riparia* (Bromeliaceae) **B.** Shorter-stemmed *P. heterophylla* illustrating its elongate green, deciduous, and persistent spiny bractlike foliage **C.** *Hippeastrum* sp. (Amaryllidaceae) with photosynthetic foliage present **D.** Heterophyllic, hemi-epiphytic aroid with leaves that failed to expand and others that developed fully to either stand free of the substrate or grow against it **E.** Extensively fenestrated leaf of hemi-epiphytic *Monstera obliqua* (Araceae) **F.** Cross-section of a root of *Anthurium paraguayense* showing the velamen and the kind of root system development commonly associated with bird's nest shoot architecture in Araceae **G.** Inflorescence, fruit, and seeds of *Anthurium gracile* (Araceae).

lifestyle. Instead of flowering after producing the usual congested array of green leaves on a short stem (Figure 7.7B), the shoot meristems of the ancestors of *P. riparia* were reprogrammed to allow their ramets to grow longer. Rather than additional leaves, however, the added nodes bear stout, spiny scalelike bracts. The leaf-bearing portion remains largely unchanged: branching still occurs close behind the shoot tip as it initiates the production of an inflorescence (Figure 7.7A,B).

The Atmospheric Bromeliads

Some 300 to 400 species, all members of *Tillandsia* and several closely related tillandsioid genera, engage in the most advanced version of bromeliad epiphytism. They do this by operating without leafy tanks or absorptive roots, subsisting instead on moisture and nutrients extracted directly from precipitation and aerosols. Their performance is what prompts the name atmospheric or *air plant,* its more colloquial equivalent (Figures 1.3, 1.4). How these most exceptional of the aerial performers in their family subsist on such meager rations hinges on truly novel structure and function.

The atmospheric bromeliads share their sympodial architecture with almost all the rest of the family, and flowers, fruits, and, seeds more or less meet the same standard (Figure 1.2C). It is the way the leaf, particularly its epidermis, and several aspects of overall body plan depart from convention that also make their kind such appealing oddities for hobbyists. Finally, none of the other bromeliads demonstrate more dramatically how evolution has altered one portion of an organism's body while leaving the rest largely unaffected (i.e., demonstrate "mosaic" evolution).

The structural modifications that make the atmospheric way of life possible are most pronounced in Spanish moss. Each of its diminutive ramets consists of just three leaves, and if fertile, a solitary terminal flower as well (Plate 3C; Figure 7.6F). Roots rarely develop beyond the few that anchor seedlings. Its less reductively modified relatives tend to be larger bodied, bear more leaves per ramet, and, as adults, produce at least occasional adventitious roots (Figure 7.6B,C,D). Only some of the lithophytes, and fewer of the epiphytes, feature longer-stemmed modules that bear hundreds of small, densely overlapping leaves (Figure 7.6E).

Comparing the atmospheric bromeliads with the rest of subfamily Tillandsioideae suggests how their much-derived condition took shape. The progression toward near complete independence of a substratum appears to have begun with an arrangement that persists today among the tillandsioids that occupy humid shady habitats. These are the species that rely on tank shoots comprising thin, soft leaves disposed in tight spirals on short stems (Figures 3.2, 5.5). Foliar trichomes are present, but their shields are narrow and rigidly held against the leaf surface (Figure 4.4 lower left). Adults are well rooted, but primarily to secure anchorage (Figure 7.6B).

The transition from reliance on the contents of leafy tanks to the atmosphere outright began while Bromeliaceae was less diverse than today, probably only within the past 5 to 10 million years. At this point, the ancestors of what would be decidedly more stress-hardy descendants experienced Darwinian selection conducive to this outcome. Perhaps climates changed as the northern Andes rose, or colonists entered longer-standing arid landscapes. Being relatively drought vulnerable, but predisposed to become less so for the reasons described below, this stem group gave explosive birth to the atmospheric bromeliads.

Not only are the atmospheric bromeliads inhabitants of seriously under re-sourced living spaces, but their manner of operation also makes their success all the more interesting. Timing is crucial because opportunities for uptake tend to be brief. Moisture and nutrients are available only while storms or mists are wetting trichome-covered foliage, events that during dry seasons may fail to oc-cur for months on end. But this is the only option for a small plant that has to operate while essentially suspended in air.

An atmospheric bromeliad would not be able to survive without its foliar tri-chomes, but this alone is probably insufficient; material savings gained by reducing investments in roots must also help (Figure 7.6). Whatever the case, these two conditions are interdependent; the existence of one requires the exis-tence of the other, and this is still inadequate. Figure 7.6 illustrates how leaves, as they evolved to assume what formerly were root functions, become thicker to store additional moisture and support moisture conserving CAM-type photo-synthesis.

The kind of evolution that brought about a shift from dependence on the con-tents of leafy tanks to the atmosphere within family Bromeliaceae is known as *heterochrony*. This mechanism involves modification of the genetic program governing the timing of the stages (*ontogeny*) that all organisms pass through as they develop from zygotes to adults (Figure 9.1). Simply put, evolution is de-monstrably heterochronous when descendants exhibit features at sexual matu-rity that their ancestors expressed as juveniles.

The mature ramets (inflorescences not shown) depicted in Figure 7.6B,C,D,F are aligned according to how deeply heterochronic evolution has affected the species that they represent. The presumed ancestral soft-leaved, tank-producing architecture is illustrated in Figure 7.6B but not by juveniles while too small to possess a tank (Figure 7.6A). The adult stages shown demonstrate heterochrony because stepwise they bear fewer leaves and tend to be smaller than their puta-tive evolutionary antecedents. Each is more "juvenilized" than its predecessor because flowering occurs following the production of fewer leafy nodes.

Subfamily Tillandsioideae also illustrates the plant-based and environ-mental circumstances that likely favored the progression from tank-supported to atmosphere-based life. Seedlings were the pivotal players, according to this hypothesis, because plant size and form assure that early juveniles encounter growing conditions avoided by adults by being large enough to secure life-sustaining supplies of precipitation and nutrient-rich litter in leafy tanks.

Seedlings of the modern, soft-leafed tank formers, being too small to maintain external reservoirs, necessarily store moisture internally to survive arid conditions, which as adults equipped with tanks they can more readily tolerate. Note in Figure 7.6A how, as the seedling of a tank former develops, it shifts rather abruptly from producing relatively succulent foliage to flatter, more broadly expanded organs capable of impounding litter and water.

It remains to be seen whether the juveniles of the thin-leafed, tank-dependent members of Tillandsioideae incorporate all the adaptations employed by their atmospheric relatives to mitigate the effects of drought. As seedlings without impoundments, they surely encounter growing conditions more like those experienced lifelong by the latter species than by their own kind after becoming tank-bearing adults. This hypothesis will rest on firmer ground if the juveniles of the impounding types prove able to conduct photosynthesis and use water more like the atmospherics than like their parents.

The emergence of atmospheric epiphytism demonstrates how major evolutionary innovation requires genetic potential plus circumstances that favor its realization by way of natural selection. In the bromeliad example, the possession of certain features concerned with foliar structure and function allowed a lineage of soft-leafed antecedents of modern subfamily Tillandsioideae to generate descendants able to colonize more demanding landscapes. Moreover, heterochrony appears to be the mechanism that fostered the replacement of structure and physiology appropriate for humid environments with an arrangement better suited for plants that operate under drier conditions.

Much of the fine-tuning responsible for the astonishing ecological variety displayed by epiphytic Bromeliaceae has occurred within the operational limits of the atmospheric way of life, which happen to be surprisingly plastic. Lineages fundamentally equipped to perform this way are not excluded from sites that pose challenges other than or in addition to drought. Quite a few of the atmospheric bromeliads normally experience what for many of their kind would be lethal humidity (Figure 4.6). Perhaps this is why the species that inhabit cloud forests tend to bear thin foliage covered with trichomes topped by unexpectedly water-repellent shields (Figure 4.4 lower right).

Araceae

It is not necessary to visit the tropics to see an epiphytic aroid or, better yet given their popularity, one of the family's more numerous secondary hemi-epiphytes. Plenty of cultivated specimens representing predominantly arboreal genera such as *Anthurium, Monstera, Philodendron,* and *Raphidiophora* long ago became familiar fixtures in private and public facilities. Indoor lighting often fails to encourage flowering, but it is good enough for shade-tolerant plants prized mainly for their decorative foliage.

Most of the 1400 or so canopy-based species that belong to approximately 2500-strong Araceae scramble over other tropical vegetation in humid, low- to mid-elevation woodlands; the rest perch on living supports free of all contact with the ground (Figures 3.1, 7.8A,B,C,D). Diversity peaks in Central America, the northern Andes, and the wet parts of Southeast Asia. More than 150 anthuriums reside in modest-sized Panama alone.

Unlike the more structurally varied and ecologically diverse arboreal bromeliads, orchids, and ferns, the aroids that share the same habitats exhibit just two closely related body plans. Either their leaves are separated by substantial internodes, as demonstrated by the hemi-epiphytes (Figures 3.1, 7.8A,B,D,G), or the shoot is condensed to form the compact rosette-type architecture that allows the "birds-nest" anthuriums and philodendrons to collect falling litter (Figures 2.5, 7.7F, 7.8C).

The arboreal aroids root adventitiously from their nodes, and what happens next depends on the identity of the plant and its circumstances. Should a root produced by one of the bird's-nest types with its telescoped shoot contact the substrate, it elongates and becomes an anchor; otherwise it remains short and more or less oriented upright to form part of the litter-impounding apparatus (Figure 7.7F). Roots are more scattered along the less compact stems of the hemi-epiphytes, but here as well, if too distant from the host, they tend to remain short (Plate 8B; Figures 7.7D,F, 7.8A,B,D,F).

Aerial roots of Araceae often possess a velamen, and they can account for more than half of a plant's body mass (e.g., *Anthurium gracile,* Plate 8B). Those further equipped with a green cortex share with the leafy epiphytic orchids modest capacities to conduct photosynthesis (Figures 4.3, 7.7F). Never, however, does the root system of an aroid fully replace the food-making function of its foliage, as occurs among the shootless members of Orchidaceae (Figure 2.2). Aroid roots can be far longer, sometimes connecting plants perched many meters high with the ground.

Most of the arboreal anthuriums, monsteras, and philodendrons, to name just three of the numerous genera that include such species, produce foliage differentiated into petioles topped by blades supplied with pinnately (feather-like) arrayed veins. Blade color, shape, and texture also vary more than usual for monocots, and sometimes to obvious advantage (Figures 7.7, 7.8). *Anthurium wendlingeri,* along with several of its relatives, possesses linear, pendent *bifacial* foliage well constructed to intercept dim light arriving from every direction.

Domed epidermal cells impart a velvet-like sheen to both surfaces, but more importantly they boost shade tolerance by focusing scattered photons on green cells located deeper inside (Figure 7.8E).

Figure 7.7F illustrates how upright, channeled leaves accompanied by masses of stubby roots position the bird's nest anthuriums and philodendrons to intercept litter, and how the more individualized appendages of an unidentified *Monstera* grow tightly against the adjacent substrate, sometimes even around its corners (Figure 7.8D). Note that several of the leaves located too distant to contact anything substantial failed to expand. Also pictured are palmately (hand-shaped) lobed organs that characterize additional anthuriums, monsteras, and philodendrons, among others.

Quite a few of the hemi-epiphytic aroids produce foliage with characteristics that defy interpretation. Perforations with no obvious utility occur among members of several genera (e.g., *Monstera obliqua,* Figure 7.7E); more clearly adaptive is another phenomenon known as *heterophylly* (*hetero* = different, *phylly* = foliage). No family compares with Araceae for on-the-spot (phenotypic plasticity) tailoring of foliage to match sun-dappled habitats or to respond to steep vertical light gradients, as described in Chapters 3 and 5 (Figure 3.1).

The heterophyllous aroids produce leaves that progressively change shape across successive nodes of individual shoots, or the transition from juvenile to adult form occurs abruptly. For example, the immature-phase leaves of *Monstera dubia* lack well-developed petioles, their blades being held tightly against the host. Later, when the ascending shoot encounters brighter light, or more precisely, when it senses an inductive ratio of red to far-red radiation, it switches to producing broader, more deeply incised blades held well above the substrate on longer petioles (see Chapter 3).

Inflorescences arise from the axils of leaves rather than terminally, as is typical for the corm-producing, terrestrial aroids in genera such as *Amorphophallus* and *Arum*. The inflorescences consist of two parts: a stout spike or *spadix* that bears densely packed, individual small flowers and a single, large, often enveloping bract called a *spathe* (Plate 6A; Figure 7.7G). Beetles and flies attracted by foul odors and dark pigments help many of the soil-rooted aroids reproduce.

The inflorescences of many of the arboreal aroids are brightly colored, and they emit pleasant fragrances, suggesting that bees and other nectar-seeking insects are their targeted visitors (Plate 6A). Sometimes a sweet-smelling, brightly colored, or nectar-secreting spadix is sufficient, the spathe having been reduced to a green, apparently inconsequential vestige. Asynchronously maturing male and female flowers located on the same inflorescence sometimes encourage outcrossing.

The epiphytic aroids offer bright red, lavender, or white berries provisioned with modest numbers of small to medium-sized seeds well suited for dispersal

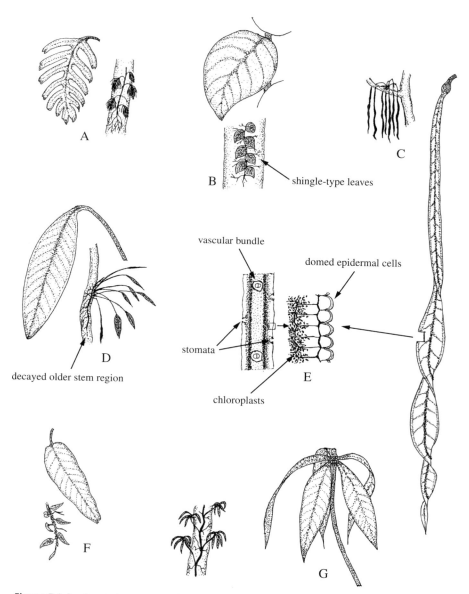

Figure 7.8 Leaf variation among epiphytic and hemi-epiphytic Araceae. **A.** *Anthurium distanti-lobum* **B.** *Raphidophora cryptantha* **C.** *Anthurium wendlingeri* **D.** *Philodendron callosum* **E.** Anatomy of a *Anthurium wendlingeri* leaf illustrating how both sides of its pendent blade are equipped to intercept scattered light in deeply shaded habitats **F.** *Anthurium trinerve* **G.** *Anthurium croatii*.

by birds (Plate 8B; Figure 7.7G). *Anthurium scandens,* like so many of its
canopy-dwelling relatives, produces pale lavender to white fruits that resemble
those of the co-occurring mistletoes, rhipsalid cacti, and some of the fleshy-fruited
bromeliads (Figure 8.1C,H,I). Often, just a slight squeeze, perhaps no more than
a foraging bird would apply, extrudes several seeds enveloped in sticky pulp.
Anthurium gracile employs red berries to launch its offspring (Plate 8B).

Amaryllidaceae and Additional Families in Order Liliales

Many of the species within Amaryllidaceae and additional families
constituting the Linnaean order Liliales feature strap-shaped foliage, rosette-
shaped shoots, and fibrous roots, all of which grant potential to adopt other
plants as mechanical supports (Table 2.8). Why this opportunity has gone so
modestly exploited is puzzling. Only 6 of the approximately 25 species of tropical Pacific *Astelia* of Asteliaceae are epiphytic, yet they possess leafy tanks that
look every bit as effective as those produced by many of the tank-forming bromeliads (Figure 10.3).

Were anyone other than an expert to encounter a tank-bearing *Astelia* in a
tropical American forest, chances are good that he or she would believe it to be
a bromeliad. Few would notice that the shoot consists of two gently spiraling
ranks of leaves rather than the single steeper or the distinctly two-ranked arrangement characteristic of the bromeliads (Figures 3.2, 5.5, 7.5). Perhaps
Astelia stands at the same threshold crossed by a more primitive Bromeliaceae
prior to generating the hundreds of litter impounders that make it one of the
most influential families in the New World tropics.

The additional liliaceous epiphytes little resemble *Astelia* or the tank bromeliads. *Hippeastrum* of Amaryllidaceae exhibits curious architecture, considering where similarly constructed plants typically grow (Figure 7.7C). Who would
anticipate a bulb-producing epiphyte? Many additional, strictly terrestrial genera in Liliales (e.g., tulips, daffodils, onions) include species equipped with the
same densely overlapping arrays of thick, scale-shaped fleshy leaves and long,
thin green appendages that often abscise to reduce the effects of drought during
dry seasons.

It's not that bulb-type architecture is totally alien to epiphytism. The shoots
of the bromeliad *Tillandsia bulbosa,* for example, qualify according to the
name, except that only one type of leaf is produced, and its base is inflated and
thin enough to house nesting ants (Figure 7.5A). A couple of drought-deciduous
pitcairnias come closer to being true bulb formers, but only *P. heterophylla*
grows with any regularity as an epiphyte (Figure 7.7B).

As foreign as a bulb-equipped plant may seem perched in the canopy of a tropical forest, this is exactly how *Hippeastrum aulicum, H. papilio,* and bat-pollinated *H. calyptratum* often occur in southeastern Brazil. Plants firmly anchored in mats of moss and humus are common sights on the trunks and thicker branches of medium to large trees in some of São Paulo state's cool, moist Atlantic forests (Figure 7.7C). Bulbs in all three cases shed much or all of their green foliage during the driest months of the year.

Most of the remaining liliaceous epiphytes belong to genera more familiar to temperate-zone botanists as terrestrials, some even as members of the so-called spring ephemeral flora characteristic of the understories of this region's deciduous forests (e.g., *Polygonatum,* Solomon's seal). Epiphytes of this third description occur where cool temperatures and abundant precipitation create favorable conditions for small herbs, whether rooted in the ground or in the crowns of trees.

8   The Epiphytic Eudicots

Although more than two-thirds of the flowering plants are *eudicots,* many fewer are epiphytic compared with the monocots (Table 2.7). Epiphytes comprise an even smaller fraction of the third and most primitive or *basal* of the three major groups of angiosperms. Except for a substantial portion of family Piperaceae, almost none of these oldest of the surviving flowering plants root above ground (Figure 7.1). The mistletoes are exclusively eudicotyledonous, and the vast majority belong either to family Loranthaceae or closely related Santalaceae.

Two of the anatomical features that differentiate most of the eudicots from most of the monocots influence some of the ways in which their epiphytes operate in aerial habitats. One of these characteristics, or more precisely its absence, makes the arboreal pteridophytes (ferns and lycophytes) decidedly more like monocots than eudicots. Only the latter possess a vascular cambium, which Chapter 1 describes as the embryonic tissue (meristem) responsible for the woodiness and attending high cost in moisture of producing the bodies of trees and shrubs. The second distinction concerns the leaf, which among the eudicots, as opposed to the monocots and the pteridophytes, has proven more amenable to modification for conducting functions distinct from and sometimes in addition to photosynthesis.

The six families profiled below include a large majority of the eudicotyledonous epiphytes, and they illustrate most of the adaptations that enable the nonparasites within this largest of the three major subsets of angiosperms to grow above ground. Additional smaller but still heavily epiphytic eudicot families, and some others with just scatterings of arboreal members, are treated in Chapter 10. Also left for later are the primary hemi-epiphytes, the carnivorous true epiphytes, most of which are eudicots, and Piperaceae, that family that best exemplifies how the most primitive of the modern angiosperms perform in aerial habitats.

Cactaceae

For most of us, the term cactus conjures up images of spiney, stout-bodied plants that populate arid, rock-strewn landscapes along with similarly drought-defying shrubs and herbs. It is an apt description for much of the family, but not the portion whose members are characterized by distinctly different ecology, form, and lifestyle. These are the species that lack the well-armed, water-storing stems that so effectively discourage thirsty animals and mitigate the impacts of prolonged dry seasons. Moreover, rather than rooting in soil, these more streamlined types spend their lives completely suspended on woody hosts, or they grow as secondary hemi-epiphytes.

What might account for the presence of a sizable contingent of arboreal species in a family dominated by slow-growing, succulent-stemmed plants that root in the ground in arid habitats? In what ways were the ancestors of Cactaceae disposed to adopt this elevated way of living? Can its modern terrestrial members shed light on this question? The occasional prickly pear (genus *Opuntia*) that anchors on bark demonstrates that hard-coated seeds enclosed in fleshy fruits and marked capacity to endure severe drought favor at least an occasional abandonment of Earth soil. Evidentially, life spent rooted to a host on a more routine basis requires more, at the very least a major departure from the compact architecture that so effectively serves the rest of the family.

Family Crassulaceae stands in stark contrast to Cactaceae, It is also dominated by succulent (thick foliage rather than stems), drought-enduring xerophytes native to warm regions, but fewer than 10 of its approximately 1500 species are epiphytes. Why such a great disparity when its membership exceeds in ecological variety that of the cactus family? In addition to the dry-growing terrestrials, Crassulaceae includes short-cycled weeds, wetland herbs, and lithophytes. Perhaps its poor showing in aerial habitats comes down to its modest capacity to disperse young. Seeds that are not particularly airworthy and the family-wide absence of fleshy fruits could make all the difference.

General Characteristics

All cacti produce shoots of two types: much-condensed axillary branches or "short shoots" called *areoles* that develop on more conventionally constructed "long shoots" known as *cladodes* or literally stem-leaves (Figure 8.1A). Areoles usually bear spines that represent leaf equivalents (*homologues*), essentially foliage modified to discourage large herbivores instead of for manufacturing food, a task performed now by the green cladodes. Members of genus *Opuntia* still produce a short-lived, tiny leaf immediately below each areole, confirming its

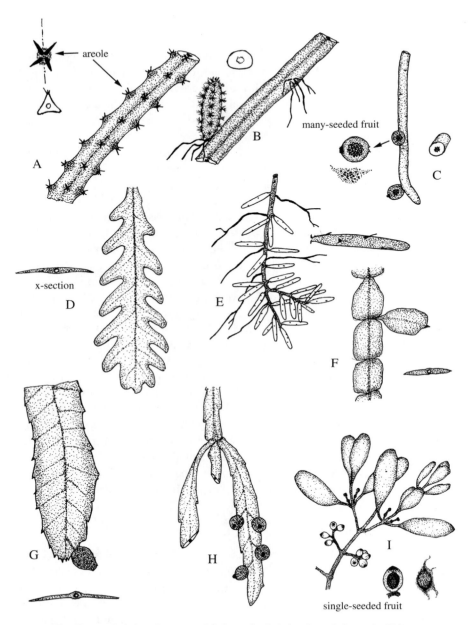

Figure 8.1. Cactus cladodes, flowers, and fruits and a fruit-bearing mistletoe. **A.** *Hylocereus* sp. with an areole magnified to provide detail **B.** *Scelenicereus inermis* **C.** *Rhipsalis horrida* **D.** *Eccremocactus imitans* **E.** *Rhipsalis mesembryanthoides* **F.** *Schlumbergera* sp. **G.** *Discocactus amazonas* **H.** Flat-stemmed *Rhipsalis micrantha* **I.** *Phorodendron flavescens* (Loranthaceae).

identity as a highly condensed, lateral branch. Species of *Pereskia,* which in many respects is the most primitive of the modern genera, demonstrate this reality even more persuasively by bearing areoles in the axils of fully developed foliage. Being shrubby and native to tropical dry forests and scrublands, they further reveal the ancestral growth habit and ecology of Cactaceae.

Adaptations for Epiphytism

Exposure to arid conditions over millions of years explains why all but the pereskioid cacti no longer produce broad-bladed foliage that by virtue of its extensive surface area expends water more freely than a thick green stem. The same history accounts for the transformation of the lateral branches into areoles and the pronounced succulence of the cladodes. All in all, the dry-growing, terrestrial membership of Cactaceae illustrates one of the most effective architectures for enduring drought that has emerged anywhere and at any time during the 450-million-year history of the land plants. The cacti further husband scarce moisture by employing CAM-type photosynthesis (see Chapter 5; Table 5.1; Figure 5.1).

The most specialized of the arboreal Cactaceae neither function like nor closely resemble their dry land relatives. Distinct body plans and cladode shapes adapt the canopy users to grow under conditions ranging from those that mark semiarid, open woodlands to the depths of dense, humid tropical forests (Figure 8.1A, B,C,D,E,F,G,H). Dozens of epiphytic cacti flourish in relatively dim light, for example, along Brazil's southeastern coast within what remains of the formerly much more extensive Atlantic rain forest. Instead of being stout, multiridged, and spiny, their cladodes are slender and round to broad and flat. Areoles usually lack spines, and while young they may secrete nectar to lure ants that discourage other insects, the group that includes most of the herbivores that prey on epiphytes.

Evolutionary History

Epiphytism has evolved at least three times in different parts of Cactaceae and in two widely separated Neotropical regions. Antecedents of tribes Hylocereeae and Rhipsalideae were most heavily involved, and no more than 30 to 40 million years ago. The few exceptions, all facultative epiphytes, occur within tribes Pachycereeae and Trichocereeae. Presumed youth for cactus-type epiphytism accords as well with the fact that both Hylocereeae and Rhipsalideae belong to Cactoideae, which is the most evolutionarily advanced of the four cactus subfamilies. The family's almost exclusive New World distribution further indicates that even its most primitive elements emerged after Africa and South America were well separated and angiosperm radiation considerably advanced.

Transitions from terrestrial to aerial life occurred in Central America–
northern South America and in what today is southeastern Brazil. Both Hylocereeae and Rhipsalideae remain most diverse within their respective ancestral
regions, but multiple migrations have produced considerable mixing. *Rhipsalis*

Figure 8.2. *Selenicereus* sp. growing as a secondary hemi-epiphyte on a street tree (*Sabal palmetto*)
in Sarasota, Florida.

baccifera holds the record for long-distance dispersal, with outlying populations in central West Africa, Madagascar, Sri Lanka, and south Florida. Its unusually fragmented range is recent, probably going back no more than a few million years following deliveries by migratory birds or more sedentary types blown off course by storms. Interestingly, predominantly epiphytic but similarly youthful and Neotropical Bromeliaeae also includes a single geographically aberrant species, although *Pitcairnia feliciana* is terrestrial and has not migrated beyond its narrowly confined range in central West Africa.

Cactus epiphytism occurs in two versions. Secondary hemi-epiphytism was the principal outcome in the north, whereas complete or holo-epiphytism remains the more prominent theme south of the Equator (Figure 8.2). No members of tribe Rhipsalideae are hemi-epiphytic, whereas a broad range of sprawling to hemi-epiphytic to fully epiphytic species occur in modern Hylocereeae. Members of more species-rich Rhipsalideae, being primarily obligate epiphytes, exhibit greater structural deviations from the arid-land, stout-bodied family norm. In all, about 10% of Cactaceae are canopy dependent in one respect or another (Table 2.7).

Stems that serve the hemi-epiphytes in genera such as *Hylocereus* and *Selenicereus* (Hylocereae) differ little in shape from those of their closest, earthbound relatives (Figures 8.1B, 8.2). Well-armed areoles continue to protect the young plant, whereas those often present on the often flatter, less prominently ridged cladodes that develop later and usually higher above ground tend to be naked. The true epiphytes, as exemplified by members of *Schlumbergera,* show less evidence of better-armed, more drought-tolerant ancestors, and their flat, thin stems more closely parallel the architecture of a typical eudicotyledonous leaf.

The two-dimensional cladodes of the Christmas cacti (*Schlumbergera*) are also more translucent than the massive organs produced by the prickly pears and barrel cacti and also the hemi-epiphytes (Figures 8.1A,B,F, 8.2). Were they thicker, the photosynthetic cells inside would not be able to harvest enough sunlight to operate in the deep shade cast by what are usually evergreen, broadleafed hosts. Many of the *Rhipsalis* species, and others in several related genera, produce pendent, trusses of thin. round cladodes (Figure 8.1C,E). Both shapes increase shoot surface to volume ratios well above what the typical desert-dwelling cactus could maintain in its more powerfully desiccating environment.

The rhipsaloid cacti illustrate a Darwinian axiom: Lose a body part through adaptive reduction, the leaf in this case, and it cannot be resurrected. It cannot be retrieved no matter how advantageous doing so might be under some new set of environmental circumstances. Instead, a remaining organ has to be reengineered to deliver the same services. The answer for the epiphytic cacti is the streamlined cladode, which especially among the flat-stemmed species resembles and operates pretty much like a robust, evergreen leaf. Like the foliage borne by structurally less reduced epiphytes in many other families, these strongly articulated, bifacial cladodes arch or hang to better capture light diminished and scattered during passage through dense overhead vegetation.

Ecology

Most of the epiphytic cacti tap pockets of suspended soil or thick layers of moisture-retaining lichens and mosses, or their typically aggressive roots penetrate rotting wood. What little is known about root structure and function is reviewed in Chapter 4. A few members of *Schlumbergera* and several species in additional genera colonize twigs where high humidity permits. At least one member of *Epiphyllum* is a regular ant-nest user. The drought-hardiest of the hemi-epiphytes root just about wherever their cladodes contact acceptable substrates. Well-established individuals can thoroughly envelop the trunks of phorophytes with networks of interwoven stems and roots, some of which reach the ground. Palms with persistent leaf bases filled with humus are especially accommodating supports (Figure 8.2).

Hot semiarid landscapes, in the case of the hemi-epiphytes, and warm, wetter woodlands for the true epiphytes host most of the arboreal cacti. Relatively few species of either description reside in cool, misty forests where the epiphytes that represent many other families such as Ericaceae and Gesneriaceae achieve their greatest diversities and abundances. Virtually nowhere does the aggregate biomass of the local epiphytic cacti rival that of co-occurring Bromeliaceae, or within a single habitat do its species ever approach the numbers contributed by Orchidaceae or the ferns.

Reproduction

Many kinds of animals disperse the arboreal cacti, and humans have domesticated several species as crops. Cultigens derived from hemi-epiphytic *Hylocereus undulatus* and a couple of its relatives produce colorful "dragon fruits" that although popular in the tropics are seldom seen in North Americans markets. Smaller berries are more typical and account for the colloquial name mistletoe cactus in the case of the white-fruited species of *Rhipsalis*. However, they contain more numerous, much smaller seeds embedded in a less sticky mucilage than the product employed by the true mistletoes to secure their offspring to bark (Figure 8.1C,I). The seeds of *Epiphyllum phyllanthus* germinate within ripe fruits (are *viviparous*), a behavior that may promote seedling success in demanding habitats (see Chapter 6).

The arboreal cacti produce many-parted, often showy flowers that present abundant sticky pollen (Plate 4A). Weak reproductive barriers among closely related species have permitted much genetic manipulation, leading in the case of the flat-stemmed epiphytes to multiple choices for flowering schedules and petal colors. The mistletoe cacti work their charm with attractive berries that range from deep pink to translucent white to yellowish (Figure 8.1C,H). The small, usually pale flat flowers that precede them contribute less appeal.

Several features grant the arboreal cacti substantial importance in woodland communities. Numerous Hylocereeae exceed just about all the other epiphytes for large, deep-throated flowers and probably the generosity of their rewards. Night bloomers are common and often bat dependent (e.g., some *Epiphyllum* spp., Plate 4A). Floral structures and daytime displays indicate generalist-type insects as the usual targets of the rhipsalid cacti and, perhaps for some species, signal spontaneous fruit set. Yields tend to be large, the berries big enough and fruiting seasons sufficiently extended to make some of these plants major resources for a variety of *frugivores* (fruit eaters). Ongoing efforts to develop crops that require little moisture and tolerate poor soils and shade, targeting hemi-epiphytes such as *Selenicereus megalanthus* and *Hylocereus polyrhiza,* suggest that Cactaceae is destined to become a more important contributor to the human diet.

Ericaceae

The most pervasive of the characteristics that favor epiphytism include CAM-type photosynthesis, adventitious rooting, and modular, inexpensive (herbaceous) construction (Table 2.8). Wind pollination, large seeds, slow development, and rigid, unitary architecture, being rare or absent among the epiphytes, almost certainly do the opposite. Every family surveyed so far accords with this hypothesis. Ericaceae fails, and by several measures. Its members are woody and mature slowly, and they lack pronounced preparation for drought. Why then do almost 700 of the family's roughly 3500 species anchor on other plants rather than in the ground (Table 2.7)?

Ericaceae is clearly at odds with several of the assumptions implicit in Table 2.8. Perhaps one or more of its entries should be deleted or qualified, or the list supplemented, or all three. Conceivably, some family-specific, less conspicuous feature cancels out the negative consequences of being woody, growing slowly, and possessing durable foliage capable of only modest rates of photosynthesis. The most intriguing of the possibilities is the novel mutualism with fungi that accounts in part for the pronounced affinity of the terrestrial ericads for substrates that most other groups of plants avoid or exploit less extensively.

No other comparably sized family of flowering plants exceeds Ericaceae for occurrence on impoverished, acidic media insofar as its soil-rooted species are concerned. This proclivity prevails from the deep tropics pole-ward to the nutrient-poor understories of boreal forests and *Sphagnum* bogs. The arboreal ericads follow suit, mostly inhabiting cool, humid tropical woodlands where substrates are similarly mossy and sodden and perhaps acidic and infertile to boot. Indeed, a sampling of the roots of ericaceous epiphytes representing several genera in a Costa Rican low montane cloud forest revealed the presence of characteristic *ericoid*-type fungal coils.

Adaptations for Epiphytism

It is reasonable to postulate that whatever allows terrestrial Ericaceae to so broadly exploit impoverished media helps their epiphytic relatives do the same thing above ground. Sprawling shoots bearing adventitious roots no doubt contribute, but the unique mutualism just mentioned could be the better part of the explanation. The challenge now is to determine whether the epiphytes engage in the same kinds of mycorrhizal relationships that assist their soil-rooted counterparts, and whether the same benefits accrue.

Chapter 5 describes plant nutrition as process that has a supply and a demand side, both of which are amenable to evolutionary adjustment to a wide range of environmental conditions. Because sluggish growth and durable leaves reduce demand, they should be adaptive in resource-poor habitats, whether aerial or terrestrial. The first trait reduces the rate at which a plant must accumulate scarce nutrients like nitrogen and phosphorus, and the second allows what is acquired to serve longer than were it invested in shorter-lived foliage (see Chapters 3 and 4).

Supply-side relief comes from any arrangement that provides a plant access to an additional source of nutrients even if its utilization requires outside assistance. Abundant nutrients are available to any epiphyte that can extract what it needs from the massive quantities of dead organic material that accumulates in aerial habitats, especially the humid kinds (Figures 2.4, 3.2). The tank-bearing bromeliads do this with the help of a host of invertebrates and microbes (Figure 7.5E). Perhaps the epiphytic ericads do the same with roots that harbor mutualistic fungi. The ericoid and *arbutoid* mycorrhizae maintained by terrestrial members of this family extract nitrogen and phosphorus directly from decomposing material, after which some ends up supporting the hosting plant.

Combine the material economy gained from slow growth and long-lived photosynthetic organs with the advantage provided by fungus-enhanced access to key nutrients, and the result could be a family well disposed for epiphytism, although only under narrowly proscribed circumstances. Potential for success above ground might be confined to sites where cool temperatures and low pH retard decomposition and, accordingly, delay nutrient release from dead organic matter. Enough moisture would also be available at such locations to permit sufficient photosynthesis to support woodiness and still meet the energy needs of symbiotic fungi that improve their partners' mineral nutrition.

The ecophysiology of the ericaceous epiphytes is otherwise not particularly noteworthy. None impound litter or house plant-feeding ants in modified stems or foliage, nor has a single species been reported to be a regular user of ant carton. A few produce tubers, but dense construction suggest nutrient rather than moisture storage. No succulent foliage or stems are present, nor has CAM photosynthesis been reported. Anchorages usually consist of large limbs and trunks covered with thick layers of debris and the mosses and lichens responsible for its production.

Epiphytism and Speciation

Rather than clustering in the manner described earlier for the epiphytes of several other good-sized families, the arboreal ericads tend to scatter among genera that also contain substantial numbers of terrestrials. About 35 include at least one arboreal member, and fewer than 10 are predominantly epiphytic if composed of 25 or more species. Additional sizable genera with strong temperate and terrestrial affinities, for example the wintergreens (*Galtheria*) and the blueberries (*Vaccinium*), contain only an occasional epiphyte. Among the exceptions are several large, exclusively tropical genera whose epiphytes far outnumber their ground dwellers (e.g., *Agapetes, Cavendishia*).

Reproductive Biology

Many of the epiphytic ericads, and particularly the rhododendrons native to New Guinea's central highlands and northern India and several neighboring Himalayan countries, produce exceptionally large, showy flowers. Numerous tropical American Ericaceae are similarly ornamental, particularly members of *Cavendischia* and *Macleania* (Plate 4B). Less colorful, small-flowered species belong to *Psammaisia, Sphyrospermum,* and *Vaccinium,* among others. The ericaceous epiphytes rely heavily on birds to exchange pollen. Others are spontaneously autogamous, judging from what happens in greenhouses (e.g., some *Sphyrospernum*). Like their terrestrial relatives, epiphytic Ericaceae produce capsules that contain dry, appendaged seeds (e.g., *Rhododendron*) and harder, smoother-coated types able to pass undamaged through the guts of animals that consume fleshy fruits (e.g., *Sphyrospernum*, Plate 8C).

Horticulture

Ericaceae ranks high among the culturally underexploited, epiphyte-rich eudicot families. Stunningly attractive, waxy, long-lived tubular red, orange, and white flowers displayed on often pendent shoots make many of the lesser-known species excellent prospects for hanging baskets and indoor planters (Plate 4B). My experience suggests that quite a few require no more than ordinary care. Epiphytic Ericaceae also warrant more attention because so many inhabit endangered ecosystems. Cloud forests are especially threatened by climate change, rising concentrations of atmospheric CO_2, and increasing supplies of plant-available nitrogen released from burning fossil fuels (see Chapter 11).

Gesneriaceae

Gesneriaceae is better known to the public for its African violets than its epiphytes, which is odd, considering that many of the latter feature showier flowers and more ornamental foliage (Plate 7A). Members of predominantly arboreal genera such as *Aeschynanthus, Columnea, Drymonia,* and *Tricantha* also far exceed the saintpaulias as candidates for hanging baskets and other alternatives to standard pot culture. Gesneriaceae warrants recognition by botanists for two additional reasons: its highly evolved, often showy tubular flowers, and its status as one of the most epiphyte rich of the eudicotyledonous families. Approximately one-fifth of its roughly 2500 species grow above ground, and of these around four-fifths are tropical American (Table 2.7).

Beyond some drymonias and a few others that also become shrubby, the arboreal gesneriads are small to medium in stature, herbaceous, and perennial (Figure 8.3A,B,D). The terrestrials are considerably more versatile, ranging from small trees to herbs, including drought-deciduous types with and without tubers (e.g., *Gloxinia*). Neither of these latter two conditions is as well developed among the epiphytes, the closest approach to seasonal deciduousness going to species such as *Columnea flaccida* and *Drymonia citrifolia* and for tubers to the few members of *Siningia,* that sometimes root above ground. *Pentadenia crassicaulis* combines partial deciduousness with thick water-storing stems. The most common condition among the epiphytes is a sprawling body comprising multiple evergreen shoots that root freely at the nodes (Figure 8.3B). Similar architecture fosters hemi-epiphytism in genus *Agamyla,* among others.

Leaf color, texture, and shape vary greatly among the epiphytic gesneriads. Weak-stemmed shoots that bear foliage of unequal size (anisophylly) are fairly common, probably because the two-dimensional architecture that results enhances the capture of overhead light by shoots that tend to arch from or creep along branches (Figure 8.3A,D). Pronounced pubescence is another family hallmark, and especially among members of genera such as *Tricantha*. Little is known about the functions performed by the gland-tipped types, but long hairs containing red to purple pigments probably help attract pollinators. Many of the brightest types co-occur with pale white to yellow relatively inconspicuous flowers.

C_3-type photosynthesis predominates within Gesneriaceae, which accords with its overall *mesophytic* as opposed to xerophytic character. However, at least one species of *Codonanthe* fixes CO_2 using a mechanism that combines characteristics associated with more than one of the photosynthetic syndromes described in Chapter 5 (Figure 5.1; Table 5.1). Leaves that possess the same tripartite internal anatomy also characterize certain members of *Aeschynanthus* and *Codonanthopsis* and additional epiphytes in a couple more families (Figure 4.1F,G). Chapter 4 and Figure 4.1G describe and illustrate the capacity of the *balloon leaves* of certain gesneriads to store exceptional amounts of moisture destined for eventual export to younger foliage. Mostly terrestrial, Old World *Boea* reputedly includes some of the few truly desiccation-tolerant flowering plants.

Adaptive Variety

The epiphytes of Gesneriaceae are less adaptively diverse than those of Bromeliaceae, the ferns, or Orchidaceae, and a rooting medium that provides abundant moisture much of the year is usually required. Several to numerous members each of *Aeschynanthus, Codonanthe,* and *Columnea* regularly anchor in ant cartons, but none here or elsewhere in the family feature shoots more than crudely configured to impound litter. Ant housing is also absent, and at this point no case can be made for mycorrhizal fungi being as important for epiphytism as proposed for Ericaceae. Ants occasionally nest in the tubers of certain *Siningia* species, but probably only after injury or disease has created cavities. In the final analysis, Gesneriaceae is more noteworthy for its aesthetic appeal than for insights on the ways in which higher plants exploit aerial habitats.

Evolutionary History

Epiphytism has evolved multiple times in Gesneriaceae, in both predominantly New World and Old World subfamilies Gesnerioideae and Cyrtandroideae, respectively. Large numbers of closely related epiphytes inhabit both regions (e.g., 100 of 110 species of tropical American *Drymonia,* and all 80 species of Paleotropical *Aeschynanthus*), suggesting once again some sort of linkage between epiphytism and prolific speciation. About 30 of the 120 or so genera that compose the family contain at least one epiphyte, but more often, canopy-based species either dominate a genus, or its entire membership is terrestrial.

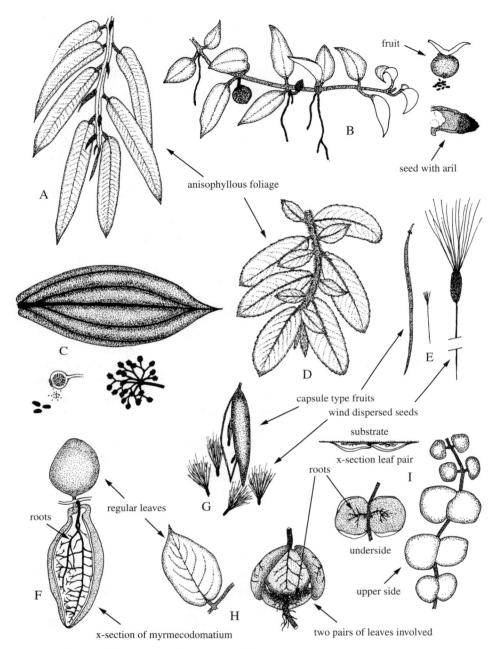

fruit

seed with aril

anisophyllous foliage

A

B

C

D

E

capsule type fruits

wind dispersed seeds

substrate

x-section leaf pair

roots

I

roots

regular leaves

G

F

underside

upper side

x-section of myrmecodomatium

H

two pairs of leaves involved

Figure 8.3. Eudicot-type epiphytes. **A.** *Drymonia decora* (Gesnericaeae) illustrating anisophyllous foliage **B.** *Codonanthe crassifolia* (Gesneriaceae) a non-isophyllous, ant-dispersed species with berry fruits and arilate seed **C.** *Medinilla* sp. (Melastomataceae) showing leaf venation characteristic of much of its family, fleshy fruits, and seeds **D.** *Columnea hirsutissima* (Gesneriaceae) showing anisophyllous foliage and dense pubescence **E.** Capsule-type fruit and seeds with hairy appendages of *Aeschyanthus* sp. (Gesneriaceae) **F.** Ordinary, strictly photosynthetic foliage of *Dischidia*

Reproductive Biology

The epiphytic gesneriads employ numerous kinds of invertebrates and vertebrates as pollinators. Flowers that exhibit the ornithophilous syndrome described in Table 6.1 indicate greater reliance on birds than most of the other angiosperm families (Plate 7A). Simultaneous openings of dozens of flowers along the pendent shoots of several columneas make especially attractive displays and easy foraging for hover fliers. Blossoms that open one to a few at a time over many days or weeks are a more common pattern. Sunbirds of family Nectariniidae substitute for hummingbirds in tropical Africa through South Asia into northern Australia. Honeyeaters and flowerpeckers provide the same service farther south and east.

Insect-pollinated *Codonanthe digna* flowers almost continuously, as do some other members of this genus of aerial scramblers. Those that associate with arboreal ants appear to be self-compatible, fruiting abundantly without assistance. Flared white petals with finely incised margins and sweet scents indicate moth reliance for some of the epiphytic gesneriads (e.g., *Paradrymonia ciliata*). Bees, flies, and possibly bats set fruit for still others. Some of the Neotropical epiphytes are serviced by the same euglossine bees responsible for much speciation in several orchid genera (see Chapter 7). Only males seeking fragrances may visit, whereas species that offer edible rewards are apt to attract both genders.

Gesneriaceae approaches Bromeliaceae for employing attractively pigmented foliage and floral bracts to signal pollinators, but unlike most members of the second family, its flowers tend to be shower. A fair number of the tropical American gesneriads bear leaves marked with red to orange patches, purportedly to keep birds alert during off-seasons that rewards lie ahead (Plate 7A). Particularly noteworthy are what look like paired eyespots, each of which consists of a pigment-free patch highlighted by a ring of red tissue (e.g., *Columnea consenguinea, C. florida,* and *C. kalbeyeriana*). Similar displays on the bodies of adult and larval moths and butterflies discourage predators.

The epiphytes of subfamily Cyrtandroideae disperse minute seeds made even more buoyant by tufts of hairs or *comas* attached at each end (Figure 8.3E). Members of subfamily Gesnerioideae that occupy similar niches in tropical America package their offspring in berries. *Codonanthe uleana* produces seeds that emit volatile attractants for ants (see Chapter 6), and it and additional members of the same genus further equip their seeds with edible appendages (Figure 8.3B). Dispersal probably requires two agents operating in succession, each

---

rafflesiana (Apocynaceae) and one of its pocket-shaped, ant-accommodating types cut open to reveal roots intruding from adjacent nodes **G.** Capsule-type fruit, seeds with hairy appendages **H.** Ordinary and myrmecodomatium-forming pairs of leaves of *Hoya darwinii* (Apocynaceae) **I.** Combination ant-housing and photosynthetic foliage of *Dischidia* sp. (Apocynaceae).

responding to a different lure, the first step being executed by birds seeking fleshy-walled fruits and the second by ants. The first leg puts distance between parent and offspring; the second provides the precision needed to target the only acceptable substrate: ant carton.

Rubiaceae

Rubiaceae ranks among the largest of the woody, predominantly tropical families with more than 13,000 members and a strong bias for moist, lowland habitats. Its approximately 450 epiphytes, about one-third of which are relatively small and soft bodied, belong to fewer than a dozen primarily Asian and Australasian genera (Table 2.7). *Chassalia petitiana* is the only species native to Africa, whereas others that represent *Didymochlamys, Hillia,* and *Notopleura,* to name just three New World genera, range through tropical America. Epiphytism has evolved repeatedly in pantropical tribe Psychotrieae and additional times elsewhere in the family.

The most notable of the rubiaceous epiphytes belong to *Hydnophytum* (about 80 members) and closely related *Myrmecodia* (about 45 members), plus a handful of similarly tuberous species assigned to three satellite genera. No other plants, arboreal or otherwise, offer ants higher quality nest sites (Figure 8.4A, B,C,E). The most elaborately constructed of the rubiaceous ant houses consist of massively swollen basal stems (actually the seedling stem or *hypocotyl*) riddled with interconnected galleries accessible through developed rather than excavated ports. Chapter 6 describes how ants choose the rough-surfaced cavities to dump refuse while reserving those with smoother walls for brood. Experiments conducted to track the movements of absorbed nutrients are discussed in Chapter 5.

Ants favor members of *Myrmecodia* over those of *Hydnophytum* at many locations. Occupancy can be low enough among some of the latter species to suggest an alternative, more primitive function with feeding by ants coming later. Figure 8.4B,C illustrates how some of the orifices located on the tops of the tubers produced by several hydnophytums seem almost certain to intercept significant amounts of precipitation. Perhaps some of what botanists consider rubiaceous myrmecodomatia function primarily to absorb water rather than animal-delivered mineral nutrients.

Several freshly collected specimens of an unidentified *Myrmecodia* dissected by this author in north central Papua New Guinea were occupied by ants assigned to genus *Iridomyrmex*. The same tubers harbored a variety of additional arthropods, and their wet walls veritably teemed with impressively large nematode worms. It was not possible to determine whether this fluid was precipitation

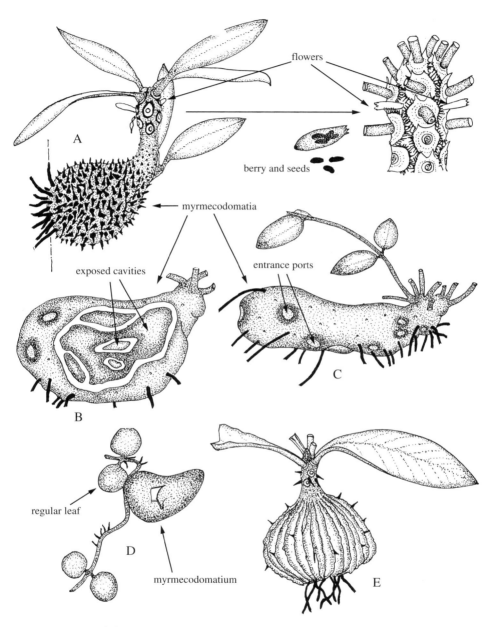

Figure 8.4. Ant-fed Apocynaceae and Rubiaceae. **A.** *Myrmecodia beccari* (Rubiaceae) with flowers, fruits, and seeds **B.** and **C.** *Hydnophytum moseleyanum* (Rubiaceae) with partially cut-away myrmecodomium to reveal chambers **D.** *Dischidia simplex* showing one of its pocket-shaped, foliar myrmecodomatia (Apocynaceae) **E.** *Myrmecodia tuberosa*.

or a plant secretion, but most likely it was the former. Tuber shape, size, and surface texture differ among species. Perhaps the spines illustrated in Figure 8.4A,E deter large-bodied ant predators.

Some of the rubiaceous epiphytes attract pollinators with showy flowers (e.g., tropical American *Hillia*), but not the tuber bearers. *Hydnophytum* and *Myrmecodia* bear inconspicuous small white blossoms in the axils of broad leaves. Depending on the species, attachment occurs flush on the stem surface or within bristly depressions (Figure 8.4A). Specimens maintained in closed quarters faithfully set fruit, sometimes more than once a year. Each small, translucent, white to pale orange berry contains several seeds embedded in a viscous pulp. Neotropical *Didymochlamys* and *Hillia* ripen capsules that release papery seeds equipped with silky comas at one end.

Melastomataceae

Melastomataceae is another of the families that contain a large portion of the eudicotyledonous epiphytes—some 650 species out of a total membership of about 4500. The arboreal melastomes, much like their counterparts in Ericaceae, root mostly in suspended, humus-based soils that provide sufficient moisture to support woody habits. However, body plans vary more here, many of the species being adventitiously rooted scramblers or climbers. Most also bear evergreen foliage that displays the prominently arced, three to five veins characteristic of much of the rest of the family (Figure 8.3C).

More than 30 of the roughly 200 melastome genera contain at least one epiphyte, but many fewer account for the vast majority of the species (e.g., *Blakea* (98/100), *Medinilla* (300/400), and *Topobea* (59/60). Such extensive clustering of close relatives accords with the idea that life above ground is exceptionally favorable for speciation, as pointed out in the treatments of Bromeliaceae, Gesneriaceae, and Orchidaceae. Melastome-type epiphytism has evolved independently in New and Old World habitats, within tribe Blakeeae in the former region and, in the latter, separately among the ancestors of *Medinilla* and *Pachycentra*.

Nothing obvious about the biology of Melastomataceae other than the tendency of its membership to grow as adventitiously rooted vines indicates why it rivals Ericaceae as one of the most successful of the woody families in aerial habitats. No special mycorrhizae have been reported, nor does the kind of primary hemi-epiphytism that enhances the fortunes of genus *Ficus* of family Moraceae prevail here. Foliage, stems, and roots contain substantial amounts of water storage tissue, sometimes enough in leaves to suggest reliance on CAM-type photosynthesis, but nothing has been confirmed. Hemi-epiphytic *Topobaea praecox* is seasonally deciduous.

While a fair number of terrestrial Melastomataceae house pugnacious ants in foliar domatia, none of the epiphytes do. Arboreal *Pachycentria glauca* accommodates in its tuberous stems what could be plant-feeding ants, but the quality of the cavities provided falls well short of the standard set by tuber-bearing Rubiaceae. This same melastome frequently roots into, or grows out of *Hydnophytum* tubers, most likely as a consequence of the foraging activities of seed-dispersing ants.

Many of the epiphytic melastomes produce showy flowers and colorful berries that can be accompanied by similarly attractive bracts. *Medinilla* is especially prized for its floral displays. *Medinilla* Gregori-Hambali produces up to hundreds of pink to magenta flowers followed by fleshy fruits in a crowded *cauliflorous* arrangement, meaning densely clustered on old stems rather than on thinner, younger growth (Plate 5B). *Medinilla alata* operates more in keeping with its arboreal habit by displaying flowers and fruits on elongate, pendent inflorescences. Small whitish berries supported by bright red pedicles indicate dispersal by birds (Plate 6B). Members of some of the other genera bear capsules that release dry seeds adapted for wind carriage.

Apocynaceae

Apocynaceae is the taxonomic home of about 140 epiphytes, most of which were formerly assigned to the now abandoned milkweed family Asclepiadaceae. DNA evidence makes this merger imperative and the surviving group even more adaptively diverse. Apocynaceae, in addition to its now greatly augmented collection of epiphytes, includes species that grow as old-field herbaceous perennials (e.g., *Apocynum, Asclepias*), desert-dwelling stem succulents (e.g., *Stapelia*), and in more hospitable locations, woody vines and shrubs. Unlike most of the other families covered in this survey, Apocynaceae, along with Rubiaceae, is better represented in the canopies of tropical Old World than American forests.

Most of the apocynaceous epiphytes belong to closely allied *Dischidia* and *Hoya*. Vine-type habits predominate, with members of the first genus exhibiting the stronger affinity for aerial substrates (60 of 90 species versus 60 of 200 species). Anchorage is accomplished with twining shoots liberally equipped with roots. More of the dischidias are adapted to house ants, and the foliage that promotes these relationships comes in three versions, the evolution of one of which required the superior malleability described earlier for the eudicot-type version of the angiospermous leaf (Figures 8.3F, 8.4D).

The pocket-shape type of leaves that house ant colonies, and sometimes precipitation in the case of *Dischidia rafflesiana,* are interspersed among the flat, strictly photosynthetic kind (Figure 8.3F). Several other ant-accommodating species bear only one kind of leaf: double-duty, concave *shingle*-like appendages, so labeled to describe how the margins of the blade tightly embrace the substrate (e.g., *D. cleistantha,* Figure 8.3I). The third version of the apocynaceous myrmecodomatium occurs in *Hoya darwinii.* Here, adjacent pairs of thickened concave leaves separated by short internodes clasp one another to form four-sided spherical organs (Figure 8.3H). Their flat, exclusively food-making counterparts are lance shaped.

Dischidia rafflesiana also exploits what ants bring home with adventitious roots that enter its myrmecodomatia from adjacent nodes (Figure 8.3F). Presumably, this arrangement and that exhibited by *Dischidia darwinii* yield enough nitrogen and phosphorus (or moisture) to justify in economic terms reassigning for this purpose resources that would yield greater energy returns if invested in strictly photosynthetic foliage. Individuals vary in the ratios of ant-accommodating to conventional leaves produced, perhaps reflecting which resource—carbohydrate or some key mineral nutrient like nitrogen—is in shortest supply (see Chapter 4). *Dischidia darwinii* compared with *Dischidia rafflesiana* grown in the same enclosure at the Marie Selby Botanical Gardens in Sarasota, Florida produces comparatively fewer myrmecodomatia.

A number of dischidias and hoyas root in ant carton the same way the ant-garden epiphytes of tropical America do. Cafeteria-style tests demonstrated clear ant preferences for the seeds of one *Dischidia* and two species of *Aeschynanthus* (Gesneriaceae) that routinely associate with ants compared with those of several others that do not. No mention was made of food rewards or the presence of chemical attractants. A subsequent survey conducted in several Southeast Asian countries confirmed that ants and epiphytes engage in similar relationships in the New and Old World tropics (see Chapter 6). A total of 18 species of ants and 51 kinds of plants were involved, and some of the pairings were consistent enough to indicate preferences by certain dispersers for the seeds of specific epiphytes.

Members of *Dischidia* and *Hoya,* as with the orchids, package their pollen in detachable organs called pollinia. Which kinds of animals make delivery presumably varies according to flower color, odor, and size (Plate 5A). Fragrances range from sweet to rank, and the pigments from bright red through pink and white to deep purple. It is unlikely that the brilliant red and scentless, but scattered, smallish flowers of *Dischidia pectinoides* and several of its close relatives produce enough nectar to satisfy metabolically demanding fliers like birds. Occasional fruiting within enclosures suggests self-compatibility, if not spontaneous autogamy. Seeds released from elongate podlike capsules bear the same tufts of coma hairs that promote wind dispersal across much of the rest of the family (Figure 8.3G).

Solanaceae

The nightshade family Solanaceae is best known for its contributions to the culinary arts that include tomatoes, chilies, the Irish potato, and eggplant. Its more numerous, mostly tropical woody species include about 60 shrubby epiphytes and hemi-epiphytes assigned to about a dozen genera, all of which are predominantly terrestrial if larger than about 10 species (Table 2.7). Fewer than two dozen of the approximately 1700 solanums are epiphytic. Interestingly, *Solanum dulcamera,* a semiwoody vine native to much of temperate North America, is one of the few perennials that occurs as an accidental epiphyte in northern Ohio.

Being at least semiwoody restricts the solanecous epiphytes to relatively moist, brightly illuminated habitats. Several species count among the modest number of eudicot epiphytes that shed their foliage seasonally (e.g., some members of genus *Merinthopodium*). Nothing else that might counter aridity in another way, such as leaf or stem succulence or pronounced hairiness, is evident. Beyond pendent inflorescences and sometimes green hold-fast roots, the solaneous epiphytes exhibit little evidence of specialization for life perched on a phorophyte. Some of the markeas and the members of several related genera produce solid woody tubers of undetermined function.

Flowers can be highly ornamental, and many are bird dependent (e.g., *Juanulloa mexicana*). Several Central American members of genus *Merinthopodium* produce nocturnal, bat-pollinated, deep purple to greenish flowers on exceptionally long, pendent inflorescences (Plate 4C). Clusters of buds repeatedly flush at their tips over several years, much as occurs in *Dischidia* and *Hoya*. Epiphytic *Dyssochroma viriflorum* of the Atlantic forest of southeastern Brazil engages two kinds of bats, one for pollination and the other to disperse its hard-coated seeds. Although fleshy and dry fruits occur within the family, the epiphytes employ only the former.

9 The Pteridophytic Epiphytes

All the epiphytes surveyed so far produce seeds, which makes them "higher" vascular plants, or what botanists call *spermatophytes*. Now it is time to consider the roughly 12,000 kinds of *pteridophytes*. Because these species reproduce more like the aquatic antecedents of the entire vascular plant complex, they represent the more primitive or "lower" of its two "evolutionary grades." The seed bearers are further differentiated into *gymnosperms* and the geologically younger *angiosperms* (flowering plants). The few thousand surviving gymnosperms in turn are divided among four subcategories: the conifers, the cycads, the relatively obscure "gnetaleans," and *Ginkgo biloba,* the sole survivor of what once was a sizable collection of species. The next chapter deals with the epiphytic gymnosperms.

A few additional comments about how the seed plants operate will put the following discussion of the epiphytic pteridophytes in broader context. The opposing terms angiosperm (*angio* = enclosed, *sperm* = seed) and gymnosperm (*gymno* = naked) describe an aspect of spermatophyte-type sexual reproduction that occurs in two versions (Figure 9.1). The seeds of the flowering plants develop inside a characteristic sex organ called a *carpel* or in an organ called a *pistil,* which consists simply of two or more carpels fused together. The seeds of the gymnosperms are borne on rather than inside equally unique appendages that differentiate the four subgroups. For example, pine tree seeds occur on the upper sides of the scales of woody cones, whereas they dangle cherry-like on short stems in the case of *Ginkgo biloba* (Figure 9.1).

Rather than seeds, the pteridophytes shed tiny spores that germinate following dispersal from minute saclike organs called *sporangia* (singular, *sporangium,* Figures 9.1, 9.2). The free-living, nonvascularized plantlets that result are called *gametophytes.* This is the life stage that produces eggs and sperm (*gametes*), which fuse to form *zygotes* that subsequently develop into the more familiar, much larger leaf- and root-bearing *sporophyte.* The sporophyte, as implied by its name, is the life stage that sheds spores to complete the higher plant's alternating, two-phased life cycle.

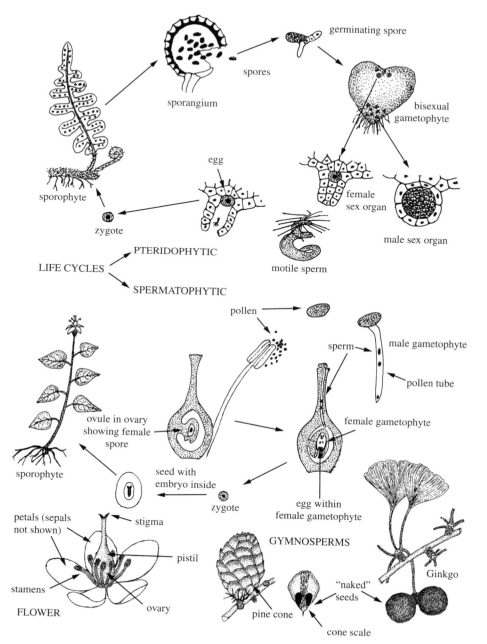

LIFE CYCLES → PTERIDOPHYTIC

→ SPERMATOPHYTIC

Figure 9.1. The life cycle of a typical angiosperm (a spermatophyte) and a fern (a homosporous pteridophyte). Also illustrated are a generalized-type flower and the seed-bearing organs of *Pinus* sp. and *Ginkgo biloba*.

Figure 9.2 illustrates how the sporangia of a large majority of the epiphytic ferns cluster in masses called *sori* (singular, *sorus*) on the undersides or margins of leaves (*fronds*). Precisely where they occur and in which of the many prevailing configurations indicate to which genus, family, and order a species belongs (Figure 9.3D,E,F,G,H). Most of the nonfern pteridophytes bear their sporangia in cones called strobili (singular, strobilus), as exemplified by the lycophytes (Figure 9.10C). Those of the first land plants were borne individually on the tips of naked, green stems (Figure 1.6).

Whereas the sporophytes of the modern pteridophytes exceed those of the earliest land dwellers for architectural complexity and drought performance,

Figure 9.2. Sporangia formed up into round sori on the underside of a frond of *Microsorium viellardi.*

membership in the lower of the two major vascular plant grades means that they still reproduce much as *Aglaophyton* did some 400 million years ago (Figure 1.6). Liquid water continues to be indispensable for the algae-like swimming sperm upon which even the most advanced of the living pteridophytes still depend (Figure 9.1). Moreover, the delicate, self-sufficient gametophytes responsible for producing them remain vulnerable to desiccation much as before.

Two additional characteristics distinguish spermatophytic from pteridophytic reproduction: the gametophytes of the seed plants are single gendered rather than bisexual, and only the male (initially in the form of a pollen grain) is dispersed into the environment. The female spore and the egg-producing gametophyte that it yields are retained by the parent sporophyte inside a minute organ called an *ovule* (Figure 9.1). Ovules become seeds when the eggs produced by their enclosed female gametophytes are fertilized. Sperm come from male gametophytes that represent the products of germinated pollen grains. Delivering pollen close enough to allow sperm to fertilize eggs is what pollination is all about.

Although the basics of the two-staged life cycle of the vascular plants have not changed in 400 million years, the seed producers, particularly those that bear flowers, have vastly improved the economy and precision of its sexual component, particularly the ways in which sperm target eggs. Most of the angiosperms no longer rely on wind to deposit pollen grains near ovules, as they have co-opted bats, birds, insects, and even the occasional nonflying mammal for this purpose. Pollen is an expensive commodity, and adopting delivery vehicles that plants can manipulate to minimize this cost is advantageous.

A flower is pollinated at the instant one or more pollen grains are deposited on the stigma located at the summit of its carpel(s) or pistil. Each grain, or more precisely each young male gametophyte, proceeds to grow a *pollen tube* that penetrates down the neck or style to deliver a pair of sperm to a female gametophyte located inside one of the ovules waiting in the ovary (Figure 9.1). One sperm fertilizes the egg to initiate a new sporophyte, and the other fuses with a second cell to produce a uniquely angiosperm-type tissue (the *endosperm*) whose purpose is the nourishment of that same young sporophyte. The act of pollination and the evolution of the pollen tube have made self-propelled sperm obsolete. Indeed, only those of the most primitive of the surviving gymnosperms such as *Ginkgo biloba* retain flagella.

The flowering plants achieve additional reproductive precision by packaging their seeds in fruits that foster dispersal by a variety of living and inanimate carriers. Reproduction is further improved by launching offspring packaged inside an organ (the seed) that usually contains enough nutrients to support the new sporophyte (seedling) until it becomes self-sustaining. Such refined pollen delivery systems and seed dispersal modes are far superior to the pteridophytic practice of dispersing tiny spores into a hostile world, destined to produce vulnerable gametophytes that launch even more desiccation-prone sperm that must locate eggs much as a predator seeks its prey.

Summarizing briefly, the pteridophytes reproduce sexually through a primitive "free-sporing" process followed by an even more archaic mode of gamete transfer that harks back to life in ancient aquatic habitats. Simply put, plants that still operate according to this long superseded style of reproduction literally cast both sexes to the wind in the form of airborne spores. To be seed bearing is to reproduce in a more economical, offspring-nurturing, and sexually precise manner. For these more advanced versions of the land plants, only the male spore must fend for itself: female spores and the egg-producing gametophytes they produce enjoy more extended and lavish parental support, as does the young sporophyte.

Such expanded parental care and elevated capacity for mate selection raises an interesting question. Despite conducting sex in what by far is the more sophisticated of the two modes practiced by the two evolutionary grades of vascular plants, why are proportionally so many fewer of the seed producers than free-sporing types epiphytic? For whatever reason, the pteridophytes have proven relatively more effective at exploiting this lifestyle than their lesser evolutionary status might lead us to believe.

The Major Groups of Pteridophytes

The modern pteridophytes belong to two subgroups, the larger and more diverse of which contains more than three-quarters of the species (Tables 2.7, 9.1). Oldest are the lycophytes or "clubmosses" because they branched off the stem vascular plant line before it gave rise to the horsetails and the ferns broadly defined, and ultimately, to the spermatophytes. Epiphytism is well developed among the tropical lycophytes, and about one-third of the ferns grow this way (Table 2.7). All of the 50 or so surviving horsetails root in the ground.

Epiphytism is probably common within the fern and lycophyte complexes for many of the same reasons that the monocot-type angiosperms engage disproportionally in the same lifestyle (see Chapters 7 and 8). Both groups consist primarily of perennial herbs with shoots and roots that grow more opportunistically (adventitiously) than those of the typical eudicot-type flowering plants, and more yet than the surviving gymnosperms.

Spores, being even smaller than the microspermous seeds produced by the orchids, further favor pteridophyte-type plants in aerial habitats (Figure 7.3). On the other hand, needing liquid moisture to reproduce sexually could be problematic. Apparently it is not, or as we will see, at least it does not present an

Table 9.1. Distribution of epiphytes within the fern complex

Subgroup within the complex	Number of epiphytic species
The psilophytes (*Psilotum* and *Tmesipteris*)	8
Ophioglossum (order Ophioglossales)	8
The lower leptosporangiates (including the filmy ferns)	500
The higher leptosporangiates (the modern ferns)	2500

Note: See Figure 9.8.

insurmountable problem. Because about 80% of the surviving pteridophytes are ferns, and by far the ferns exceed the lycophytes in adaptive variety and biological importance, it makes sense to treat them first.

The Ferns

All too often the ferns are dismissed as a relatively inconsequential collection of rather primitive plants most of which bear feather-shaped leaves and grow in moist, shaded locations. In fact, members of this group meet the challenges posed by demanding and more permissive environments alike and no less so above than on the forest floor. While the ferns make up only about 3% of the higher plant species overall, they account for approximately 10% of the epiphytes.

The absence of woodiness has not impeded fern diversification any more than it has the monocot-type angiosperms. Sizes and proportions range from palm treelike to miniscule, the greatest dimensions of the smallest of the aquatic species measuring in millimeters. Members of the water fern genus *Azolla,* the most diminutive of all, have become reduced to floating, rootless green *thalli* that resemble certain nonvascular plants more than their dry land relatives. In essence, the fern sporophyte has proven itself exceptionally plastic in its historical response to ecological opportunity, adjusting its form and function to match all sorts of growing conditions.

Many of the terrestrial ferns possess elongated rhizomes bearing fronds separated by lengthy internodes (Figures 9.3B, 9.4A,B,C,E,F,G,H). For others the same organs are inserted in dense rosette arrays on shorter, more upright axes. The epiphytes share both arrangements and virtually every condition between. The resulting body plans range from those well suited to creep along twigs and small branches to others better disposed for static postures on stouter anchorages, as illustrated by the compact bird's nest aspleniums and platyceriums (Figure 9.5). Shoots meters long support secondary hemi-epiphytism in numerous genera.

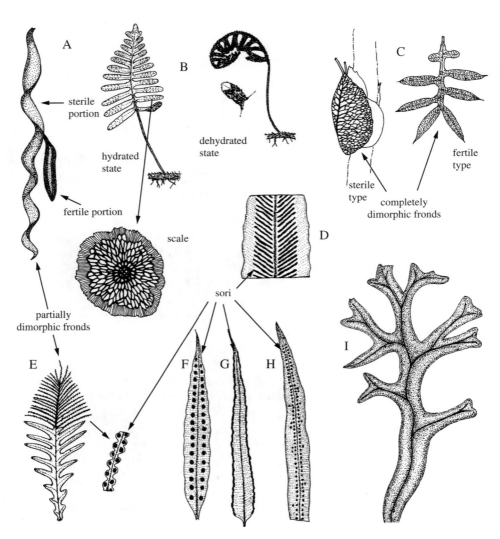

Figure 9.3. Fern fronds. **A.** Dimorphic frond of *Ophioglossum pendulum* **B.** Poikilohydrous (desiccation-tolerant) *Pleopeltis polypodioides* in wet and dehydrated conditions with one of its foliar trichomes magnified **C.** *Drynaria bonii,* a debris-impounding species that produces two kinds of fronds, one type that functions primarily to collect litter and a second type that bears sori and conducts photosynthesis. Note the reticulate venation illustrated by the former **D.** *Asplenium* sp. showing linear sori **E.** *Aglamorpha meyeniana* **F.** *Olendra pistallaris* **G.** *Scyphularia simplicifolia* **H.** *Polypodium fraxiniifolium* **I.** *Pyrrosia longifolia* showing dichotomous leaf venation.

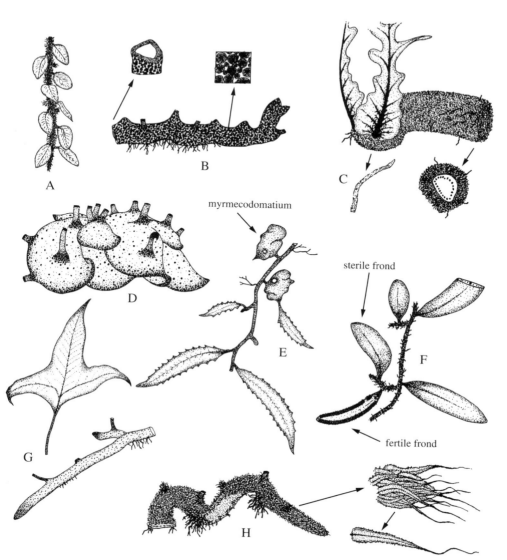

Figure 9.4. Fern fronds and rhizomes. **A.** *Microgramma* sp., a small creeping species that often occurs as a twig epiphyte **B.** *Lecanopteris sinuosa* with its robust, ant nest-accommodating rhizome densely covered by scale-shaped trichomes **C.** *Microsorum linguliforme* showing its extensive coat of woolly trichomes **D.** *Lecanopteris celebica* demonstrating a succulent rhizome and scattered scale-shaped trichomes **E.** *Solanopteris* sp. bearing two myrmecodomatia on short lateral branches **F.** *Pyrrosia piloselloides,* a CAM-performing fern with modestly succulent, dimorphic fronds **G.** *Microsorium viellardi* with naked rhizome **H.** Flat-stemmed *Icogramma meglophylla* with its dense covering of strap-shaped trichomes.

Rhizomes also range from thin and wiry to broad and fleshy and from round to flat in cross section (Figure 9.4). The most bizarre of the two-dimensional types (e.g., *Lecanopteris*) fairly envelop their substrates. Others appear almost modular, as if sympodial, like so many of the monocotyledonous epiphytes (Figure 1.2). Shapes that have evolved to attract ants that nest in plant cavities are described below.

Hairs and scales (trichomes) are common and occur in multiple shapes, sizes, and densities. Those borne on the unusually thick rhizomes of species of *Lecanopteris* and several other genera are scattered, seated in shallow depressions, and topped by symmetrically constructed caps (Figure 9.4B,D). Some of the more elongated types occur at concentration high enough to obscure the entire plant except for its foliage (e.g., *Polypodium aureum,* Figure 9.6). The rhizomes of still other species are completely naked (e.g., *Microsorium viellardii*).

The root is least noteworthy of the vegetative organs that make up the sporophytic body of an arboreal fern. The words tough, wiry, and profuse best describe all roots but those of *Ophioglossum,* which instead are fleshy, densely mycorrhizal, and produced at far lower rates per shoot. None comes close to possessing anatomical refinements equal to the velamen that serves thousands of aroids and orchids. Those that develop into tangled masses intercept considerable quantities of litter, although shield-shaped foliage performs the same function and often probably more effectively (Figure 9.3C). The root system is much diminished to entirely absent among the filmy ferns (Figure 9.7).

The fern frond exceeds the rhizome for structural variety (Figures 9.3A, B,C,D,E,F,G,H,I, 9.4A,C,E,F,G). At one extreme, those of *Pyrrosia longifolia* resemble flattened versions of the dichotomously branched trusses of naked stems that conducted photosynthesis and bore sporangia for some of the earliest of the vascular plants (Figures 1.6, 9.3I). More often it consists of a petiole (stipe) and blade, the latter equipped with veins that range from dichotomously branched and primitively open-ended at the margins to closed-reticulate like those of most of the seed plants (Figure 9.3C,I).

Frond dimorphism occurs on two levels of body organization among the epiphytic ferns. Either the individual appendage is divided into discrete sterile and reproductive (sporangia-bearing) portions, or the entire organ is devoted exclusively either to photosynthesis or to spore production (Figure 9.3A,C,E). The unusually stiff, short-lived but persistent sterile fronds of *Drynaria* and *Platycerium* form basket-like impoundments from which the more deeply dissected green, fertile appendages extend (Figures 9.3C, 9.5). Only the tank bromeliads and a scattering of additional seed plants exceed the ferns for collecting exploitable debris with leaves.

Figure 9.5 A large *Platycerium* sp. supporting *Ophioglossum pendulum* in Papua New Guinea.

Although far fewer in number, the epiphytic ferns match the angiosperms for mitigating the three greatest challenges faced by plants on land: drought, shade, and marginal supplies of key nutrients. The litter collectors have already received their due; others host plant-feeding ants (Figure 9.4B,E). Additional species jettison foliage to avoid drought, or they tolerate extreme desiccation without injury (Figures 9.3B, 9.6). Old World genus *Pyrrosia* contains succulent-leaved members that perform CAM-type photosynthesis (Figure 9.4F). At the opposite extreme are the ultra shade-tolerant, filmy ferns whose fronds are so delicately constructed that you can read newsprint through them (Figures 9.7). Chapter 4 includes a more detailed account of the water relations of the ferns.

The hardiest of the arboreal ferns thrive alongside the most drought-defying of the epiphytic bromeliads and orchids. Members of *Pleopeltis* and *Lecanopteris* bear scales with the same umbrella shape as those that allow the gray tillandsias to forgo roots for all but mechanical anchorage (Figures 4.4, 4.5, 9.3B, 9.4B,D). Whether these scales can absorb moisture like those of the atmospheric bromeliads is not known. Denser mantles of coarser, more erect trichomes

Figure 9.6. *Polypodium aureum* in its leafless, dry season condition in a Costa Rican deciduous forest. Note the dangling spent frond and thick covering of rhizomes by hairs.

Figure 9.7. A colony of filmy ferns (*Trichomanes polypoidioides*) growing near the base of the trunk of a rain forest tree. Photo by Bruce K. Holst

probably assist water balance in many ferns simply by sponging up and holding precipitation for slower but more significant uptake by nearby roots (Figures 9.4C,H, 9.6). While dry they slow dehydration.

How the ferns counter aridity during the gametophytic phase of the life cycle has not been given sufficient thought. Deciduousness is not possible without leaves, nor have succulence or CAM-type photosynthesis been reported. Being small and cheaply constructed would work if they allow a gametophyte to mature and produce sporophytes during the course of a single wet season (Figure 9.1). Several dozen higher ferns make a case for another mechanism: tested for tolerance, their gametophytes proved capable of surviving desiccations sufficient to kill the sporophytes of more typical vascular plants.

The sensitivities to drought of gametophytes almost certainly influence the growing conditions required by the memberships of several of the more primitive groups of ferns. Epiphytes and terrestrials alike representing genera such as *Ophioglossum* and *Psilotum* produce notoriously slow-growing, chlorophyll-free mycorrhizal gametophytes, and they never occur on any but substrates able to insulate their users during extended bouts of dry weather (Figures 9.5, 9.9, 9.11).

Members of a modest-sized subset of epiphytic ferns root in cartons constructed by ants. The angiosperms that operate in the same way engineer their associations with this medium by producing seeds that the six-legged architects find attractive enough to incorporate into covered runways in addition to their living quarters (see Chapters 6 and 8; Figures 3.1, 3.3, 6.2). Whether any of these ferns utilize these same substrates as faithfully as their seed-bearing companions, and, if so, whether by similar means, remain to be seen.

Rhizomes that house ant nests take several forms. Members of genus *Solanopteris* produce hollow, potato-like mymecodomatia at the tips of short lateral branches (Figure 9.4E). Colonies commonly occupy the spaces beneath and within the thick rhizomes of several species of *Lecanopteris* and *Phymatodes,* respectively (Figure 9.4B,D). Users either mine out cavities in the first case, or, the soft tissue initially present breaks down spontaneously.

The ferns are not as closely related as their shared name implies. Common attributes that suggest otherwise, such as a pinnately compound frond that bears sporangia, evolved repeatedly during early vascular plant history. Other, less universal and more recently evolved aspects of foliage, like the dimorphism that distinguishes different parts of the same organs, or separate organs borne by the same individuals, are also redundant. These and many other characters indicate that the plants lumped together under the heading *fern* belong to multiple lineages separated by much geologic time and considerable genetic distance (Figure 9.8).

Fern-type epiphytism also has considerable taxonomic breadth, having evolved in most of the Linnaean orders and many of the families that make up the group according to its broadest definition (Table 9.1; Figure 9.8). These repeated emergences of arboreal descendants from terrestrial ancestors followed different pathways, some discernible by studying survivors. For example, secondary hemi-epiphytism preceded obligate epiphytism in family Davalliaceae, and accompanying this transition was a shift from a round, elongate rhizome to a shorter, flatter organ and from widely separated to densely congested foliage.

A large majority of the living ferns, some 9000 species to be more exact, are designated "modern" because the attributes that define their kind, which are relatively young by geologic standards, have been layered over the features that have characterized their clade since more ancient times (Table 9.1; Figure 9.8). The most advanced portion of the fern complex consists of what taxonomists label the core *polypodiaceous group.* Add the 600 or so filmy ferns that make up most of the lower "leptosporangiate" species (Table 9.1), an even larger portion of which grow above ground, and the dominance of the epiphytic pteridophytes by the most highly evolved of the ferns is shown to be even more pronounced.

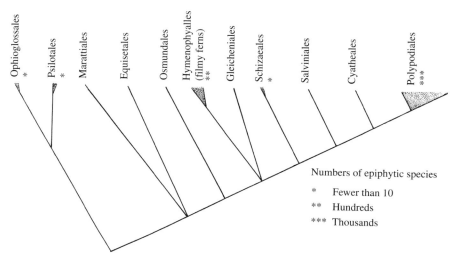

Figure 9.8. The phylogeny of the non-lycophyte pteridophytes with the groups to which the epiphytes belong identified (adapted from Smith et al. 2006).

The best place to look for a filmy fern is on the lower trunk of a rain forest tree (Figures 3.1, 9.7). Some of these most delicately constructed of the species rival the most advanced of the atmospheric bromeliads for diminished root systems, leaf specialization, and the effects of moisture on survival. Here is where the similarity ends. Whereas the heavily trichome-covered bromeliads suffocate if kept wet too long, the typical filmy fern requires continuously high humidity (Figure 4.6). Naked foliage thin enough to render functional stomata superfluous desiccates in short order when exposed to anything much less than fully saturated air.

The filmy ferns are too diverse to dismiss the entire lot as exceptionally drought vulnerable, predominantly epiphytic, and restricted to the depths of tropical rain forests. A few occur in temperate North America and Eurasia, and some of the tropical species are decidedly poikilohydric, although perhaps less than described for *Pleopeltis polypodioides* in Chapter 4. Shade tolerance is a more universal attribute, as is perhaps their capacity to take up moisture through foliage in addition to, or instead of by roots. Finally, some of the tropical species are hemi-epiphytic.

Another, more modest-sized and primitive collection of ferns that only remotely resemble the core polypodiaceous and filmy types make up the Linnaean order Ophioglossales (Figure 9.8). All of its even fewer epiphytes belong to genus *Ophioglossum,* and, as described above, favored anchorages are deep pockets of humus and other soil-like media (Table 9.1). Figure 9.5 illustrates *Ophioglossum pendulum* hanging from among the shield-shaped, debris-accumulating leaves of a large *Platycerium* specimen in Papua New Guinea. The ribbon-shaped, lobed frond illustrated in more detail in Figure 9.3A inspired the colloquial name "hand fern."

Even less like the higher ferns are the half dozen or so species assigned to phylogenetically ancient, yet structurally specialized *Psilotum* and *Tmesipteris* (Table 9.1; Figures 9.8, 9.9, 9.10A,B, 9.11). The sporophytes of the members of both genera lack roots and leaves, their bodies consisting of nothing more than trusses of naked stems that bear massive, fused sporangia. Epiphytism is the prevailing lifestyle, and its challenges may account for the group's exceptionally simplified anatomy, as suggested in Chapters 5 and 7 for the shootless orchids and the most simple bodied of the atmospheric bromeliads. Least fern-like within the clade are the horsetails.

A growing body of evidence attributes the existence of so many modern ferns to the rise of the woody angiosperms beginning during the late Cretaceous-early

Figure 9.9. *Psilotum nudum* growing on a fire-damaged bald cypress trunk in southwest Florida. Photo by Bruce K. Holst

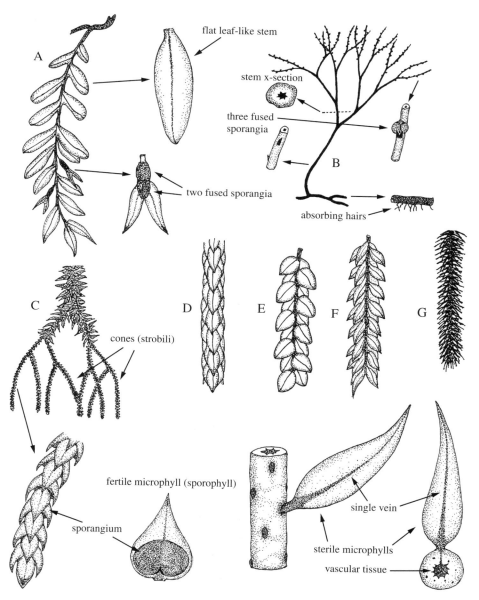

Figure 9.10. *Psilotum, Tmesipteris,* and a variety of epiphytic lycophytes. **A.** *Tmesipteris tannensis* displaying its leaflike, short lateral branches and two-parted fused sporangia **B.** *Psilotum nudum* showing stem anatomy, dichotomous branching, and its characteristic three-parted, fused sporangia **C.** *Huperzia phlegmaria* shoot bearing multiple terminal strobili. Part of a strobilus and a single microsporophyll with its axillary sporangium are also shown **D.** Sterile *Huperzia carinatum* shoot **E.** Sterile *Huperzia nummularioides* shoot **F.** Sterile *Huperzia proliferum* shoot with a single microphyll magnified and its stem anatomy displayed **G.** Sterile *Huperzia squarrosa* shoot.

Figure 9.11. *Tmesipteris tannensis* growing in a mantle of adventitious roots clothing the trunk of a tree fern in New Zealand.

Tertiary periods some 80–60 million years ago. This truly landscape-altering event was instrumental because it massively expanded a kind of living space that is particularly well suited for pteridophytes. In essence, the over-occurrence of epiphytism among the polypodiaceous and filmy ferns is an evolutionary consequence of an even more momentous breakthrough accomplished by the flowering plants.

If what might be called the recent arrival hypothesis is correct, the label *modern* is especially appropriate for the polypodiaceous ferns because they diversified subsequent to and because of the angiosperms' rise to near worldwide prominence after appearing tens of million of years earlier. The modern ferns, despite their ancient manner of reproduction, are actually newer in terms of the characteristics that define their kind, compared with those marking the most anciently derived of the surviving angiosperms (the basal families in particular). The adjective *modern* is ultimately justified by the older beginnings of all the other of the lineages that make up the fern complex (Figure 9.8).

A wholly unrelated phenomenon probably provided additional impetus for the radiation of the modern ferns: the acquisition around the same time of a novel hybrid photoreceptor that boosts shade tolerance. This key signaling molecule can be considered part of what was an exceptional "Darwinian opportunity." The pigment in question responds to certain wavelengths of light by setting in motion a mechanism that causes the *chloroplasts* (the tiny bodies where photosynthesis occurs; Figure 7.8E) inside green cells to orient in a way that boosts a deeply shaded leaf's capacity to conduct photosynthesis. Another mechanism known as *phototropism* that operates on a grander scale causes entire organs (leaves and shoots) to orient toward the brightest sectors within their environments.

Even if the emergence of this novel light-sensing molecule helped foster the adaptive revolution just described, the ferns still owe their current vitality in large measure to an evolutionary breakthrough accomplished earlier by another group of plants. If this is true, then a key biochemical innovation, along with the late Cretaceous-early Tertiary expansion of the angiosperms, granted a group of fundamentally older, smaller-bodied plants a new lease on life. Had these fortuitous events not occurred, the ferns presumably would be many fewer in number and far less important as epiphytes than they are today.

The Lycophytes

More than 200 million years ago, division Lycophyta included trees that, along with similarly oversized horsetails and the earliest of the gymnosperms, dominated our planet's first true forests. The lycophytes that survive today are strictly herbs, but being small does not alter their status as the geologically and phylogenetically oldest of the living vascular plants. This is why the epiphytes about to be described possess a uniquely uncomplicated body plan, foliage of primitive simplicity, and a spate of lesser, but equally ancient novelties.

Unlike the *megaphyllous*-type leaf that serves almost all the other higher plants, the lycophytes employ *microphylls* that represent superficial outgrowths or *enations* from the surfaces of what were naked stems borne by ancestors (Figures 2.4, 9.10F). Those with sporangia located in their axils that usually overlap to form cones on the ends of branches are called *microsporophylls* (Figure 9.10C). The presence of these elongated reproductive organs combined with the sterile microphylls that clothe the remainder of the shoot account for the widely applied misnomer "clubmoss."

About two-thirds of the living lycophytes are either terrestrial or aquatic. Shoots that creep over or partially below ground are typical for the dry land species, and like the sympodial monocots, they senesce from rear to front. Growth forward is punctuated by regular *dichotomous* divisions that yield two equal-sized branches, one destined to become a determinant, ramet-like module bearing one or more cones and the other a continuation of the advancing rhizome (Figure 1.2C).

Most of the several hundred arboreal lycophytes are tropical, with the few exceptions filling similar niches in temperate rain forests (Table 2.7). Contrary to the scrambling habit that characterizes the terrestrials, the epiphytes lack elongate rhizomes and so remain compact bodied, as befits their typically more cramped quarters (Figure 2.4). While some of the ground-hugging tropicals live weedy existences in recent cleared forest openings and along roadsides, none of the arboreal types occur in any but nearly to fully mature woodlands.

Epiphytism among the lycophytes is nearly always associated with the more primitive *homosporous* version of the pteridophytic cycle depicted in Figure 9.1. Species that engage in *heterospory* disperse two kinds of spores that differ by size, numbers produced, and gender. The relatively massive *megaspores* and tiny *microspores* yield egg- and sperm-producing gametophytes, respectively. Recall that the seed plants also operate this way, except that the megaspores and their female products reside within ovules, whereas the microspores (pollen grains) are moved from plant to plant at the behest of pollinators (Figure 9.1).

Despite heterospory being the more seed-plantlike version of the pteridophytic life cycle, homospory prevails among the arboreal lycophytes. Only about 10 heterosporous species, all members of genus *Selaginella,* compared with several hundred homosporous types, normally root on phorophytes rather than in the ground. Additionally, *Selaginella* includes about 700 members, and the total for the homosporous species is fewer than 500. Nothing else, such as dissimilar tolerance of shade or drought, explains this odd asymmetry.

The presence of drought-sensitive gametes does not explain the disproportionate participation in epiphytism by the homosporous versus heterosporous lycopods, because both groups employ free-swimming sperm. Any impediment posed by heterospory is more likely related to the lopsided ratio of microspores to megaspores, this number being many thousands to one. Perhaps too few eggs, hence new sporophytes, are produced to allow the heterosporous species to maintain populations in any but the most pteridophyte-friendly habitats (see Chapter 3). The relatively low dispersibility of megaspores compared with that of homospores may exacerbate the problem.

The high incidence of epiphytism among the homosporous lycophytes and the modern ferns amply illustrates the continuing viability of the more ancient of the two basic modes of vascular plant reproduction. Being arboreal and equipped with bisexual gametophytes does not preclude vigorous speciation either, or the capacity of epiphytic ancestors to produce terrestrial descendants. A particularly impressive example of the latter, which accounts for more than 50 recently differentiated alpine meadow species, was fostered by the North Andean uplift (orogeny) that began fewer than 20 million years ago.

The surviving homosporous lycophytes exhibit architecture that had already proven exceptionally durable several hundred million years ago. Even their long-extinct arborescent relatives, despite being gigantic by modern standards, bore the same spirally arranged, simple microphylls and shed spores from club-shaped cones. The herbaceous version of the lycophyte body plan has proven exceptionally enduring, but rigid as well. Little, for example, beyond microphyll shape and orientation distinguishes the cultivated huperzias (Figure 9.10C,D,E,F,G).

The inflexibility of the lycophyte body has limited the group's capacity to diversify in aerial habitats. Its 1200 or so living members exhibit little of the functional and structural variety achieved by the arboreal ferns and seed plants. None produces a tank, engages ants in mutualisms, is deciduous, or stores significant amounts of water in succulent foliage or stems. The quillworts perform CAM-type photosynthesis, but as a response to scarce CO_2 rather than drought in certain types of aquatic habitats.

Finally, the presence of hundreds of epiphytic lycophytes in the modern flora is probably another consequence of the late Cretaceous-early Tertiary rise of angiosperm-dominated tropical forests. If so, it is a muted response compared with that of the polypodiaceous ferns. No reports indicate emergences of anything like a novel photoreceptor to improve the hospitality of dark woodlands for small herbs. It seems that the lycopods just never evolved the capacity for either the structural or functional innovations achieved by the higher ferns and flowering plants.

Quite a few of the arboreal lycophytes perform well in cultivation. Provided abundant moisture, well-drained humus-rich soil, and partial shade, they make excellent choices for hanging baskets. There is one serious drawback, however: while most of the higher ferns are easily propagated from spores, the same cannot be said of the lycophytes. The fact that their gametophytes are often obligately mycorrhizal rather than photosynthetic does not help. Cuttings will suffice, but only if they include the root and bud-producing lower portion of a shoot.

10 Miscellaneous Epiphytes

This final installment of our survey begins with Piperaceae, which is one of the basal angiosperm families because its antecedent stem linage branched off the main flowering plant line before those that gave rise to the modern or *crown* monocots and eudicots (Figure 7.1). Fuller analyses of the carnivorous epiphytes and primary hemi-epiphytes come next, followed by profiles of the few arboreal gymnosperms. The chapter ends with some additional families of flowering plants that seldom receive recognition as having epiphytic members.

Piperaceae

Piperaceae is the last to be considered of the families that contain hundreds or more epiphytes. It stands alone, however, in having all but about a dozen of its approximately 700 arboreal species assigned to a single genus, which, including its terrestrial membership, tops 1500. Such a massive clustering of closely related species suggests that *Peperomia* is still expanding, although by what means is not clear. Its monotonously simple flowers and inflorescences stand little chance of fostering the kind of pollinator-assisted speciation that helps explain why the orchids are so numerous (see Chapter 7; Figure 10.1A,B).

The epiphytic peperomias range across the tropics, with a fair number of endemics on midocean islands such as the Hawaiian Archipelago. Tropical America hosts the highest number of species. Africa is comparatively impoverished, with fewer than two dozen. Tropical Asia and Australasia fall between these extremes. Cultigens abound, most of which are derived from arid-land, rather than arboreal stock.

The wetter growing peperomias include facultative and obligate canopy users and weak-stemmed, secondary hemi-epiphytes, most confined to tropical lowland habitats. A substantial number of the terrestrials experience drier, sunnier conditions, in some cases assisted by pronounced succulence and peculiar leaf anatomy. About a dozen or so of the family's arboreal members, mostly hemi-epiphytes, belong to similarly oversized and widely distributed genus *Piper*.

The shoots of the epiphytic peperomias root adventitiously and usually sprawl, creep, or hang from mossy perches (Figure 10.1A,B). One to five sometimes

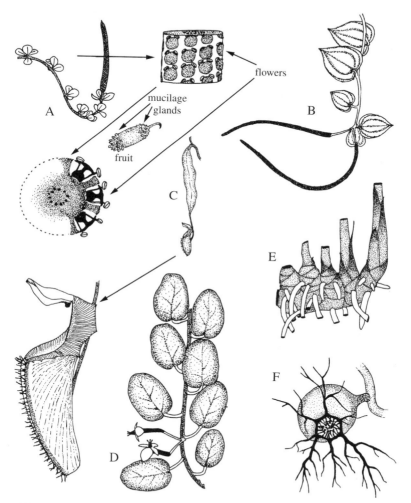

Figure 10.1. Miscellaneous epiphytes. **A.** and **B.** *Peperomia* spp. (Piperaceae) showing the family-wide spike-type inflorescence in three views, the clustered few-parted flowers, and an adhesive, single-seeded fruit **C.** Pitfall-type trap of the carnivorous epiphyte *Nepenthes veitchii* (Nepenthaceae) **D.** Pendent flowering shoot of *Begonia* sp. (Begoniaceae) **E.** Sympodial architecture of *Hedychium villosa* (Zingiberaceae) **F.** A suction trap with trigger appendages of *Utricularia* sp. (Lentibulari-aceae), maximum dimension 3–5 mm.

quite ornamental leaves arise at each node. Those of the odd, terrestrial xerophytes just mentioned can be folded and fused into pod-shaped organs topped by translucent windows that allow light to reach the photosynthetic tissue inside. None of the epiphytes exhibits more than moderate succulence.

Several members of *Peperomia* manufacture sugar by way of an oddly mixed photosynthetic syndrome instead of being either strict C_3, C_4, or CAM types (see Chapter 5). Species like *Peperomia camptotricha* fix CO_2 in leaves that consist of a colorless water-storing upper hypodermis, a considerably thinner, deep green central zone provisioned with vascular bundles, and a thick lower hypodermis comprising pale green, CAM-performing cells (Figure 4.1F,G). The only other epiphytes reported to possess this kind of anatomy belong to family Gesneriaceae (see Chapter 8).

The minute, few-parted flowers of *Peperomia* densely crowd slender spikes resembling the spadix-type inflorescences of family Araceae minus the leafy spathe (Plate 6A; Figures 7.7G, 10.1A,B). Not much is known about how these plants reproduce. A study of eight species conducted in Brazil's Atlantic rain forest recorded visits by syrphid flies and exchanges of airborne pollen by the two self-incompatible subjects observed. Wind transport of pollen has not been reported for any other epiphyte.

Fruit set was consistently high among the eight monitored subjects, owing in part to spontaneous autogamy, and perhaps also to *apomixis*. Apomixis is the technical term for asexual reproduction, and when flowers are involved, the results look and appear to germinate like genuine seeds or fruits containing real seeds. Propagules generated via apomixis lack true embryos, which by definition are the products of fertilized eggs, as illustrated in Figure 9.1.

Even less has been published about how the piperaceous epiphytes disperse. The small, single-seeded fruits of *Peperomia* readily separate from the infructescence and are adhesive—another rarity among the epiphytes, most of which rely on ants, wind, birds, or bats to put distance between parents and progeny (Figure 10.1A). The numerous, easily ruptured, mucilage-filled glands that cover part to most of the fruit are responsible for its stickiness. Note also how the style that remains prominent on the example illustrated in Figure 10.1A has grown into a hook, presumably to further facilitate carriage by animals. Time spent studying these modest-sized, largely overlooked epiphytes will likely reveal some interesting quirks of reproduction.

The Carnivorous Epiphytes

Botanical carnivory has fascinated naturalists for centuries. No less a luminary than Charles Darwin devoted an entire volume to its study. The notion that a plant feeds on animals rather than the other way around is nothing short of counterintuitive. How could such a mechanism evolve, and given the abundance of potential prey, why hasn't this happened more often? Recent studies explain its rarity, or more to the point, the infrequent occurrences of the environmental conditions under which carnivory represents an economically viable way for a plant to make a living.

Botanical carnivory is sustainable only in certain kinds of wetlands and similarly infertile upland habitats, including some as-yet undetermined portion of those occupied by epiphytes. Cost-effectiveness is the key determinant. The substantial investments a plant must make to produce the traps and other accoutrements required to capture and process prey must be paid back, and profits gained after that. This is not possible where roots, which are cheaper, have access to abundant supplies of key nutrients like nitrogen and phosphorus.

In addition to being chemically impoverished, sites suitable for the botanical animal-prey users have to be moist and sunny, meaning well suited in other ways to support vigorous photosynthesis. Why this is so can be appreciated by using the same logic employed in Chapter 4 to explain why certain characteristics of foliage, such as its anatomy and longevity, predict the nature of a plant's water supply, and to explain how moisture is used to support photosynthesis (see Chapter 4; Figure 4.2). Energy is the decisive currency in both situations.

It is difficult to determine where the epiphytes are most likely to encounter all three environmental conditions that make prey dependence a workable strategy. Cloud forests are humid enough, but persistent fog and mist may reduce sunlight below acceptable levels. Lowland habitats are typically better illuminated, but being warmer, apt to be too droughty to sustain botanical carnivory. Not enough is known about the fertility of woodland canopies to generalize about nutrients.

Carnivory is not the only option for obtaining nitrogen and the other key nutrients that most nonparasitic plants extract from Earth's soil. Thousands of epiphytes depend on similarly unconventional sources such as impounded litter and plant-feeding ants. Additional kinds of habitats lack the same nutrients in the right places to fully meet the demands of vegetation dependent solely on roots (e.g., the rocky homes of the lithophytes). These circumstances as well have fostered adoption of alternatives to roots and of replacements for terrestrial soil (see Chapters 3 and 5).

Observing where the plants that utilize prey occur is the best way to determine where botanical carnivory is sustainable. While hundreds of such species in more than a dozen genera root in the ground or under water, fewer than 50 in just 4 genera feed on animals in aerial habitats. Prey use is also a less mechanistically varied phenomenon among the epiphytes. One of the most extensively studied species employs a crude, passive trapping and processing device instead of one of the more dynamic options that serve so many of the terrestrial and aquatic carnivores (Figures 5.5, 10.1F).

Catopsis berteroniana (Bromeliaceae) was described in Chapter 5 as engaging in a form of carnivory that represents little more than an embellished version of the mode of nutrition employed by hundreds of its relatives (Figures 5.4, 7.5E). Rather than impounding organic debris to meet its needs, the upright, yellow, highly light-reflective shoots of *Catopsis berteroniana* intercept and consume flying insects. Restriction to sunny, relatively litter-poor microsites helps explain the switch from a predominantly vegetarian to an animal-based diet.

Two additional more species-rich groups of carnivorous eudicots also include epiphytes. Most spectacular are the pitcher plants of genus *Nepenthes* of family Nepenthaceae (Figure 10.1C). The majority of its approximately 60 members are tendril-climbing vines or secondary hemi-epiphytes. The more compact-bodied species range from terrestrial, to facultative, to fully epiphytic. One of the soil-based types subsists on intercepted litter, illustrating the exact opposite of the evolutionary progression imputed for *Catopsis berteroniana.*

Unlike *Catopsis berteroniana,* with its rudimentary, multifunctional traps fashioned from spirally inserted, tightly overlapping, upright foliage, *Nepenthes* produce pitcher-like organs at the tips of broad green *phyllodes* that represent the bases of what are now dual-tasked pseudoleaves (Figure 10.1C). Each trap is equipped with a lid to deflect rain and an often red to deep purple, slippery, sometimes nectar-secreting rim around the orifice. Unlike the tank bromeliads, all of which rely on precipitation, *Nepenthes* secrete the fluid contained in their pitchers. Digestive enzymes, also of plant origin, make the trap even more stomach-like. The same glands absorb nutrients following their liberation from degrading prey.

Even more specialized for carnivory are the bladderworts of genus *Utricularia* (family Lentibulariaceae). Most of its approximately 200 species inhabit moist soil, or they grow submerged except for showy snapdragon-like flowers. Bright red-petaled *Utricularia humboltii* subsists on tiny aquatic organisms inhabiting the sodden layers of humus and mosses that cover the trunks and larger branches of trees in certain rainy, cool South American habitats. It and several relatives also thrive in the water-filled leaf base chambers of co-occurring bromeliads (Figure 2.7).

Two species of the otherwise ground-based genus *Pinguicula* (also Lentibulariaceae) are epiphytic, one as a Cuban endemic. Gland-studded, yellowish "flypaper" leaves provide all 60 or so species the means to immobilize and digest small invertebrates. By contrast, the bladders of *Utricularia* operate by abruptly inflating to suck in small crustaceans, insect larvae, and anything else that swims close enough to brush the trigger hairs ringing the entrances of its numerous submerged traps (Figures 2.7, 10.1F).

The Stranglers and Other Primary Hemi-epiphytes

A tall tree growing in a dense forest is better positioned to obtain what a plant needs to grow than a shorter statured neighbor. Being rooted in the ground and having foliage positioned high in the canopy guarantees access to abundant sunlight above and plentiful soil moisture and nutrients below. Should its lesser companion be epiphytic, that individual stands a far greater chance of experiencing drought and scarcer supplies of nutrients; if terrestrial, it faces the prospect of substantial shading (Figure 3.1).

When it comes to conducting photosynthesis and acquiring essential minerals, the primary hemi-epiphytes operate more like trees than like either full-blown epiphytes or understory herbs. Germinating above, but soon to root below, they face the drought-for-sun trade-off only temporarily. They also position their foliage in strong sunlight from the start and at lower cost than a free-standing tree. Best equipped of all for competition are the stranglers (Figures 2.8, 3.1).

For a young tree to grow tall enough to occupy space in the upper canopy, it has to manufacture a substantial amount of mechanical and water vascular tissue (wood). Realizing its full potential also requires luck—specifically an accident that creates a forest gap. The less fortunate sapling remains tucked deep below unbroken vegetation, perhaps to survive for a few years, but unless released by a wind-throw, a lightning strike, or some other canopy-rending event, it eventually starves for lack of enough sunlight.

Primary hemi-epiphytism has evolved in several dozen families, but few of the products are equipped to marshal the wood necessary to seriously impede, let alone dispatch a large phorophyte. It's a different story for the species that possess more active vascular cambia. Under favorable circumstances, hemi-epiphytes of this more robust kind generate pseudotrunks comprising thick, anastomosing roots (Figure 2.8). Victory for these individuals amounts to complete takeovers of the sunny spaces formerly occupied by their hosts.

Shade cast by dense evergreen foliage is the strangler's most effective weapon, and the species best equipped to use it belong to genus *Ficus* of the fig family (Moraceae). Rarely is a support killed by interference with the expansion of its trunk. Success can also come without a loser. South Asian *F. bengalensis* and *F. regligiosa,* for example, can dispatch good-sized phorophytes, but many of their kind germinate and achieve full size without ever contacting a host.

Pantropical genus *Ficus* consists of nearly 1000 species, many of which produce woody aerial roots that fuse to form rigid networks (Figure 2.8). This capability is sufficiently pervasive across the genus to have fostered the strangling habit numerous times and on five continents. *Ficus hochstetteri* is a widespread African example. Mexico has *F. podifolia* and *F. mexicana,* among others. *Ficus indica* is a conspicuous element in many Malaysian landscapes, as is *F. aurea* in Florida. Australia and South America have their indigenous stranglers as well. Forests in Southeast Asia host unusually high concentrations of species, more than two dozen at some locations. Requirements for anchorages that vary on the basis of exposure to sun, height above ground, and substrate texture and orientation differentiate the resident figs into noncompeting groups (guilds) at some sites.

Humans are responsible for the ongoing spate of invasions by stranglers in part, because some of the most aggressive of the figs are prized ornamentals and others produce valuable timber. Asian *Ficus microcarpa* is a widespread pest in Hawaii and rapidly achieving similar status in central and south peninsular Florida. At the same time, older problems continue, such as the dismantling of ancient stoneworks by native *Ficus* species at important archaeological sites distributed from South Asia to Central America.

About one-half of the *Ficus* species are stranglers or less robust hemi-epiphytes, but the canopy dwellers come in additional versions. *Ficus paraensis* is a shrubby ant-garden specialist in Amazonia. It, like about a dozen members of additional families, relies on methyl-6-methylsalicylate and similarly volatile lures to entice certain kinds of arboreal ants to sow its seeds (see Chapter 6). Still other species are root climbers, suggesting that *Ficus* also includes accidental and facultative secondary hemi-epiphytes. Neotropical *Coussapoa* of the same family includes almost 50 species, primarily hemi-epiphytes, but not usually stranglers.

Primary hemi-epiphytes in several more families occasionally overwhelm their hosts. *Clusia* (Clusiaceae) is a distant second to *Ficus* in this respect. It too is a prolific producer of robust aerial roots, some of which hang freely from shoots positioned tens of meters above ground. Unlike the figs, however, *Clusia* includes CAM-equipped hemi-epiphytes, some of which switch to C_3-type photosynthesis during the rainy season. Several of its shrubby members are true epiphytes and, like the hemi-epiphytes, produce suspended in addition to trunk-hugging roots.

Primary hemi-epiphytes that reach considerable size, yet rarely kill, are even more numerous and diverse. *Grisellina* of Cornaceae (the dogwood family) is a sturdy hemi-epiphyte in New Zealand and in Chile's temperate rain forests. *Gibsoniothamnus* and *Schlegelia* of the catalpa family Bignoniaceae, *Marcgravia* and related genera in Margraviaceae, *Metrosideros* (Myrtaceae), *Cosmibunea,* and *Posoqueria* (Rubiaceae), *Hydrangia* (Saxifragaceae), *Juanulloa, Lycianthes,* and *Markea* (Solanaceae) also include woody species that begin life above ground and end up with roots embedded in terrestrial soil. *Fragraea* (Longaniaceae) and *Burmeistera* (Campanulaceae) each contain scramblers that sometimes grow as hemi-epiphytes, as do several additional families.

The Gymnosperms

If the 8 to 10% figure estimated to represent the portion of the vascular plants that qualify as arboreal applied as well to its major taxa, then 160 to 200 of the gymnosperms would be epiphytic. In fact, the count is only five, with all but one species belonging to the most mysterious of the four surviving subgroups: the gnetophytes (Table 2.7). Epiphytism may never have been as important for the naked-seeded plants as for the ferns and angiosperms, but we cannot be sure. The gymnosperm evolutionary tree has more than four branches, including the sometimes epiphytic seed ferns that went extinct many millions of years ago (Figure 1.7).

Scattered individuals that represent a number of conifers native to cool, wet habitats end up growing on phorophytes, but rarely do they reach maturity there. Living this way in places like the mossy temperate rain forests of the Pacific Northwest of North America is made possible primarily by local climate-driven convergences of soil and bark as rooting media; no special plant adaptations are involved. The fact that many of these same species use toppled, rotting tree trunks as seedling nurseries does not make their occasional canopy users more than accidental epiphytes either.

Why so few of the gymnosperms are epiphytic on a more regular basis is evident from the information contained in Table 2.8. Several of the impediments listed on the right side of the table characterize the entire gymnosperm complex, whereas others occur only in some of its modern subgroups. Additional attributes unique to these most primitive of the surviving seed plants count as well. Perhaps more interesting than why so few of the naked-seeded species are regularly arboreal is why even one grows this way.

Like the conifers, the lone surviving ginkgophyte (*Ginkgo biloba*) is terrestrial, as likely were its numerous extinct, similarly woody relatives. Just one cycad, *Zamia pseudoparasitica,* of the more than 250 surviving species composing this similarly ancient collection resembling unusually slow-growing palm trees, occurs as a humus epiphyte, or perhaps its frequent production of a long taproot makes it a facultative primary hemi-epiphyte.

The remaining gymnospermous epiphytes belong to the vaguely angiosperm-like gnetalean genus *Gnetum.* Its 50 or so other members grow as vines, shrubs, or small trees. Not enough is known about these reproductively most advanced of the living naked-seeded plants to speak confidently about how they operate in tree crown habitats. They produce modest-sized seeds with fleshy outer coats, but so do *Ginkgo,* the cycads, and the taxalean yew-type conifers (Figure 9.1).

At this point, it is fair to assume that most of the gymnosperms lack body plans and patterns of growth conducive to epiphytism. Virtually all are woody and of substantial size at maturity, not that either characteristic precludes aerial life, as hundreds of epiphytic Ericaceae and Melastomataceae amply testify. The multiple years required by most of the gymnosperms to mature probably constitutes a more serious impediment, and perhaps even more so, their rigidly programmed architectures. None of the cycads, conifers, or *Ginkgo* come close to the pteridophytic and angiospermous epiphytes for branching and rooting opportunistically.

The gymnosperms are further ill disposed for epiphytism by the way they reproduce. Like many of the angiospermous epiphytes, the cycads, *Ginkgo,* and the yew-type conifers produce seeds with edible coats, but what's inside is more problematic. Although somewhat less so for the gnetaleans, the seeds of gymnosperms contain small, rudimentary embryos provisioned with a primitive type of nutrient-rich tissue (the remains of the female gametophyte) that among the angiosperms has been replaced by a more readily available source called endosperm. Consequently, the seeds of the gymnosperms germinate slowly, and their seedling do not become nutritionally self-sufficient for months or longer.

Pollination raises yet another barrier, and it may well be among the two or three most limiting in relation to lifestyle options. Conifers wind-pollinate, and so engage in a practice that exacts a steep price in energy and in key nutrients like nitrogen. It also requires that interfertile individuals grow close together. All the angiospermous epiphytes, except for a few peperomias, use animals to exchange pollen. Some of the terrestrial cycads entice beetles and flies for this purpose, as do members of *Gnetum,* but these associations lack the precision and material economy characteristic of the epiphytic bromeliads, gesneriads, orchids, and their kind (see Chapter 7 and 9).

So the mystery continues: Why does just one member of the third largest of the 10 cycad genera grow as a rain forest epiphyte or hemi-epiphyte and then only through such a small range, entirely within northern Panama? Does something about this plant at once differentiate it from its consistently terrestrial relatives and account for its epiphytism? Might special circumstances within its narrow habitat be responsible for its provocative lifestyle?

Additional Oddities

Most of the families and genera cited below include epiphytes and secondary hemi-epiphytes that operate unassisted by special features such as leafy tanks or velamentous roots. *Begonia* (Begoniaceae), with its several dozen humid forest epiphytes, *Fuschia* (Onagraceae), with about the same number, and five *Impatiens* (Balsaminaceae) warrant mention primarily because of their horticultural prominence.

A few individual epiphytes bear mention in this survey because they constitute odd outliers in sizable, otherwise terrestrial families, for example, a *Thallictrum* in Ranunculaceae and several species of *Pyrus* in Rosaceae. Encountering one epiphyte each in *Agave* and *Yucca* (Agavaceae) and a half-dozen more in *Drimys* of primitive, woody Winteraceae is also unexpected. Two grasses, one each in *Microlaena* and *Tripogon,* root on phorophytes frequently enough to exceed accidental status. Several sedges (Cyperaceae) do the same thing.

Urticaceae, which is best known for the stinging hairs borne by the nettles, also includes about 40 epiphytes in *Elatostoma, Pilea,* and *Procis.* The ginger family Zingiberaceae, with about the same number of arboreal members, some of which possess drought-deciduous foliage, is also predominantly terrestrial. All its epiphytes branch sympodially, as do a majority of the other arboreal monocots. The persistent bases of the two-ranked leaves of *Hedychium villosa* overlap to produce stout storage organs that resemble the pseudobulbs of orchids (Figure 10.1E).

Epiphytism predominates in a couple of small families largely confined to humid tropical woodlands. Palmlike Cyclanthaceae is exclusively Neotropical, with about 200 species, approximately half of which are either secondary hemiepiphytes or humus-type true epiphytes. *Asplundia* accounts for more than half, most of which exhibit vining habits and fan-shaped, pleated foliage. Being monocots, members of Cyclanthaceae produce no wood, so their shoots die from the rear as they grow forward. Typically compact inflorescences made up of unisexual flowers attract insects, and the brightly colored fruits contain bird-dispersed seeds (Plate 6C). Dense tangles of greatly elongated styles often resemble the silk of young ears of corn.

Exclusively Old World Pandanaceae, which is best known for its terrestrial screwpines (*Pandanus*), fills the same niches occupied by Cyclanthaceae in tropical America. Both families exploit aerial habitats as root climbers and secondary hemi-epiphytes and less often as shrubby epiphytes. Most of the canopy dwellers belong to genus *Freycinetia.* Flowers are small, often numerous, and densely aggregated, as are the resulting dry to fleshy fruits. Pollinators include bats, birds, insects, and possibly wind. Numerous species are dioecious.

The family Marcgraviaceae is similar to Cyclanthaceae in being small (125 species), exclusively Neotropical, vining, adventitiously rooted, and the home for more than its share of secondary hemi-epiphytes. It differs in being heavily bird pollinated and woody (Plate 5C). Most of the hemi-epiphytes belong to *Marcgravia* and *Marcgraviastrum.* Shoots are often heterophyllic, the juvenile-

Figure 10.2. *Burmannia kalbreyeri* (Burmanniaceae) in Venezuela rooted in humus adhering to the trunk of a palm tree with persistent leaf bases. Photo by Bruce K. Holst

type foliage being two-ranked and held shingle-like against the substrate. Adult leaves tend to be more robust, spirally arranged, and held aloft on longer petioles. Epiphytic shrubs to small trees in addition to woody hemi-epiphytes also occur in Bignoniaceae, mostly in *Gibsoniothamnus* and *Schlegelia*. About 20 similarly woody arboreal species also occur in Myrcinaceae, mostly in *Grammadinia* and *Myrcine*.

Araliaceae could have been included among the families mentioned in the section above devoted to primary hemi-epiphytism. About 10% of its nearly 1000 members grow as facultative or obligate epiphytes or as hemi-epiphytes, both the primary and secondary types. Hemi-epiphytism is favored by the group's generally semiwoody construction and bias toward root-clinging shoots. Compound leaves, insect pollination, and fleshy fruits are nearly universal. More than half the arboreal species belong to 200-member *Schefflera,* which is a source of numerous cultivars engineered for use in building interiors. Habitats tend to be moist, but not necessarily tropical. *Pseudopanax laetevirens* penetrates to 50°S in Argentina and Chile.

Family Rapateaceae parallels Bromeliaceae in being similarly aged at about 65 million years and strictly Neotropical except for West African genus *Maschalocephalus*. Likewise, its crown radiation occurred in the ancient Guyana Shield region of northern South America beginning 10–12 million years ago. A large majority of its approximately 100 members still grow where their stem group diversified, and consequently they share the same acidic, nutrient-poor, highly weathered soils with many of the oldest of the surviving bromeliads.

All six rapateaceous epiphytes belong to closely related *Epidryos* and *Stegolepsis*. Sympodial shoots bearing two-ranked leaves equipped with inflated bases characterize both genera. Despite their similar beginnings in terms of body plan, ecology, timing, and place, Bromeliaceae far exceeds Rapateaceae for size and geographic range in addition to success above ground. Had CAM-type photosynthesis, a more effective tank shoot, and absorbing trichomes evolved in the lesser of these two families as well, the two groups likely would be more comparable in size and ecology today.

Perhaps the oddest of the epiphytes belong to Burmanniaceae, a small monocot family best known for its chlorophyll-free terrestrials that parasitize fungi that in turn extract nutrients from the roots of green plants. Genus *Burmannia* includes the few photosynthetic species, two of which occur as epiphytes in tropical America (Figure 10.2). Both *Burmannia foliosa* and *B. kalberyeri* root in humus and bear pendent shoots equipped with lax, ribbon-like foliage; neither has been examined to determine whether it obtains some of its sustenance from the same sources that sustain its fully parasitic relatives.

Figure 10.3. Tank-type *Astelia* sp. (Asteliaceae) growing as an epiphyte in North Island, New Zealand.

Cochliostema of Commelinaceae (about 700 species) also belongs in this survey, even though it accounts for only two of the epiphytes, both tank producers. A second pair of nonimpounding types occur elsewhere in the family. *Cochliostema,* along with *Astelia* (and recently recognized *Collospermum*) of Asteliaceae (within the lily complex), illustrate how sharing a device that helped foster exuberant speciation in one family does not guarantee the same outcome elsewhere (Figure 10.3). Why Commeliniacae and Asteliaceae have failed to exploit epiphytism more expansively, despite being equipped with a shoot much like that possessed by well over a thousand bromeliads, is anyone's guess.

11 Threats and Conservation

Conservationists paint a bleak picture of what lies ahead for the world's most environmentally sensitive flora, a group that includes many of the epiphytes. Expanding urban development and mounting numbers of people and livestock are bound to continue the current wholesale destruction of tropical woodland habitats. Moreover, changing climates and artificially elevated supplies of two key plant nutrients will increasingly challenge whatever manages to escape this fate. It is hard to imagine, short of some stunning turn of human events, that more than a modest fraction of the surviving epiphytes will still be growing in the wild by the end of this century.

The Convention on International Trade in Endangered Species (CITES) confirms that the epiphytes rank high among threatened flora, although perhaps more by coincidence than by design. Appendices I and II list only two sizable families in close to their entirety: Orchidaceae, which contains more than half of the vascular epiphytes, and Cactaceae, a considerably smaller but still a substantial source of species that share many of the same aerial habitats. Whatever the thinking responsible for this decision, overlisting the epiphytes is more than justified by their extraordinary vulnerability to several of the most biodisruptive aspects of a modern phenomenon known as "global change."

This final chapter begins with a brief review of the ecosystem services provided by the epiphytes, especially their extraordinary capacity to improve living conditions, and particularly their provisions of food and shelter for organisms ranging from microbes to large vertebrates. All these subjects have come up in previous chapters, but not juxtaposed with the issue of plant conservation versus extirpation. Next comes an assessment of global change, including how some of its components unquestionably and others with near equal certainty imperil wild-type vegetation, especially the kind to which this book is devoted.

How Epiphytes Influence Microclimates

Chapters 3 and 6 describe a number of direct and more circuitous ways that the epiphytes affect the fortunes of their neighbors. Some have sweeping consequences. Chapter 3, for example, points out how plants that grow above ground may reduce the capacities of their hosts to recycle scarce nutrients, all the while increasing the fertility of the hosting ecosystem. A largely ignored phenomenon that belongs in the same high-impact category concerns the moderation of climates in wooded landscapes by dense populations of certain types of epiphytes.

Being capable of impounding thousands of liters of precipitation per hectare, the tank-equipped bromeliads are especially well disposed to benefit heat- and drought-sensitive organisms. Only the arboreal mosses and leafy liverworts, when present as abundantly as illustrated in Figure 3.2, can hold more moisture aloft. These same epiphytes and others representing numerous additional taxonomic groups enhance the capacities of woodlands to intercept *occult* (mist, fog) moisture in addition to airborne nutrients, and sometimes with major off-site effects. Many a cloud forest would be less able to supply a drier downstream ecosystem were its canopy epiphyte-free.

All that is required to appreciate how powerfully plants can cool and humidify air is to make a quick detour from an open field into an adjacent stand of tall, dense vegetation on a hot, sunny day. Studies have shown that certain kinds of epiphytes perform especially well on this score, enough in some situations to prompt investigators to label their kind the "air conditioners" of tropical forests.

Contributions to Biodiversity

The term biodiversity alludes to the totality of life that resides within a given physical space, be that space a rotten log or the entire biosphere. To an ecologist, biodiversity has multiple dimensions that interact in complicated and still poorly understood ways. Plants contribute most straightforwardly to biodiversity simply by being part of a community. Epiphytes can add mightily to a tropical forest's species richness, accounting for more than one-third of its inventory of resident vascular plants. Impacts on its *carrying capacity*—an ecosystem's ability to support organisms in addition to providing living space—are far greater and more difficult to quantify compared with tallying kinds of occupants.

Epiphytes heighten the carrying capacities of many humid woodland ecosystems by expanding a living area that at drier sites may be just as heavily populated, but is typically far smaller in spatial extent. The floor of a forest to a depth of about 50 centimeters literally teems with soil-dwelling invertebrates and microbes. The many trunks and branches arrayed immediately above constitute a more expansive, but far less hospitable habitat except when supplemented by thick layers of clinging, moisture-retaining humus and arboreal flora (Figures 2.4, 3.2, 9.7). Many terrestrial fauna, even earthworms, often thrive many meters up into the canopies of forests liberally colonized by epiphytes.

Epiphytes elevate another dimension of biodiversity by operating in ways different from those of their neighbors. Many obtain moisture and mineral nutrients from unconventional sources, and some employ food-making mechanisms foreign to their arborescent companions, as described in Chapters 2 to 5. This ability is necessary because, lacking contact with the ground, they experience the same sites differently. Epiphytes that anchor on twigs and naked bark on more robust axes, for instance, endure desert-like conditions even in rain forests (Figures 2.2, 2.3, 3.1). Those equipped with tanks that impound precipitation and solids, or with roots that penetrate suspended soils, tend to conduct their internal affairs more in the way of the forest dominants on which they depend for mechanical support (Figures 2.4, 5.5, 7.5B,C,E).

No vascular plant that resides in a humid forest other than an epiphyte is apt to synthesize sugar via the CAM mechanism. Likewise, none is likely to be as tolerant of desiccation as some of the arboreal ferns. No others maintain aquatic microcosms high enough in the canopy to allow animals with gill-equipped larvae to spend their entire lives without having to come down to the ground. Finally, none of the other botanical residents add as many unusual twists and turns to the paths that nutrients and energy ply as they respectively cycle within and move through woodland ecosystems (Figure 3.1). Who else helps decompose spent biomass in leafy tanks, entices plant-feeding ants, helps secure their carton nests, or reduces opportunities for trees to retrieve shed nutrients?

Less clear is the extent to which any epiphytes present can influence the nutrient budgets, water use efficiencies, and photosynthetic outputs of an entire ecosystem (see Chapter 3). To what degree might they enhance the capacity of a forest to capture and retain key nutrients? No better addressed is the question whether woodlands use sunlight or scarce nutrients more effectively to manufacture biomass when they harbor this or that type of arboreal flora. These are not trivial issues when it comes to developing management strategies for fragile ecosystems that include endangered organisms.

Global Change

Earth scientists have determined that CO_2 liberated by burning fossil fuels is warming our planet. Biologically usable or *reactive* nitrogen released during the same process is beginning to impact biological communities through an entirely different mechanism. Contributing to global change as well are the toxic chemicals manufactured from the same hydrocarbons that meet the bulk of society's energy needs. And as if these activities and certain land use practices that elevate heat trapping methane and other gasses in the atmosphere weren't insult enough, humans are further altering the face of the planet by encouraging alien organisms to displace natives in natural ecosystems.

Why believe that global warming threatens the epiphytes? While it is true that climatologists predict a planet-wide average rise of several degrees Celsius by the end of this century, most of this change is expected to occur well poleward of where almost all the plants described in this book grow. Concern is indeed warranted, because altered precipitation more than rising temperature threatens tropical vegetation, and especially the epiphytic kind (Table 3.1; Figure 3.4). Moreover, the amount of rain delivered needn't change, only when and how it arrives.

Our planet's land areas are zoned into living spaces circumscribed by temperature and precipitation and inhabited by *associations* or *biomes* of correspondingly adapted fauna and flora. Latitude most powerfully determines where the biomes occur, with elevation becoming increasingly influential toward the Equator. Because temperature fluctuates less at lower than higher latitudes, precipitation, and particularly its distribution through the year, largely determines where different kinds of tropical organisms live. Continuously high humidity is the reason the tropical rain forest biome wins top billing for species richness. Its desert equivalent, although just as warm, supports many fewer species, and they exhibit far less structural and functional variety.

Being hypersensitive to moisture supply explains why the epiphytes compared with terrestrial vegetation are poised to over-respond to climate change (Table 3.1; Figure 3.4). Imagine the vulnerability of a drought-deciduous orchid that relies on photoperiod to cue its most water-expensive activity, which happens to be C_3-type photosynthesis (see Chapter 4). How would it fare were its foliage to continue to flush and senesce on about the same calendar dates while the dates marking the beginnings and endings of the dry and wet seasons change? Plants routinely adjust to naturally evolving climates, but keeping pace with the at least tenfold faster change currently under way exceeds biological capacity.

Germination is usually among the most drought-vulnerable stages of a plant's life cycle, and this could be especially so for the epiphytes. Alter the timing, intensity, or duration of a rainy season, and reproduction could fail, even though every other aspect of this process such as fruit set and seed dispersal continue as before. Recognizing failure early on presents a special challenge to the conservationist, given its usually slow onset. Minor changes in plant performance that fall within the bounds of normal variation may or may not portend extirpation.

Extinction is forever, but getting there as a victim of climate change is apt to be more gradual than abrupt.

CAM-type epiphytes native to upland habitats compared with warmer-growing species that operate in the same physiological mode may respond adversely to rising temperatures in addition to more, or less, or differently scheduled precipitation. Experiments have demonstrated that the capacities of some of the plants that conserve moisture by synthesizing malic acid from CO_2 after sundown may diminish as the Earth's atmosphere heats up. Nights that no longer cool as much as before could reduce or eliminate much of a CAM plant's ability to accumulate enough nocturnally fixed carbon to manufacture adequate amounts of sugar during daylight hours (Figure 5.1).

High-elevation epiphytes are adapted to climate in additional ways that increase vulnerability to global warming. Cloud forest inhabitants should rank among the most sensitive because they live where shade limits photosynthesis and bathing mists constitute a major if not the primary source of moisture. Rising earth surface temperatures predicted to drive cloud zones up mountainsides will seriously complicate this picture. Photoinjury inflicted on fundamentally shade-adapted species by unfiltered sunlight alone might be enough to eliminate species. Add the effects of higher rates of transpiration driven by warmer air in the absence of a former source of moisture, and chances of failure rise even higher.

Two studies support the presumption that cloud forest epiphytes have lower thresholds for survival than most other kinds of tropical plants. The Puerto Rican tank bromeliad *Werauhia sintenisii* monitored for two years in a dwarfed cloud forest reproduced, which is one of the most energy-expensive of plant activities, as if adapted to avoid deficits caused by seasonal cloudiness. Modest differences in daily solar irradiance and minimum temperatures two to three months prior to flowering markedly affected the number of flowers borne per plant, suggesting high sensitivity to both aspects of climate.

A transplant experiment conducted in a Costa Rican cloud forest further demonstrated how small changes in climate impact targets rendered hypersensitive by adaptation to specific conditions along the steep environmental gradients that characterize tropical montane regions. Most of the members of a diverse collection of local epiphytes perished within a few months following relocation to a site fewer than 100 meters downslope. Imagine how the populations of these bromeliads, orchids, and ferns would respond if their habitats warmed by a degree or two or cloudiness gave way to sunny weather during a different time of year.

Climate change will create additional problems to the extent that it interrupts vital relationships between interdependent organisms. Numerous pollen and nectar seekers fly during the same few weeks to months each year, which means that their botanical partners must coordinate to secure essential services. Should climate change alter either party's schedule of activity too much, one or both will pay a price determined by who depends on whom and for what. Certain migratory birds and plants are similarly coupled relative to seed dispersal.

Excess Nutrients

Burning fossil fuels emit CO_2 and water just as occurs during the natural carbon cycle, only much faster. Additional byproducts include gases that contain nitrogen atoms liberated after millions of years as components of long-dead organisms—tiny seagoing protozoa for oil and, for coal, ancient vascular plants. Plant-usable nitrogen, as always, comes from lightning discharges and the activities of certain bacteria. It is the new and growing input attributable to human activity that is cause for alarm. The contribution from this still-mounting source has more than doubled the global supply that prevailed during preindustrial times. Atmospheric CO_2 has risen about 35% during the same interval.

Reactive nitrogen illustrates how too much of what plants need can destabilize an ecosystem. Augment the baseline supply, and growth quickens but not uniformly (see Chapter 3). Should this challenge persist, species richness is apt to fall because the more aggressive residents of an ecosystem, and these are usually the individuals most markedly inhibited by infertility, displace their less nitrogen-responsive neighbors (Figure 3.7). Carbon dioxide, being a plant nutrient as well as a heat-trapping gas, has much the same effect. Just as vegetation responds unevenly to nitrogen, some plants grow more vigorously than others in air supplemented with CO_2. There is no reason to assume that the same does not apply to the epiphytes.

Air containing elevated CO_2 also influences the economy with which plants expend water to make food, and again not uniformly across species (see Chapter 4). Enough is known about this phenomenon to anticipate that the epiphytes differ on this basis as a consequence of possessing different photosynthetic syndromes. Those that perform C_3-type photosynthesis are the better candidates for growing faster and using water more economically; anticipating what the CAM-types will do is more problematic, but it probably will not be the same. Perhaps rising supplies of CO_2 and nutritive nitrogen are already affecting some of the epiphytes, but how much and to what end, only time will tell.

Plant Invasions

Few epiphytes have managed to establish viable populations beyond their native ranges, despite many having had ample opportunity to do so. Although thousands of arboreal bromeliads, cacti, orchids, and members of additional families have multi-decade-long histories of outdoor cultivation well beyond their native ranges, only the rare exception has managed to establish a feral population, that is, has become "naturalized." Most successful on this score are several strangling figs, probably none of which were recognized by the individuals responsible for their introductions as being such aggressive competitors in alien (to them) ecosystems.

Things might change, of course, and what lies ahead could be troublesome if a situation recently reported on the Hawaiian island of Oahu is prophetic. *Guzmania lindenii*, a large South American bromeliad with spectacularly deep purple and green–banded foliage, was recently discovered growing on the ground and on woody vegetation along a windswept ridge far removed from any known seed source. Hundreds of individuals, ranging from fruiting adults to seedlings, had to be destroyed to abort what appeared to be the early stage of a robust escape from cultivation.

Slow maturation helps explain why so few of the epiphytes have managed to establish reproducing populations beyond their home ranges. Bark probably contributes as well, being too hostile for all but the more stress-tolerant species except when well clothed with abundant mosses and lichens. For these same reasons, communities of epiphytes have been spared losses of biodiversity similar to those experienced in many terrestrial settings. Immunity on this score is poor compensation, however, considering how being arboreal heightens vulnerability to climate change and a variety of other threats of human origin.

The rising popularity of sustainable forestry is also threatening the epiphytes, because so many of the selections that yield more valuable timber than the natives they displace make less acceptable phorophytes. Particularly unfortunate is the inhospitality of the crowns of plantation stocks derived from species of *Eucalyptus* and *Pinus*. On the other hand, mature to declining groves of cacao, citrus, and coffee, among the orchard types, often support abundant and diverse communities of epiphytes.

Habitat Loss

Loss of habitat currently threatens the epiphytes above all else, but how seriously differs by region and biome. More of what was dry than humid tropical woodland has already been converted for agriculture; the threat to cloud forest is more recent, its utility for this purpose being more limited. Relatively localized phenomena and the subject's biology further influence the vulnerabilities of individual species. The likelihood of extirpation generally scales inversely with population size and area occupied, with capacity to recover from fire and severe weather and appeal to collectors coming into play as well. Conservation status ranges from severely endangered to totally immune to extirpation; identifying who falls at the two extremes is easy, but not so those somewhere in between.

Tillandsia recurvata (Bromeliaceae) is a prolific colonizer of diverse kinds of trees and shrubs in peninsular Florida and southward through much of Latin America, so its future is secure (Figure 1.4). Some of the more fastidious and highly insular species are also reasonably well off because it takes considerable human skill and climbing equipment to reach them, or they occupy remote or low-value real estate. Promontories that discourage all but the most determined plant enthusiasts and agile livestock insulate their epiphytic and lithophytic floras from just about every conceivable human intervention other than those imposed through global change.

To be spared one threat can mean heightened vulnerability to another. Many of the species that avoid fire, humans, and hungry livestock by anchoring on rocky outcrops depend on mists that form nightly as air warmed and humidified at lower elevations cools upon rising. Remove this source and what had been a sustaining refuge becomes intolerably dry. Epiphytes on small islands are less vulnerable. Much of what remains of Costa Rica's undisturbed deciduous forest, along with its relatively stress-tolerant arboreal flora, occurs on small islets maintained as picnic sites for shiploads of tourists cruising in the Gulf of Nicoya.

Scattered trees left standing to shade cattle or anchor fence wire often host abundant epiphytes, but how faithfully these communities reflect past conditions is debatable. Heightened exposure to strong light and better ventilation post forest clearing may have eliminated the most drought sensitive of the original inhabitants while lifting the fortunes of their hardier former companions and any newcomers recruited since from nearby drier woodlands.

Finally, epiphytes are most protectable where they occur naturally (*in situ* conservation). Relying on botanical gardens (*ex situ* conservation) would require not only keeping millions of specimens alive generation after generation under artificial conditions, but accurately documented as well. Eventual failure is certain even under the most favorable circumstances. Only secured preserves made valuable to local citizens stand much chance of permanent success. Designating projects such as these acceptable investments in a global carbon-offset market would help. In any case, urgency calls for more concerted and better-financed efforts than anything in place today. We owe this much to posterity.

Glossary

Abscission: a process that causes the shedding of short-lived organs such as leaves and produces a clean, healed break where separation occurred.

Accidental epiphyte: a plant that is anchored on another plant, but is a member of a normally terrestrial species (Figure 1.1).

Adaptation: an attribute of an organism that suits it for growth under certain growing conditions.

Adaptive radiation: the proliferation of species (*lineages*) from a common ancestral stock. The *derived* species diverge in the sense that they usually become adapted to grow under a variety of environmental conditions (Figure 2.1).

Adaptive strategy: the sum total of the adaptations possessed by a plant or species that allow it to operate under certain growing conditions or pursue a particular kind of lifestyle (e.g., a humus epiphyte versus a twig epiphyte).

Adaptive trade-off: a condition that prevails when the presence of one performance-enhancing attribute requires the reduction of another aspect of performance (e.g., heightened capacity for photosynthesis versus diminished water economy).

Adaptive type: a term used in this book to describe a group of species that share the same adaptations for epiphytism or use the same kinds of rooting media and with the same frequency (Tables 2.1–2.6).

Adventitious roots or buds: rather than arising from a conventional location (e.g., a bud from the axil of a leaf), the adventitious root or bud arises more randomly (e.g., roots that originate at the nodes along the stems of many epiphytes).

Aglaophyton: a quasi-vascular, leafless, rootless land plant that lived about 400 million years ago. Its body was only crudely differentiated into shoot and root systems (Figure 1.6).

Air plant: an epiphyte that appears to be subsisting entirely on moisture and nutrients extracted from the atmosphere—a member of the *atmospheric* type (e.g., ball moss, Figure 1.4).

Alien: a relative term used to describe an organism or species not living within its natural geographic range. The opposite of *endemic* or native.

Allelopathy: a phenomenon whereby one plant inhibits the growth of another individual of a different species by releasing toxic chemicals.

Allogamy: sexual reproduction resulting in progeny with two parents. Allogamous plants outcross rather than self-pollinate, as is the habit of the *autogamous* types.

Angiosperm: a flowering plant, a member of division Magnoliophyta (Figure 7.1).

Anisophylly: a condition characterized by the presence of unequal-sized leaves on the same shoot, usually resulting in the two-ranked architecture illustrated in Figure 8.3A,D.

Anthocyanins: a class of water-soluble biochemicals that impart blue to red color to a variety of plant organs such as fruits and petals.

Ant-house epiphyte: an epiphyte that bears stems or leaves (*myrmecodomatia*) modified (chambered) to house ant colonies (e.g., Figure 8.4).

Ant-nest epiphyte: an epiphyte that roots in an ant-nest *carton* (Figure 3.3).

Apical meristem: the tissue comprising embryonic stem cells located at the tips of shoots and roots that mediate growth in length, and in the case of the shoot also produce axillary buds, leaves, and reproductive organs.

Arboreal: growing as an epiphyte, not to be confused with arborescent, which means treelike.

Areole: the condensed lateral shoot characteristic of the cacti. Spines that represent modified leaves are common on the aeroles of desert-dwelling species but often missing (lost) among the epiphytes (Figure 8.1A).

Aril: an edible appendage associated with a seed that promotes its dispersal by an animal. The arils of the ant-dispersed epiphytes are small and rich in fats and protein and represent a special type of aril known as an elaiosome (Figure 8.3B).

Atmospheric epiphyte: an epiphyte that normally extracts moisture and mineral nutrients directly from precipitation and aerosols, a member of the atmospheric adaptive type. Most of these plants are highly specialized bromeliads or orchids (Figures 1.3, 1.4, 2.2).

Autogamy: self-fertilization; to be autogamous is to self-pollinate.

Autotrophy: *free-living* as applied to green plants because they manufacture all their food using solar energy and simple inorganic raw materials, specifically CO_2, water, and mineral nutrients.

Axenic: a tree that never harbor epiphytes in a region where epiphytes are common.

Axil: the acute angle formed where the petiole of a leaf joins the stem at a node and where axillary or lateral buds occur (Figure 1.2A).

Bark epiphyte: a plant that routinely anchors on branches and trunks that lack layers of humus thick enough to insulate an epiphyte's roots (Figure 2.3).

Basal angiosperm: a member of one of the families of flowering plants whose ancestors diverged from the stem angiosperm line before it gave rise to the *monocots* and *eudicots* (Figure 7.1).

Berry: a fleshy-walled, multiseeded fruit.

Biogeochemical cycle: the movement of a substance, specifically, a nutritive element like phosphorus, as it circulates among the living and physical compartments that make up an ecosystem (Figure 3.1).

Biomass: the organic material that makes up organisms.

Biome: a major geographic region characterized by a specific kind of climate and populated by organisms adapted to that climate, for example, tropical rain forest biome, temperate deciduous forest biome.

Body plan: the architectural organization of a plant body (e.g., *monopodial, sympodial;* Figure 1.2C,D). Different plans are distinguished by characteristics such as pattern of branching and degree of modularity.

Bract: a scalelike organ borne on stems and inflorescences, basically a leaf but much reduced in size or modified to provide a service other than photosynthesis or in addition to photosynthesis (e.g., Plate 1).

Breeding system: the mechanism that allows plants to control mate choice and thereby the parentage of their offspring (Table 6.1). See *dioecy, pollination syndrome,* and *self-compatibility.*

Bryophyte: a member of the plant division Bryophyta, a moss or liverwort.

Bud (terminal vs. **axillary** vs. **adventitious):** a young, unexpanded shoot usually located at the tip of a shoot or in the *axil* of a leaf (Figure 1.2A).

C_3 plant: a plant that fixes CO_2 the primitive way: directly into sugar using only the C_3 photosynthetic pathway (Figure 5.1).

C_3-type photosynthesis (syndrome): the light-driven fixation of CO_2, the immediate stable product of which is the simple sugar glucose (Figure 5.1; Table 5.1).

Calyx: the term for all the *sepals* on a flower (Figure 9.1).

CAM plant: a plant equipped to conduct photosynthesis using the CAM mechanism (Table 5.1; Figure 5.1).

CAM-type photosynthesis (syndrome): the type of photosynthesis characterized by nighttime assimilation of CO_2 from the atmosphere into malic acid prior to its internal regeneration the next day, followed by its refixation into sugar using light energy (Table 5.1; Figure 5.1).

Capsule: a dry-walled, multiseeded fruit that splits open to release its contents.

Carbon fixation: describes all reactions involving enzyme-mediated condensation of CO_2 into an organic compound such as glucose or malic acid. See *C_3-type photosynthesis* and *CAM-type photosynthesis.*

Carpel: the primitive version of the female reproductive organ of the angiosperm flower. Two or more carpels fused together make a *pistil*—a derived condition.

Carton: the composite material that certain ants fabricate from a variety of materials, including wood fiber and soil, to construct their nests and covered trails (Figures 3.3, 6.2).

Character: a term used interchangeably with *feature* in this text in reference to an attribute of an organism or a species, such as petal color. For this example the character states could be white, red, and yellow.

Chloroplast: one of the subcellular bodies that occur in large numbers within green cells. Chloroplasts contain the biochemical machinery used to fix CO_2 during photosynthesis (Figure 7.8E).

Clade: all the species derived from a single ancestral lineage (ancestor) and thus constitute a monophyletic group (Figure 2.1). See *monophyletic*.

Cladode: a photosynthetic stem that is the functional equivalent of a leaf in Cactaceae and in succulent-stemmed species in several other families (Figure 8.1).

Climate change: the ongoing modification of Earth's climates attributable to increasing concentrations of CO_2 and other heat-trapping gases in the atmosphere.

Cloud forest: a forest high enough above sea level to be invested by clouds on a regular basis. Cloud forest vegetation is adapted to cool temperatures, high humidity, and low light intensities.

Coma: hairy appendage that promotes seed dispersal.

Commensalism: a relationship between two unrelated organisms in which one benefits by virtue of that association while the other remains unaffected.

Community: a collection of co-occurring organisms that exhibits a certain amount of functional and structural integration. The compositions of biological communities tend to be predictable according to the qualities of the corresponding habitats.

Complex (noun): loosely used in this book to describe an undefined, high-ranking taxonomic group of organisms such as the angiosperms or ferns.

Cone: a type of reproductive organ that bears *sporangia* and *spores* for *pteridophytes,* or seeds for seed plants (e.g., Figures 9.1, 9.10C). See *strobilus*.

Convergent evolution: a pattern of evolution (*homoplasy*) characterized by the independent acquisition by separate lineages of features that serve the same purpose, but are not *homologous* (lack a common genetic basis, i.e., are analogous) (Figure 2.1). See *parallel evolution*.

Corolla: the collective term for the petals of a flower (Figure 9.1).

Cultigen (cultivar): a cultivated and usually genetically improved version of a wild-type plant (species).

Cuticle: the thin layer of wax that covers the aerial portion (the shoot) of a land plant.

Cycad: a member of a group of about 250 species of primitive *gymnosperms,* characterized by palmlike foliage and thick trunks. Only a single species is epiphytic.

Deciduous: describes an organ, usually a leaf with a relatively short life, less than a year in the case of the foliage of a perennial plant (e.g., Figures 2.6, 7.2A). The opposite of *evergreen*.

Decomposer: a microbe that lives by reducing litter and other kinds of dead biomass to their component inorganic elements while extracting the chemical energy also present.

Derived: refers to species and the attributes of species: the state of being evolved from an ancestral lineage or of being a *character* state derived from an earlier state of the same character.

Detritivore: an invertebrate animal that feeds on litter, thereby contributing to its decomposition (Figure 7.5E).

Dimorphic: occurring in two forms, for example, two kinds of leaves on the same plant (Figure 9.3C).

Dioecy: a type of breeding system of certain seed plants whereby the individuals that make up a species bear either pollen or seeds; that is, they are individually unisexual, the two genders being relegated to separate plants.

Diploid (chromosome number): the condition in which cells contain two sets of chromosomes, hence two copies of each gene (locus). This condition is characteristic of the cells that make up the body of the *sporophyte* phase of the higher plant life cycle (Figure 9.1).

Disturbance (ecological): a term used by ecologists to describe physical disruptions in habitats that displace or kill resident organisms, thus creating conditions that tend to increase species richness by reducing the chances that aggressive populations will exclude those of their weaker competitors (Figure 3.7).

Division: the category or rank within the Linnaean taxonomic hierarchy just above *order* and immediately below kingdom. The suffix of a division is -phyta (Figure 2.1).

Drought-avoiding: describes plants that shed their foliage at the beginnings of dry seasons in order to prevent lethal desiccation.

Drought-enduring: describes plants that continue photosynthesis through dry seasons, but avoid serious dehydration by using moisture sparingly and maintaining large reserves in organs such as succulent leaves.

Dry forest: the type of forest characteristic of tropical regions that experience pronounced dry seasons. Most or all of the resident trees and some of the perennial herbs are deciduous, and rainfall ranges from about 700–1500 mm per year.

Ecological succession: a somewhat orderly and predictable process whereby biological communities develop on barren substrates (primary succession) or regenerate (secondary succession) following disturbance.

Ecosystem: a more or less self-contained physical space and the organisms that live there. Ecosystems scale in inclusiveness from local, to regional, to the entire global biosphere (Figure 3.1).

Endemic: a relative term used interchangeably with *native* to describe an organism or species living within its natural geographic range. The opposite of *alien* or nonnative.

Endosperm: a storage tissue inside the seeds of most flowering plants that allows the embryos inside to become nutritionally and otherwise self-sufficient, that is, to produce green organs and roots.

Epidermis: the outer layer of cells on organs such as leaves and roots, often highly specialized among the epiphytes as an adaptation to the often stressful conditions that prevail in aerial habitats.

Eudicot: a member of the eudicotyledon group of flowering plants, as opposed to being a *monocot* or a basal *angiosperm* (Figure 7.1).

Evergreen: describes ephemeral plant organs, usually leaves, with lives that exceed one year, the opposite of *deciduous*.

Ever-wet forest: woodlands that during normal years receive enough precipitation to spare the local vegetation even short-term moisture stress; includes rain forest (Figure 7.4).

Evolutionary grade: describes a group of organisms (*species*) that share the same level of functional and structural sophistication (e.g., the *pteridophytes* versus the more advanced plants that reproduce by seeds rather than by naked *spores*).

Exodermis: a single layer of cells located immediately beneath the *velamen* of an aerial orchid root (Figure 4.3). Specialized passage and aeration cells present in this barrier tissue help mediate the absorption of mineral nutrients and moisture and allow gas exchange between the root core and the surrounding atmosphere.

Exotic (plant or animal): describes an organism when it occurs outside its native range, where it is not *endemic,* but an *alien.*

Facultative epiphyte: a species whose members often root in tree crowns and on rock or the ground (Table 2.5).

Family: the rank within the *Linnaean hierarchy* just below *order* and immediately above *genus.* The suffix for family is -aceae (Figure 2.1).

Feature: see *character.*

Filmy fern: one of the roughly 600-member group of ferns characterized by unusually thin fronds and that inhabit mostly dark, moist tropical forests (Figures 9.7, 9.8).

Flora: all the plants that occur within a circumscribed geographic area.

Free-living: self-feeding by way of photosynthesis instead of being parasitic. See *autotrophy.*

Frugivore: an animal that feeds primarily on soft-walled fruits.

Gamete: a sex cell, either an egg or a sperm (Figure 9.1).

Gametophyte: the physical embodiment of the haploid phase of the two-staged, higher plant life cycle. Its body is made up of cells that contain *haploid* (single) sets of chromosomes, and it produces *gametes* that fuse to form *zygotes* that become *sporophytes* (Figure 9.1).

Gene pool: the sum of the genes possessed by all the members of a species or a lesser population of interbreeding individuals.

Genome: all the different genes possessed by a single organism.

Genotype: another way of describing the *genome* of an individual.

Genus: the rank in the Linnaean hierarchy located just below *family* and immediately above *species* (Figure 2.1).

Geologic time: time measured in Earth history (Figure 2.1).

Global change: a term used to describe the ongoing, altering effects of human activity on the biosphere, such as climate alteration and production of nutritive nitrogen as consequences of fossil fuel use.

Gnetophyte: a group of about 60 species of somewhat flowering, plantlike *gymnosperms,* a small number of which are epiphytic.

Gymnosperm: plants that produce seeds in or on organs other than the flowering plant *carpel* or *pistil,* as opposed to *angiosperm.* Includes conifers, *Ginkgo,* and the cycads, among others (Figure 9.1).

Habit (or growth form): describes the general structure and lifestyle of a plant, examples being trees, shrubs, herbs, and epiphytes (which can also be shrubs or herbs).

Haploid (chromosome number): the halved number of chromosomes (just one set rather than two) characteristic of the cells that make up the *gametophyte* phase of the higher plant life cycle (Figure 9.1).

Haustorium: the invasive organ of a mistletoe or root parasite that extracts water and nutrients from a host (Figure 5.8).

Hemi-epiphyte: a plant that regularly spends either the early part (the primary type, Figures 2.8, 3.1) or the second part of its life (the secondary type, Figures 3.1, 7.8A,B,D) anchored on a host.

Herbivore: an animal that feeds on plants.

Herbivory: consumption of plant material.

Heterochrony: a type of evolution effected by alterations of the genetic program that controls development (*ontogeny*), resulting in *derived* species (descendant species) with attributes that their ancestors expressed at different stages of their life cycles (Figure 7.6A–D).

Heterophylly: a condition of leaves that change form and function along a single shoot, usually becoming progressively larger and more structurally elaborate, common among secondary *hemi-epiphytes.*

Heterospory: one of the two conditions of the *pteridophyte* life cycle, distinguished by the production of two kinds of spores (megaspores and microspores) that produce strictly female or male gametophytes, respectively. See *homospory* for a description of the opposing, more primitive condition.

Heterotrophy: nutrition based on the consumption of biomass rather than the manufacture of food from simpler substances in the manner of the photosynthetic autotrophs (green plants).

Higher plant: a vascular plant as opposed to a nonvascular plant such as a moss or alga, not to be confused with higher versus lower vascular plants (i.e., seed-producing versus free-sporing plants; Figure 9.1).

Homologous: describes attributes possessed by different species or different attributes by the same species that share the same genetic basis (e.g., leaves and bracts).

Homoplasy: the independent evolution of similar biological attributes that serve similar purposes in different lineages. Includes parallel and convergent evolution, and the loss and multiplications of specific kinds of organs (e.g., the replacement of leaves with cladodes in Cactaceae and several additional families).

Homospory: one of the two conditions of the *pteridophyte* life cycle, distinguished by the production of only one kind of spore, which upon germination produces a bisexual gametophyte. See *heterospory* for a description of the opposing condition.

Humus epiphyte: an epiphyte (or species) that normally roots in suspended humus (Table 2.2; Figure 2.4).

Hydrophilic: readily wetted, having high affinity for water.

Hyphae: the basic structural unit of the body of a fungus, consisting of an elongated single cell or long chains of attached cells (Figure 7.2 upper left).

Hypodermis: a water storage tissue located just within the epidermis, usually most extensively developed beneath the upper surface of a leaf, comprising large, thin-walled, and collapsible colorless cells (Figure 4.1B).

Inflorescence: that part of the shoot system of an angiosperm that is specialized to bear flowers.

Infructescence: an inflorescence after its flowers have produced fruits.

Keystone species: plant or animal species that plays an inordinately influential role in its hosting ecosystem.

Land plant: a vascular or higher plant, although some authorities include the mosses and liverworts (bryophytes) in this category.

Life history: the totality of the events that occur during the course of a plant's life cycle and their calendar dates, such as when and how it reproduces, goes dormant and reactivates if perennial, and the length of its normal life span.

Lifestyle or **strategy** or **habit:** the way a plant or a species lives in a specific kind of habitat (e.g., as an epiphyte, deciduous tree, or forest understory herb).

Lineage: a population (or gene pool) envisioned as a self-perpetuating entity that evolves as it progresses through geological time (Figure 2.1).

Linnaean classification: the formal Latin taxonomic hierarchy that includes all the species known to science. Its ranks include species, genera, families, and orders (Figure 2.1).

Lithophyte: a plant that routinely grows anchored on rocks (Figure 1.5).

Litter: the dead, shed parts of plants (e.g., leaves, twigs, flower parts; Figures 2.5, 7.5E).

Lower plant (or **nonvascular plant**): a plant that lacks vascular tissue, such as an alga or moss. See *bryophyte.*

Lower vascular plant: see *pteridophyte* (Figure 9.1).

Lycophyte: a member of the pteridophytic division Microphyllophyta (Figure 9.10C–G).

Malic acid: a common four-carbon fruit acid. By synthesizing malic acid, CAM plants can capture CO_2 from the atmosphere at night (Figure 5.1).

Mating system: the mechanism possessed by plants that determines the parentage of their sexually produced offspring (e.g., *dioecism, self-incompatibility*). See *Breeding system.*

Meristem: that part of the plant body made up of embryonic (meristematic) stem cells that produce tissues and organs. *Apical meristems* produce leaves, stems, roots, and reproductive organs. See *vascular cambium,* which is a lateral meristem.

Mesophyll: the tissue that fills the interior of a leaf exclusive of its vascular tissues (e.g., Figure 4.1C,D).

Microphyll: the primitive, single-veined leaf of the *lycophytes* (Figure 9.10C–G).

Microsperm (dust seed): the unusually diminutive seed produced by orchids and some parasitic plants (Figures 7.2 upper left, 7.3).

Mineral nutrient: one of the elements (e.g., nitrogen, magnesium) that all plants require and mostly obtain from the ground.

Mistletoe: a parasitic plant that attacks the shoots of its hosts. Most mistletoes are partial (hemi-) rather than total (holo-) parasites (Figure 5.7).

Modern fern: a member of the core "polypodiaceous" group of ferns that underwent a relatively recent spurt of evolution and speciation and today account for more than three quarters of the living species (Figure 9.8).

Moist forest: a type of tropical woodland that receives more precipitation annually than a dry-type forest, but less than an ever-wet forest.

Monocot: a member of the monocotyledon group of flowering plants (Figure 7.1).

Monophyletic: describes a group of species, all of which share a common ancestor (Figure 2.1). See *clade, paraphyletic, polyphyletic.*

Monopodial: describes plants equipped with shoots that grow to considerable lengths by adding many *phytomeres* produced by long-lived *apical meristems.* Shoot growth is therefore relatively indeterminate (Figure 1.2D).

Mutualism: a mutually beneficial and physically close relationship involving members of different species, a type of *symbiosis.*

Mycorrhiza (plural mycorrhizae) (mycorrhizal fungus): a mutualistic relationship that prevails between many kinds of plants and certain root-inhabiting fungi. The fungi receive food while providing the host plant with certain mineral nutrients, particularly phosphorus, obtained from the environment. Some of the relationships that receive this label more closely approach parasitism than mutualism (e.g., those involving orchids; Figure 7.2 upper left).

Myrmecodomatium: a leaf or stem that possesses a chamber evolved to house a colony of plant-feeding or plant-protecting ants (Figures 8.3F, 8.4A–E).

Myrmecophyte: a plant that closely associates with ants by harboring ant colonies in its body or by rooting in an ant nest.

Myrmecotroph: a plant that depends heavily on nutrients provided by ants (e.g., Figure 8.4 A–E).

Neotropics: the tropical latitudes of the Americas. See *Paleotropics.*

New World: a geographic term that refers to the land masses that make up the Americas. See *Old World.*

Niche: a term used by ecologists to describe the role played by an organism or a population in an ecosystem which in turn reflects growth requirements, life history, and more. Much about an organism makes sense only in the context of its niche.

Node: the part of a shoot where one or more leaves and axillary buds are attached (Figure 1.2A). See *phytomere.*

Nutritional piracy: a way that epiphytes obtain nutrients by interdicting flows of substances between the crowns of trees and the ground as part of the biogeochemical cycling process (Figures 3.1, 3.8).

Obligate epiphyte: an epiphyte that consistently grows in aerial habitats and typically dies soon after falling to the ground.

Old World: a geographic term that refers to the region beyond the Americas. See *New World.*

Ontogeny: the development of an organism from *zygote* to maturity. See *heterochrony.*

Order: the taxonomic rank in the *Linnaean system* between *class* and *family.*

Ovary: the swollen chamber that makes up the base of a *carpel* or *pistil* and houses the *ovules* and the resulting seeds (Figure 9.1).

Ovule (as compared with seed): an ovule contains a female *gametophyte* that produces an egg, which following fertilization converts that ovule into a seed (Figure 9.1).

Paleotropics: the tropical latitudes of the Old World. See *Neotropics.*

Paraphyletic: describes a taxon (e.g., genus, family) that contains fewer than all the species that make up a clade (Figure 2.1). See *clade, monophyletic, polyphyletic.*

Phenotype: the external manifestation of the *genotype.*

Phenotypic or **developmental plasticity:** a process whereby aspects of the phenotype can change to better accommodate a plant to its growing conditions (Figures 3.5, 3.6).

Phloem: the vascular tissue responsible for transporting the products of photosynthesis within the body of a higher plant (Figure 1.2B).

Phorophyte: a woody plant that serves as a host for an epiphyte, literally its mechanical support. Used interchangeably with the term "host" in this volume.

Photosynthetic syndrome: a suite of structural and physiological attributes that support photosynthesis of a specific kind (Figure 5.1). See *CAM* and *C_3-type photosynthesis.*

Phototropism: directional growth toward a source of light, usually mediated by a pigment system that responds to the blue component of sunlight.

Phylogenetic constraint: a condition imposed on a *lineage* by its genetic legacy that limits options for additional evolutionary change.

Phylogeny: the evolutionary history of a *lineage* or group of lineages through geologic time (Figure 2.1).

Phytomere: the basic, repeating structural unit of the vascular plant shoot. A phytomere consists of one node and the attached leaf or leaves and the axillary bud(s) and the internode located above that node (Figure 1.2A).

Phytotelma: a plant cavity in which a *phytotelmata* resides (e.g., a bromeliad tank).

Phytotelmata: the watery contents of a *phytotelma* (Figure 7.5E).

Pistil: the female reproductive organ that occupies the center of most flowers and houses the *ovules* and eventually seeds. It receives pollen (on its *stigma*). The fact that the ovules and seeds are contained in its swollen base (the *ovary*) accounts for the name *angiosperm* (covered seed) assigned to the flowering plants (Figure 9.1).

Pneumathode: a region in the *velamen* that ventilates the living root core by resisting engorgement with water during wet weather (Figure 4.3).

Poikilohydrous: describes plants that dry out quickly during droughts and rehydrate even faster when wetted; desiccation tolerant, resurrection plant (Figure 9.3B).

Pollination syndrome: a suite of plant characteristics that facilitate pollination by a specific kind of pollinator (e.g., bats, birds, moths; Table 6.1).

Pollinium (plural pollinia): a detachable male organ produced by most orchids and some members of family Apocynaceae that contains large numbers of individual pollen grains (Figure 7.2 upper right).

Polyphyletic: describes a taxon (e.g., genus, family) made up of species representing some of the species from two or more *clades* (Figure 2.1). See *monophyletic, paraphyletic*.

Population: used in various ways, including interchangeably with species, also groups of individuals that represent fewer than the complete species, such as all the individuals representing a species present in a particular community or ecosystem.

Primitive: the ancestral condition compared with its more advanced state when applied to a single character. If used to describe a species or higher taxonomic group, it means that the members of that group exhibit a preponderance of antecedent rather than *derived* character states.

Pseudobulb: a round to cylindrical, stout stem region produced by many *sympodial* orchids. The number of nodes (*phytomeres*) that make up a pseudobulb varies from one to many depending on the species (Figures 1.2C, 7.2A,C,D).

Pteridophyte: the category of lower vascular plants made up of the ferns, horsetails, and lycophytes. Pteridophytes are free-sporing rather than seed-producing (*spermatophytes*), and their *sporophyte* and *gametophyte* stages live independently (Figure 9.1).

Rain forest: the type of forest that grows where conditions, especially rainfall, are conducive for continuous plant growth. Tropical rain forests typically receive at least 2000 mm of precipitation annually and never less than about 50 mm per month (Figure 7.4).

Ramet: one of the serially produced subdivisions of the shoots produced by plants that branch *sympodially*. Each ramet consists of a more or less set number of leafy nodes (*phytomeres*); after producing these, it flowers once (is *determinate*) and branches to form a replacement ramet (Figures 1.2C, 7.2A,C,D).

Reaction wood: woody host tissue that develops in tumor-like fashion around the site of penetration by a mistletoe *haustorium* (Figure 5.7).

Resurrection plant: a desiccation-tolerant plant (Figure 9.3B). See *poikilohydrous*.

Rhizome: a horizontal stem that grows at or below ground level, common among herbs that exhibit *sympodial* branching (Figures 1.2C, 7.2D).

Saprophyte: an organism that feeds on dead biomass (e.g., many bacteria and fungi).

Scape: a leafless axis upon which flowers are borne (Plate 6A,B).

Seed fern: a member of a group of primitive gymnosperms that bore fernlike foliage and reached peak diversity and importance during the Paleozoic era, after which the group became extinct (Figure 1.7). At least a few species were epiphytes.

Self-incompatibility versus **self-compatibility:** the opposing conditions of being unable or capable, respectively, of setting seeds with self-pollen. See *allogamy, autogamy, breeding system.*

Sepal: the organ that forms the outermost ring of appendage around most flowers (collectively, *calyx;* Figure 9.1).

Skototropism (negative *phototropism*): growth away from light as a means by which the shoots of certain vines and secondary hemi-epiphytes locate objects to climb such as a tree trunk.

Sorus (plural **sori**): a cluster of *sporangia* produced on the underside of the leaves of many ferns. Sorus shape and location on a frond indicate relationship among the modern ferns (Figures 9.2, 9.3D–H).

Speciation: the process whereby one *lineage* produces two daughter lineages (Figure 2.1).

Sporangium (plural **sporangia**): the tiny saclike organ in which spores are produced following a type of cell division (meiosis) that allows diploid mother cells to give rise to *haploid* daughter cells (Figures 9.1, 9.2).

Spore: the single-celled reproductive unit of the *sporophyte* of the vascular plants. It contains only one set of chromosomes, and when it germinates, it gives rise to a *gametophyte* (Figure 9.1).

Sporophyte (versus **gametophyte**): the stage in the plant life cycle (alternation of generations) characterized by cells that contain two sets of chromosomes. This is the stage organized into leaves, stems, and roots. It produces the *gametophyte* stage from spores that contain only one of the two sets of chromosomes (hence the name sporophyte, literally spore-producing plant; Figure 9.1).

Stigma: the pollen-receptive portion of a *carpel* or *pistil* in a flower (Figure 9.1).

Stoma (plural **stomata**): the minute apparatus on the surface of a leaf dominated by two guard cells that control its aperture and thus determine the porosity of leaf surface to gases (Figure 4.1A,E).

Strobilus (plural **strobili**): see *cone.*

Succulent: pertaining to organs much thickened by the presence of water storage tissue in foliage or in swollen stems when the subject is a cactus (Figures 4.1C,D,F,G, 8.1A–H). See *cladode.*

Symbiosis: an enduring, physically close association between two unrelated organisms, includes *commensalisms, mutualism,* and *parasitism.*

Sympodial branching (or body type): describes plants and individual shoots that branch as a result of the activation of successive axillary buds short distances behind aborted terminal buds (Figure 1.2C). The resulting strongly modular shoots consist of series of interconnected *ramets,* as demonstrated by many epiphytic orchids (Figure 7.2D).

Tank epiphyte: an epiphyte that collects litter and moisture in an impoundment (*phytotelma*) fashioned from a rosette of leaves with tightly overlapping bases, as in *Astelia,* many bromeliads, and ferns, among others (Figure 7.5B,C,E).

Taxon (plural **taxa**): the term applied to any of the categories in the hierarchy of Linnaean taxonomic ranks such as genus or family. It is most often used to refer to a specific group of related species (e.g., Bromeliaceae or one of its component genera or subfamilies; Figure 2.1).

Terrestrial: describes plants that grow on the ground.

Transpiration: the process whereby plants lose water through their *stomata* while conducting photosynthesis (Figure 4.1E).

Transpiration ratio: a measure of water use efficiency expressed as the amount (mass) of water lost relative to *biomass* gained during photosynthesis.

Trash basket: a tangle of aerial roots produced by certain aroids, orchids, and some other epiphytes to collect debris as a source of nutrients.

Trash basket epiphyte: an epiphyte that collects litter in a basket-like array of aerial roots (e.g., numerous ferns and orchids, among others; Figure 2.6).

Tribe: a taxonomic rank within the *Linnaean system* between subfamily and *genus*.

Trichome: a hair or scalelike epidermal appendage. Function varies from the absorption of moisture and nutrients to protection from herbivores or damaging exposures to sunlight (Figures 4.5, 9.3B).

Twig epiphyte: an epiphyte that habitually grows on twigs rather than anchored to more robust branches and trunks; a member of the twig-type category of epiphytes (Table 2.2; Figure 2.2).

Unitary: describes the structural organization of plants characterized by discrete shoot and root systems that tend to grow upright, such as trees (Figure 1.2A). See *sympodial* as an example of a more modular-type body plan.

Vascular cambium: a cylindrical layer of embryonic (*meristematic*) stem cells within stems and roots that causes them to thicken by adding vascular tissue, mostly wood (*xylem*). Herbaceous plants lack vascular cambia, hence, do not become woody.

Vascular plant: a plant equipped with *xylem* and *phloem* vascular tissues, a higher plant.

Velamen: the special multilayered epidermis covering the roots of many orchids and aroids, particularly those that normally operate exposed to air. This tissue and the underlying endodermis alternately insulate the organ from rapid water loss and enhance plant hydration depending on circumstances (Figure 4.3).

Vivipary: premature germination of seeds before they are dispersed, usually within a fruit.

Water relations or management: a term used to describe the ways in which a plant acquires, stores, retains, and uses moisture.

Water use efficiency: see *transpiration ratio*.

Wood: the type of *xylem* tissue that thickens the stems and roots of woody plants. See *vascular cambium*.

Xeromorphic: describes a plant or its parts that exhibit structure denoting adaptation to drought (e.g., succulent foliage).

Xerophyte: a plant adapted to grow in arid environments. The associated adjectives describe the different strategies that the xerophytes employ to cope with drought (Table 2.4). See *drought-avoiding, drought-enduring*.

Xylem: the water-vascular tissue of the land (vascular) plants. See *wood*.

Zygote: a fertilized egg and the beginning of the *sporophyte* (diploid phase) of the two-staged life cycle of the higher plants (Figure 9.1).

References

Adams, W. W., III, and Martin, C. E. 1986. Morphological changes accompanying the transition from juvenile (atmospheric) to adult (tank) forms of the Mexican epiphyte *Tillandsia deppeana* (Bromeliaceae). *American Journal of Botany* 73:1207–1214.

Andrade, J. L., and Nobel, P. S. 1997. Microhabitats and water relations of epiphytic cacti and ferns in a lowland Neotropical forest. *Biotropica* 29:261–170.

Angiosperm Phylogeny Group. 2003. An update of the angiosperm phylogeny group classification for the orders and families of flowering plants: APG II. *Botanical Journal of the Linnean Society* 141:399–436.

Barthlott, W., Schmit-Neuerburg, V., Nieder, J., and Engwald, S. 2001. Diversity and abundance of vascular epiphytes: a comparison of secondary vegetation and primary rain forest in the Venezuelan Andes. *Plant Ecology* 152:145–156.

Benner, J. W., and Vitousek, P. M. 2007. Development of a diverse epiphyte community in response to phosphorus fertilization. *Ecological Letters* 10:628–636.

Bennett, B. 1992. Uses of epiphytes, lianas, and parasites by the Shuar people of Amazonian Ecuador. *Selbyana* 13:99–114.

Benzing, D. H. 1981. Bark surfaces and the origin and maintenance of diversity among angiosperm epiphytes. *Selbyana* 5:248–255.

Benzing, D. H. 1981. The population dynamics of *Tillandsia circinnata* (Bromeliaceae) in cypress crown colonies in southern Florida. *Selbyana* 5:256–263.

Benzing, D. H. 1990. *Vascular epiphytes*. New York: Cambridge University Press.

Benzing, D. H. 1997. Vulnerabilities of tropical forests to climate change: the significance of resident epiphytes. *Climate Change* 39:519–540.

Benzing, D. H. 2000. *Bromeliaceae: profile of an adaptive radiation*. New York: Cambridge University Press.

Bush, S. P., and Beach, J. H. 1995. Breeding systems of epiphytes in a tropical montane wet forest. *Selbyana* 16:155–158.

Cavelier, J., Soltis, D., and Jaramillo, M. A. 1996. Fog interception in montane forest across the central cordillera of Panama. *Journal of Tropical Ecology* 12:357–369.

Chase, M. W. 1987. Obligate twig epiphytes in the Oncidiinae and other Neotropical orchids. *Selbyana* 10:24–30.

Chia-chun, H., Hong, F.-W., and Kuo, C.-M. 2002. Epiphyte biomass and nutrient capital of a moist subtropical forest in Northeastern Taiwan. *Journal of Tropical Ecology* 18(5):659–670.

Clark, K. L., Nadkarni, N. M., Schaeffer, D., and Gholz, H. L. 1998. Atmospheric deposition and net retention of ions by the canopy of a tropical rain forest, Monteverde, Costa Rica. *Journal of Tropical Ecology* 14:127–145.

Condit, R., Hubbell, S. P., and Foster, R. B. 1996. Changes in a tropical forest with shifting climate: results from a 50 ha permanent census plot. *Journal of Tropical Ecology* 12:231–256.

Crayn, D. M., Winter, K., and Smith, J. A. C. 2004. Multiple origins of crassulacean acid metabolism and the epiphytic habit in the Neotropical family Bromeliaceae. *Proceedings of the National Academy of Science USA* 101:3703–3708.

Davidson, D. W. 1988. Ecological studies of Neotropical ant gardens. *Ecology* 69:1138–1152.

De Figueiredo, R. A., and Sazmia, M. 2007. Phenology and pollination biology of eight *Peperomia* species (Piperaceae) in semideciduous forests in southeastern Brazil. *Plant Biology* 9(1):136–141.

Dejean, A., and Olmstead, I. 1997. Ecological studies of *Aechmea bracteata* (Swartz) (Bromeliaceae). *Journal of Natural History* 31:1313–1334.

Dejean, A., Olmstead, I., and Snelling, R. R. 1995. Tree-epiphyte-ant relationships in low inundated forest of Sian Ka'an Biosphere Reserve, Quintana Roo, Mexico. *Biotropica* 27:57–70.

Diesel, R., and Schuh, M. 1993. Maternal care in the bromeliad crab *Metopaulias depressus* (Decapoda) maintaining oxygen, pH, and calcium levels optimal for larvae. *Behavioral Ecology and Sociobiology* 32:1–15.

Dressler, R. L. 1981. *The orchids.* Cambridge, MA: Harvard University Press.

Ehleringer, J. R., and Marshall, J. D. 1995. Water relations. In: *Parasitic plants,* ed. M. C. Press and J. D. Graves, 125–140. London: Chapman and Hall.

Flores-Palacios, A., and Ortiz-Pulido, R. 2005. Epiphytic orchid establishment on carton termite trails. *Biotropica* 37:457–461.

Foster, P. 2002. The potential negative impacts of global change on tropical montane cloud forests. *Earth Science Reviews* 55:580–586.

Frank, J. H. 1986. Bromeliads as oviposition sites for *Wyeomyia* mosquitoes: form and color influence behavior. *Florida Entomologist* 69:728–742.

Freiberg, M. 2001. The influence of epiphyte cover on branch temperature in a tropical tree. *Plant Ecology* 153:241–250.

Gentry, A. H., and Dodson, C. H. 1987. Diversity and biogeography of Neotropical vascular epiphytes. *Annals of the Missouri Botanical Gardens* 69:557–593.

Gravendeel, B., Smithson, A., Slik, F. J., and Schuiteman, A. 2004. Epiphytism and pollinator specialization: drivers for orchid diversity? *Philosophical Transactions of the Royal Society of London B: Biological Sciences* 359(1450):1523–1535.

Griffiths, H., and Smith, J. A. C. 1983. Photosynthetic pathways in the Bromeliaceae of Trinidad: relations between life-form, habitat preference, and the occurrence of CAM. *Oecologia* 60:176–184.

Heitz, P., and Briones, O. 1998. Correlation between water relations and within canopy distributions of epiphytic ferns in a Mexican cloud forest. *Oecologia* 114:305–316.

Heitz, P., Wanek, W., and Popp, M. 1999. Stable isotope composition of carbon and nitrogen content in vascular epiphytes along an altitudinal transect. *Plant, Cell and Environment* 22:1435–1447.

Heitz-Seifert, U., Heitz, P., and Guevara, S. 1996. Epiphyte vegetation and diversity on remnant trees after forest clearance in southern Vera Cruz, Mexico. *Biological Conservation* 75:103–111.

Huxley, C. R. 1980. Symbiosis between ants and epiphytes. *Biological Review* 55:321–340.

Ingram, S. W., and Nadkarni, N. M. 1993. The composition and distribution of epiphytic organic matter in a Neotropical cloud forest, Costa Rica. *Biotropica* 25:370–383.

Kaufman, E., and Maschwitz, U. 2006. Ant gardens of tropical Asian rain forests. *Naturwissenschaften* 93(5):216–227.

Kaufman, E., Weissflog, A., Hashim, R., and Maschwitz, U. 2001. Ant garden on giant bamboo *Gigantochloa scortechinii* in West Malaysia. *Insectes Sociaux* 48:125–133.

Kernan, C., and Flower, N. 1995. Differential substrate use by epiphytes in Corcovado National Park, Costa Rica. *Journal of Ecology* 83:65–73.

Lasso, E., and Ackerman, J. D. 2003. Flowering phenology of *Werauhia sintenisii*, a bromeliad from the dwarf montane forest of Puerto Rico: an indicator of climate change? *Selbyana* 24(1):95–104.

Lesica, P., and Antibus, R. K. 1991. Canopy soils and epiphytic richness. *National Geographic Research and Exploration* 7:156–165.

Lugo, A. E., and Scatena, F. N. 1992. Epiphytes and climate change research in the Caribbean: a proposal. *Selbyana* 13:123–130.

Martin, C. E. 1994. Physiological ecology of the Bromeliaceae. *Botanical Review* 60:1–82.

Maxwell, K., Griffiths, H., Borland, A.M., Broadmeadows, S. J., and Fordham, M. C. 1995. Short-term photosynthetic responses of the C_3-CAM bromeliad *Guzmania monostachia* var. *monostachia* to tropical seasonal transitions under field conditions. *Australian Journal of Plant Physiology* 22:771–781.

Montaña, C., Diroz, R., and Flores, A. 1997. Structural parasitism of an epiphytic bromeliad upon *Circidium praecox* in an intertropical semiarid ecosystem. *Biotropica* 29:517–521.

Nadkarni, N. M. 2000. Colonization of stripped branch surfaces by epiphytes in lower montane cloud forest, Monteverde, Costa Rica. *Biotropica* 32:358–363.

Nadkarni, N. M., and Matelson, T. J. 1989. Bird use of epiphyte resources in Neotropical trees. *Condor* 91:891–907.

Nadkarni, N. M., and Solano, R. 2002. Potential effects of climate change on canopy communities in a tropical forest: an experimental approach. *Oecologia* 131:580–586.

Neider, J., Prosperi, J., and Michaloud, G. 2001. Epiphytes and their contribution to canopy diversity. *Plant Ecology* 153:51–63.

Nishio, J. N., and Ting, I. P. 1978. Carbon flow and metabolic specialization in the tissue layers of the crassulacean acid metabolism plant *Peperomia camptotricha*. *Plant Physiology* 84:600–604.

North, G. B., and Nobel, P. S. 1994. Changes in hydraulic conductivity for two tropical epiphytic cacti as soil moisture varies. *American Journal of Botany* 81:46–53.

Nyman, L. P., Davis, J. P., O'Dell, S. J., Arditti, J., Stephens, G. C., and Benzing, D. H. 1987. Active uptake of amino acids by leaves of an epiphytic vascular plant *Tillandsia paucifolia* (Bromeliaceae). *Plant Physiology* 83:681–684.

Ozanne, C. M. P., Anhuf, D., Boulter, S. L., Keller, M., Kitching, R. L., Korner, C., Meinzer, F. C., Mitchell, A. W., Nakashizuka, T., Silva Diaz, P. L., Stork, N. E., Wright, S. J., and Yoshimura, M. 2003. Biodiversity meets the atmosphere: a global view of forest canopies. *Science* 301:231–256.

Paoletti, M., Taylor, R., Stinner, B., Stinner, D., and Benzing, D. 1991. Diversity of soil fauna in the canopy and forest floor of a Venezuelan cloud forest. *Journal of Tropical Ecology* 7:373–383.

Pett-Ridge, J., and Silver, W. L. 2002. Survival, growth, and ecosystem dynamics of displaced bromeliads in a montane cloud forest. *Biotropica* 34:211–224.

Pierce, S., Maxwell, K., Griffiths, H., and Winter, K. 2001. Hygrophobic trichome layers and epicuticular wax powders in Bromeliaceae. *American Journal of Botany* 88:1371–1389.

Pittendrigh, C. S. 1948. The bromeliad-Anopheles-malaria complex in Trinidad. I. The bromeliad flora. *Evolution* 2:58–89.

Pryer, K. M., Schuettpelz, E., Wolf, P. G., Schneider, H., Smith, A. R., and Cranfill, R. 2004. Phylogeny and evolution of ferns (monilophytes) with a focus on the early leptosporangiate divergences. *American Journal of Botany* 91:1582–1598.

Rains, K. C., Nadkarni, N. M., and Bledsoe, C. S. 2003. Epiphytic and terrestrial mycorrhizas in lower montane Costa Rican rain forest. *Mycorrhiza* 13:257–264.

Reich, A., Ewel, J. J., Nadkarni, N., Dawson, T., and Evans, D. R. 2003. Nitrogen isotope ratios shift with plant size in tropical bromeliads. *Oecologia* 137:587–590.

Richardson, B. A. 1999. The bromeliad microcosm and the assessment of faunal diversity in a Neotropical forest. *Biotropica* 31:321–336.

Rico-Gray, V., and Thein, L. B. 1989. Ant-mealbug interactions decrease reproductive fitness of *Schomburkia tibicinis* (Orchidaceae) in Mexico. *Journal of Tropical Ecology* 5:109–112.

Rothwell, G. W. 1991. *Botryopteris forensis* (Botryopteridaceae), a trunk epiphyte on the tree fern *Psaronius*. *American Journal of Botany* 64:1254–1262.

Schneider, H., Schuettpelz, E., Pryer, K. M., Cranfill, R., Magallón, S., and Lupia, R. 2004. Ferns diversified in the shadow of angiosperms. *Nature* 428:553–557.

Schrimpff, E. 1981. Air pollution patterns in two cities in Colombia, S. A. according to trace substance content of an epiphyte (*Tillandsia recurvata* L.). *Water, Air and Soil Pollution* 21:279–315.

Schuetpelz, E., and Trapnell, D. W. 2006. Exceptional epiphyte diversity on a single tree in Costa Rica. *Selbyana* 27:65–71.

Seidel, J. L., Epstein, W. W., and Davidson, D. W. 1990. Neotropical ant gardens I. Chemical constituents. *Journal of Chemical Ecology* 16:1791–1816.

Smith, A. R., Pryer, K. M., Schuettpelz, E., Korall, P., Schneider, H., and Wolf, P. G. 2006. A classification for extant ferns. *Taxon* 55(3):705–731.

Still, C. J., Foster, P. N., and Schneider, S. H. 1999. Simulating the effects of climate change on tropical montane cloud forest. *Nature* 398:608–610.

Stuntz, S., Ziegler, C., Simon, U., and Zotz, G. 2001. Diversity and canopy structure of the arthropod fauna within three canopy epiphyte species in Central Panama. *Journal of Tropical Ecology* 18:161–176.

Stuntz, S., Simon, U., and Zotz, G. 2002. Rain forest air-conditioning: the moderating influences of epiphytes on the microclimate in tropical tree crowns. *International Journal of Biometeorology* 46:53–59.

Sugden, A. M., and Robins, R. J. 1979. Aspects of the ecology of vascular epiphytes in Colombian cloud forest. I. The distribution of the epiphyte flora. *Biotropica* 11:173–188.

Thorne, B. L., Haverty, M. I., and Benzing, D. H. 1996. Association between termites and bromeliads in two dry tropical habitats. *Biotropica* 28:781–785.

Turton, S. M., and Sexton, G. J. 1996. Environmental gradients across four rain forests: open forest boundaries in northeastern Queensland. *Australian Journal of Ecology* 21:245–254.

Wake, D. B. 1987. Adaptive radiation of salamanders in middle American cloud forests. *Annals of the Missouri Botanical Gardens* 74:242–264.

Wania, R., Heitz, P., and Wanek, W. 2002. Natural N^{15} abundance of epiphytes depends on position within the forest canopy: sources, signals, and isotopic fractionation. *Plant, Cell and Environment* 25:581–589.

Watkins, J. E., Jr., Mack, M. C., Sinclair, T. R., and Mulkey, S. S. 2007. Ecological and evolutionary consequences of desiccation tolerance in fern gametophytes. *New Phytologist* 176(3):708–717.

Watson, D. M. 2001. Mistletoe—a keystone resource in forests and woodlands worldwide. *Annual Review of Ecology and Systematics* 32:219–249.

Wikström, N., Kenrick, P., and Chase, M. 1999. Epiphytism and terrestrialism in Neotropical *Huperzia*. *Plant Systematics and Evolution* 218:221–243.

Winter, K., Wallace, B. J., Stocker, G. C., and Roksandic, Z. 1983. Crassulacean acid metabolism in Australian vascular epiphytes and some related species. *Oecologia* 57:129–141.

Young, A.M. 1979. Arboreal movements and tadpole-carrying behavior of *Dendrobates pumilio* (Dendrobatidae) in northern Costa Rica. *Biotropica* 11:218–219.

Youngsteadt, E., Nojima, S., Häberlein, C., Schulz, S., and Schal, C. 2008. Seed odor mediates an obligate ant-plant mutualism in Amazonian rain forests. *Proceedings of the National Academy of Science USA* 105:4571–4575.

Yu, W. 1994. The structural role of epiphytes in ant gardens. *Biotropica* 26:217–221.

Zotz, G. 1997. Substrate use by three bromeliads. *Ecography* 20:264–270.

Zotz, G. 2005. Vascular epiphytes of the temperate zone—a review. *Plant Ecology* 176:173–183.

Zotz, G., and Bader, M. Y. 2009. Epiphytic plants in a changing world: global change effects on vascular and nonvascular epiphytes. *Progress in Botany* 70:147–170.

Zotz, G., and Heitz, P. 2001. The physiological ecology of vascular epiphytes: current knowledge, open questions. *Journal of Experimental Botany* 52:2067–2078.

Zotz, G., and List, C. 2003. Zufallsepiphyten-flanzen auf dem weg nach oben? *Bauhinia* 17:25–37.

Zotz, G., and Richter, A. 2006. Changes in carbohydrate and nutrients throughout the reproductive cycle indicate that phosphorus is a limiting factor in the epiphytic bromeliad *Werauhia sanguinolenta*. *Annals of Botany* 97:745–754.

Zotz, G., and Thomas, V. 1999. How much water is in the tank? Model calculations for two epiphytic bromeliads. *Annals of Botany* 87:183–192.

Subject Index

Taxon Index